ANDY RODDICK BEAT ME WITH A FRYING PAN

ANDY RODDICK BEAT ME WITH A FRYING PAN

Taking the Field with Pro Athletes and Olympic Legends to Answer Sports Fans' Burning Questions

Todd Gallagher

THREE RIVERS PRESS
NEW YORK

This book is dedicated to the loving memory
of my grandmother, Laura Ciotti.

Published in the United States by Three Rivers Press, an imprint of
the Crown Publishing Group, a division of Random House, Inc., New York.
www.crownpublishing.com

Three Rivers Press and the Tugboat design are
registered trademarks of Random House, Inc.

The photographs used in this book are printed with the permission of the following:
Stephen Andrew Skinner: p. 6 (Trevor Butler), p. 9 (Butler and Washington Capitals),
p. 220 (Jed Donahue and DeShawn Stevenson), p. 225 (Brendan Haywood and Donahue)
Lisa Donovan: p. 16 (Josh Davis and Todd Gallagher), p. 17 (Davis and Gallagher), p. 48
(Maurice Greene and Donahue), p. 51 (Greene and Donahue), p. 58 (Byambajav
Ulambayar, Bayanbat Davaadalai, and Gallagher), p. 61 (Ulambayar, Davaadalai, and
Gene Miranda), p. 67 (Paul Lim and Gallagher), p. 69 (Gallagher and Lim), p. 152
(Ismael Paez), p. 187 (Jose Canseco)
Naomi Hiltz: p. 34 (Amanda Mitts)
Joseph Lamb: p. 78 (James White)
Ryan Chiang: p. 94 (Paul Abbott and Gallagher)
Molly Hayden: p. 131 (Pete Weber)
Steven Stanziani: p. 195 (Matt Reis and Gallagher)
Veronica Ferrari: p. 243 (Gallagher and Andy Roddick), p. 246 (Roddick)
St. Paul Saints: p. 255 (Dana Kiecker), p. 257 (Leroy the Phone Guy)

Library of Congress Cataloging-in-Publication Data

Gallagher, Todd.
  Andy Roddick beat me with a frying pan : taking the field with pro athletes and olympic
legends to answer sports fans' burning questions / Todd Gallagher.—1st ed.
  1. Sports—Miscellanea.   I. Title.
  GV707.G35 2007
  796—dc22   2007017845

ISBN 978-0-307-35280-4

Printed in the United States of America

Design by Joseph Rutt

10 9 8 7 6 5 4 3 2 1

First Edition

CONTENTS

Introduction   ix

Question 1   Could a morbidly obese goalie shut out
               an NHL team?   1

Question 2   Could an Olympic swimmer doggie-paddle
               and still beat a regular guy?   11

Question 3   How many tough men could Mike Tyson
               defeat in one night?   19

Question 4   Would a major league batting champion
               dominate in Wiffle ball?   26

Question 5   How easy is it for pro athletes to get laid?
               And how easy is it for a groupie to bag a
               pro athlete?   33

Question 6   What kind of handicap would it take to
               beat an Olympic sprinter?   45

Question 7   Would sumo wrestlers make great NFL
               linemen?   53

Question 8   Are dart professionals great beer pong
               players?   64

Question 9   Can basketball players really "make
               change" off the top of the backboard?   71

Question 10   How would a psychic do in a Rock,
                Paper, Scissors tournament?   80

Question 11   Are there pro athletes who have to
                pinch pennies?   87

Question 12   Can fans hit as well as pitchers?   91

Question 13   Do pro athletes really play high?   99

Question 14   How big is the gap between male and
                female athletes?   104

Question 15   Are there great players who never got
                a shot at the pros?   121

Question 16   How would a pro bowler do at skee-ball?   130

Question 17   How many Tampa Bay Devil Rays can the
                average major leaguer name?   134

Question 18   How good are pro golfers at miniature golf?   138

Question 19   Could any celebrities play in the pros?   144

Question 20   Playing one-handed, could a pro billiards
                player beat an amateur?   150

Question 21   Are those guys really athletes?   155

Question 22   Do athletes think about their statistics
                while they're playing (or, Can I trust these
                guys to put my fantasy team above their
                real team)?   164

Question 23   Can I do that? If I practiced, couldn't
                I be as good as the pros?   173

Question 24   Does a six-fingered pitcher have an
unfair advantage?   191

Question 25   How easy is the transition from soccer
player to NFL kicker?   193

Question 26   What would happen if the NBA raised
the basket to 12 feet?   201

Question 27   Is it as easy to cheat at poker as they
made it look in *Rounders*?   210

Question 28   Could a non-basketball player beat an
NBA player in free throws?   217

Question 29   How long before NASCAR drivers are
replaced by AI (Artificial Intelligence,
not Allen Iverson)?   231

Question 30   Could Andy Roddick beat an average
tennis player with a frying pan?   237

Question 31   Would a team of midgets be the greatest
offense in baseball history?   249

Acknowledgments   266

Index by Joe Queenan   271

INTRODUCTION

As any sports fan knows, the debates can be almost as interesting as the games themselves . . . unless you're a Tampa Bay Devil Rays fan, in which case they're much more interesting. And as any sports fan will tell you, the most enjoyable debates aren't the same tired ones that sportswriters and media personalities rehash ad nauseam. They're the ones that rage on in living rooms, locker rooms, and barrooms around the world. (Full disclosure: I have not actually been around the world to confirm this.)

You've probably had a bunch of these kinds of debates with your friends. I definitely have. Many drunken nights have been spent trying to figure out what kind of absurd handicap I'd need to be able to compete against an elite athlete or arguing whether a glue-sniffing neighbor's outlandish strategy really would revolutionize a sport. When I was coaching in the USBL, arguing about the validity of urban legends being peddled in cheap magazines turned long bus rides into the barbershop scene from *Coming to America.* And back when I was doing interviews for ESPN, the best conversations I'd have with coworkers were the ones that could never be discussed on the air, in the magazine, or on the website without getting someone fired.

But there are limitations to being a fan beyond the limiting shame of screaming support for people dribbling a basketball who don't even know you. No matter how fun these debates are, arguing in and of itself is never enough to settle them in a satisfactory way. If you've been insisting for years that pro tennis players are so good that Andy Roddick could play with a frying pan and still crush your buddy who thinks tennis is easy, you can't just call up Andy and throw a skillet in his hand. If you believe a 1,000-pound goalie would dominate the sport of hockey, NHL teams aren't lining up to shoot on your rotund ringer to prove you right. If you think a writer is just making things up in claiming LeBron James can touch the top of the backboard, you can't get BronBron to set the record straight. And if your coworkers are adamant that a Division I women's basketball player would whip your ass in a game of one-on-one, there's not much you can do but say you respectfully/disrespectfully disagree. In many ways, you're always on the outside looking in.

The bigger problem for fans who want answers is that no one on the "inside" is trying to settle these debates either. Working in sports as a basketball coach, writer, and TV producer, I found out why firsthand. Many times fans (of sports, not of me) approached me with questions they couldn't answer. Eventually I became so overwhelmed by how often certain questions came up, and was so curious about ones from my own life, that I turned to peers in the sports media to see what we could do. The good news was that they'd invariably say they had been bombarded with many of the same questions and were dying to know the answers themselves. The bad news was that they'd tell me to forget it; answering the questions would be too expensive, too time-consuming, and no athlete would ever participate.

It doesn't take an insider to understand the time and money limitations. Media outlets are businesses and want to maximize profits, and having talking heads blabber about the hot topic of the day is a lot more cost effective than staging events and doing research.* To be honest, at ESPN we used to have a hard enough time getting players to do fifteen-minute interviews about their favorite music (except for Kenny Anderson, who told me he'd rather win a Grammy than an NBA MVP award).

---

* On a sports landscape littered with opinions that are both loud and worthless, anything that requires a substantive response or more than a "take" for resolution is usually ignored. It's why we get filler: articles that endlessly recycle the same storylines, ten weeks of NFL draft coverage where announcers furiously debate the merits of players they have never seen, lifestyle segments that are nothing more than an excuse to fit in product placements, and *Around the Horn*.

But I always believed that the questions fans posed were so much more interesting than what athletes typically get asked—or, at the very least, what I had to ask them—that they'd be happy to participate. So through the years I always kept the idea of answering these questions in the back of my mind.

To the rescue came Three Rivers Press, which was bound by neither hard daily deadlines nor the same budgetary concerns that limit media outlets looking to take advantage of the twenty-four-hour news cycle. They had the money to cover my expenses, I made the time to do the legwork, and you, the fans, had the imagination, so I went out to get the answers we've always wanted.*

As tempting as it was just to give my own blustery opinions on these questions and spend the rest of the year in Hawaii, I turned to the people who could really settle the debates: the players. As I had hoped would be the case, the questions struck enough of a chord with the athletes that many of the best in the world were happy to put them to the test on the field of play. Andy Roddick actually did play with a frying pan, the NHL's Washington Capitals really did shoot on a rotund goalie, and many others participated as well: the National League batting champion, a two-time Olympic gold medalist sprinter, a PGA golfer, a three-time Olympic gold medalist swimmer, a former American League MVP, America's #1 darts player, a bowling Hall of Famer, and one of the greatest dunkers in basketball history, to name a few.

It wasn't just the events the athletes enjoyed. One of the most refreshing parts of this project was to see pro athletes who have been barraged with the same boring questions over and over again have their deadened eyes light up at the chance to have a fun, thoughtful, albeit ridiculous, conversation about the sport they have dedicated their lives to. I grilled everyone from LeBron to Johan Santana to Dwyane Wade to Eddie George to "The Black Widow" Jeanette Lee, and instead of rolling

---

* Oh, and try to sell a ton of books too. Next book, I would like to have the money and someone else can have the goddamn time. Please be aware, however, that you will still be handling "imagination" in an unpaid role.

their eyes at me like Steve Nash used to at the dopey questions I was forced to ask, or screaming at me like a two-year-old like Stephon Marbury did, they were happy to oblige.

As much time as I put into this project flying around the country, renting out airport terminals, and importing sumo wrestlers from Mongolia, this was more than just work. I'm as obsessed with sports as many of the fans who have approached me with questions, having wasted countless hours of my life playing and watching everything from basketball to baseball to tennis to soccer to pool. So it was insanely fun to be able to get into it with an NBA coach about his team's questionable moves, try to convince a loopy Mike Tyson to fight ten "tough men" in a single night, talk to Mike Cameron about how he has patrolled center field while drunk, listen to Wade and Carmelo Anthony call out Gilbert Arenas for keeping track of his stats during games, and try to start a bidding war between major league general managers for a midget baseball player.

Even when throwing myself into the action crushed my fantasy that a pro career was only a couple of trips to the batting cage away or blew a long-held belief to pieces, it was the most fun I ever had in sports.

Then again, how couldn't it have been? After twenty years of arguing with my dad, I finally settled whether a team of midgets could beat my beloved Pirates.

A Note on the Questions

Like most questions that sports fans debate, the questions covered in this book typically fall into a handful of categories:

- *The outlandish strategies:* Would your friend's insane plan to "change the game" really work or does he just need to get out of the house more often?

- *The proposition bets on handicap matches:* A coworker swears a pro golfer could play with a toothpick instead of a golf club and still crush you, or something equally amazing in magnitude. We find out just how good these guys really are.

• *The myth busters:* Discerning sports fans call "bullshit" on some of the remarkable, yet undocumented, athletic feats and stories described by old-timers, sportswriters, and publicists. We put these myths to the test to separate fact from fiction.

• *"_____ can't be that hard":* Countless armchair athletes think that their own laziness, indifference, or lack of opportunity is keeping them from athletic glory, or at the very least, from being a pro bowler. If they put in the time and really, really tried their hardest, how far off are these slobs from being the pros themselves?

• *The life:* Is the glamour of being a pro athlete that we see on TV a fair representation? Just how often is it really made to rain, and can "I'm Keith Hernandez" actually be a successful pickup line for a professional athlete?

• *The controversies:* Those questions everyone but the fans themselves tiptoes around, such as, *Was Bobby Riggs vs. Billie Jean King really the final word on the "battle of the sexes"?*, and other subjects that can get people in the media fired when they discuss them openly and honestly.

COULD A MORBIDLY OBESE GOALIE SHUT OUT AN NHL TEAM?

I t's not hard to imagine an owner looking for an unfair advantage to "break" the rules of a sport. Baseball owner Bill Veeck famously batted 3'7" Eddie Gaedel at leadoff in a baseball game despite, or more accurately, because of, his diminutive strike zone. Charlie Finley employed Olympic sprinter Herb Washington as a pinch runner for his Oakland A's. Chicago Bulls GM Jerry Krause once shaved a gorilla and put it in a Bill Wennington uniform in order to get more power in the post. For hockey, the question is simple and has been asked thousands of times by hardcore sports fans and casual observers, from sportswriters like ESPN's Bill Simmons (in an article entitled "33 Ways to Make Sports Better") to Rob Lowe's and Bradley Whitford's characters on *The West Wing:* Why not go out and find the fattest goalie you can to block the net?

As strange as it may sound to anyone with a sense of decency, there is actually sound reasoning behind it. Because of the geometry of the game, the potential for one mammoth individual to change hockey is staggering. Simply put, there is a goal that's 6 feet wide and 4 feet high, and a hockey puck that needs to go into it in order to score. Fill that net completely, and no goals can possibly be scored against your team. So why hasn't it happened yet?

One answer is that professionalism and fair play prevent many sports teams from doing whatever it takes to win. This is also known as "having no imagination." Additionally, in hockey the worry of on-ice reprisal from bloodthirsty goons would weigh heavily on the mind of any player whose very existence violated the game's "unwritten rules." In other words, had Eddie Gaedel worn a St. Louis Blues uniform rather than one of the St. Louis Browns, his heartwarming story may have instead been a cautionary tale.

Also, advertising money is a strong motivation for professional sports leagues to keep a sense of legitimacy to their made-up games. But considering that no one wants to advertise with the NHL to begin with, I started thinking there must be a simpler explanation. Maybe it was just against the real rules.

Looking for answers, I followed a path blazed by draft dodgers and drug-addicted football players and headed north to Canada. Actually, since it was the dead of winter, I just bought a five-dollar international phone card and called the NHL offices in Toronto to speak with Johanna Kytola. Johanna, not surprisingly, was appalled by the idea. However, after some prodding she was forced to concede that the NHL rulebook doesn't put any physical constraints on the size of players . . . which I suppose could have been surmised just by looking at Zedno Chara.

I had checked Johanna into the boards, but then she dropped her gloves. There are, she said, nonnegotiable restrictions on the size of goalie pads, and no regulation goalie pads would even come close to covering the body of a man who makes John Goodman look svelte. In practical terms this means a mammoth net-minder would have to absorb quite a bit of punishment on his exposed body from hard rubber pucks hurtling toward him at upward of 100 miles per hour. To pull this off, a team would not only have to find a uniquely fat guy, they'd have to find a total masochist.*

Then Johanna threw a Tie Domi haymaker: "A man of that size would have a very hard time passing a physical. If he did and it became a problem for the league, the issue would then go through the commissioner and governor's office until a solution was reached."

What do you mean by "solution"? Are you going to have Scotty Bowman put together a death squad or something?

"No comment."

From Johanna's veiled threats it was clear that this idea had merit, so I decided to continue researching how to ruin pro hockey forever. And no, that doesn't mean seeing if I could get their Versus deal extended.

It made sense that a guy who can't get out of bed might have trouble passing a physical or possibly even making it to the physical, but would a failed physical be enough to bar him from being forklifted into action? To find a legal loophole big enough for our fat goalie to be greased up and shoved through wouldn't be easy, since the NHL has more lawyers than fans. I didn't have a team of lawyers on retainer to go head to head with the NHL's, but David needed only one attorney to win the right to fight Goliath. The stone in my sling was Gilbert Geilim, a lawyer in Los Angeles who thought we sort of had a case against the philistines in the league office: "The NHL would eventually figure out a way to keep a man who is a health risk off the ice, but if they looked like they were making the criteria for a physical to exclude a certain segment of

---

* Or more than one. While a morbidly obese goalie may not be able to take the punishment for an entire game, a group of four rotated in shifts when in severe pain or suffering low blood sugar could probably do the trick.

society, even the morbidly obese, you might luck out and get a judge to issue a temporary injunction."

No matter the odds, one thing was clear: That we could even potentially win a legal battle made it my duty to press on.

For ostensible humanitarian reasons, I needed to determine whether an obese goalie could handle the physical demands of playing professional hockey. Jacob DiCesare, a doctor at the University of Pittsburgh Medical Center, told me, "When people get into the weight range you're referring to—one thousand pounds and above—it is rarely because of body fat. People in that class of weight are nearly always retaining fluid somewhere in their body, often in the abdomen, although there have been cases where a majority of weight . . ." and that's when I tuned out.

Finally, he switched from medical mumbo jumbo and addressed the far more interesting aspect of fat men getting hit in the gut with a puck. "Well, it would really hurt, especially because the padding wouldn't cover a lot of the body. At best you're looking at some severe bruising. Not to mention the incredible risk the morbidly obese would have just getting out on the ice. But theoretically if they had no cardiopulmonary issues or other health issues, once they were sat down in front of the net, and if they could deal with the pain, then sure, they'd do fine."

With that ringing endorsement, it was time to see whether obese people might agree to be pelted with hockey pucks and circus peanuts. I spoke with a friend of mine who had packed on the pounds since high school—we'll just call him Mr. XL—and asked whether he'd be willing to gain enough weight to fill a net if an NHL contract were on the line. Since Tony . . . oops, Mr. XL . . . wasn't even aware that the NHL still existed, he was skeptical. I insisted that with some real commitment he could be bathing in gravy in no time.

Now he was intrigued: "So how much weight exactly would I have to gain?"

Roughly 800 pounds.

"Um . . ."

That was as close to a yes as I needed. At all times there is a wealth of morbidly obese men in the world, all of whom are financially limited by their condition and have few ways of acquiring the Ho Hos and powdered doughnuts required for their survival. Undoubtedly at least one of them would be willing to take the physical abuse and mental anguish for the right kind of money. Millions of dollars can help a bruised ego and a broken sternum; that's what therapists and painkillers are for.

We were getting close. Now that the futzing around with feelings and rules was out of the way, the true test was almost at hand: actually putting a big fella in the net. My insurance doesn't cover obese-goalie-related death, so horror-movie director George Romero's special-effects school constructed a heavy foam fat suit to replicate the exact measurements of our mountain of a man. To test the limits of fat-goalie domination, they used the dimensions of the pear-shaped Robert Earl Hughes, one of the heaviest men in history at 1,069 pounds, who reportedly had a waistline of 122 inches, and then, to account for the carbo-loading regimen an NHL team would put this kind of goalie through, beefed him up a little more. (Romero's people declined my request to exhume and totally zombify Hughes, however.) This translated to an overall width of about 3½ feet. Sitting him in front of a 6-foot goal would reduce the area available to score to 2½ feet, or about 15 inches on either side of our goalie. Add in our man's arms, legs, pads, blocking glove, and catching glove, and the goal would be reasonably full.

The only way to fully test this theory was to get an NHL team to

Hi, friends! Will you let me play?

shoot against the faux fatso. My esteemed editor, Jed Donahue, got in touch with a fellow Georgetown graduate who was doing nearly as well as he is: Ted Leonsis, billionaire owner of the Washington Capitals, whom the *Sporting News* once called one of the twenty most powerful people in sports. Leonsis, who made his fortune in the world of telecommunications and technology, is a bit of a visionary. And while his vision may not have originally included allowing the professional hockey team he owns to take slapshots at a guy in a fat suit, he saw the potential and gave the stunt the green light.

With a team of highly skilled shooters in place, we needed someone to get in the suit. I certainly wasn't going to do it (insert fake injury/ailment/note from my mom here), so I enlisted George Mason University goalie Trevor Butler. Once everything was set, I threw the suit in a rented white molester van and headed for D.C., the whole time glancing nervously in my rearview mirror, imagining how I'd explain what I was doing to an officer who thought he was pulling over the Beltway Sniper.

After the monumental chore of getting Trevor in the suit and pads, we hit the ice—literally. To get him some level of comfort in the fat suit, I took him onto an unused rink adjacent to the one the Caps were playing on, and within seconds he fell flat on his fake fat stomach. Panic set in as we tried to pull him up, but finally a team of five men was able to drag him off the ice and get him on his feet again. Had this been an actual 1,000-pound man instead of an athletic goalie in a fat suit, the game would have been called on account of fatness.

While Trevor prepared for his grand entrance, I checked in with the Caps. Their reactions were even less encouraging than Johanna's icy responses were. Most players wanted nothing to do with an elephantine goalie. Defenseman Ben Clymer was so ashamed of being associated with the tub that he tried to identify himself with a fake name (he used center Kris Beech's). Winger Dainius Zubrus put it bluntly: "It would be embarrassing if there was a goalie that big." Defenseman Steve Eminger confirmed my worst fears about how our big man would be received when he said opposing teams would simply try to run him over in the net. The Real Kris Beech had an even more depressing comment for our new star: "You might spear him and see if chocolate came out."

But if a half-ton wonder could bring the Stanley Cup to Washington, then it sounded like everyone would be as sweet as can be. Well, *barely tolerant* is probably a more accurate description, but it's a start. As Zubrus put it, "If he was dominant it'd be fine. That's the goal, to win, right?" Beech agreed, but with a reservation: "That'd be good as long as I didn't have to go to dinner with him."

As I saw it, this was as close as we were going to get to support, so it was time to unveil the heavy artillery. Trevor took to the ice on the Capitals' official practice rink with as much grace as he could possibly muster. A full crowd was in attendance to watch their sporting heroes that day, and as Trevor waddled to the net, children laughed and pointed, adults covered their heads in shame, and the Capitals stared, jaws agape.

We got Trevor situated in front of the net, though it took a good five minutes of work, including tying his torso to the crossbar . . . probably a disturbing sight, given that very few people were clued into the fact that this was not an actual 1,000-pound man. Trevor's goalie crouch was itself unnerving: butt on the ice and legs splayed out in front of him—really the only way someone that large could be situated. There were certainly places to score around his head and shoulders, but he filled most of the net and made it difficult to see the goal line.

I watched in horror as the Caps began to shoot, but Trevor blocked every single one of their first eleven shots, including a glove save he may not have even been aware of that drew cheers from the crowd. After one particularly brutal slapshot that ripped off the fat suit's overalls, I checked on Trevor to see how he was doing. "My knee hurts and I can't breathe." Great, Trevor! Keep up the good work!

As our session progressed, the Caps went through a number of drills and shot from various angles. They began methodically testing the fattie's limited ability to move, trying breakaways, two on ones, and one-timers. Caps winger Matt Bradley seemed bothered as a particularly good wrister was easily stopped, while Trevor kept complaining about his inability to lift his arms or breathe. This led me to believe that real science was occurring, because it didn't seem like anyone was having fun.

From our practice session some easy conclusions could be drawn. Breakaways, in particular, were death for Trevor. An NHL player will score every time from close in on a goalie who can't move unless the goalie is large enough to literally cover the entire net. Angles and wraparounds were also extremely problematic

He'd be even better if he could actually move.

since Trevor could not move to close the open gaps. But when the shots were coming from straight on in five-on-five game situations, Trevor pretty much shut them down.

So what does that equal?

Well, not much, in Trevor's opinion. He said that in a real game a portly net-minder wouldn't stand a chance. "You're kind of a sitting duck in net like that. And if that was my skin instead of padding I would be in the emergency room or dead right now." Pussy.

Unfortunately, I couldn't so easily dismiss the Capitals' harsh assessments just by pretending to be tough. Their scouting report on my new superstar showed there were indeed some on-ice problems. Ben Clymer's review was less than glowing: "The hardest part [to score on] was through his body, 'cause he's pretty fat. The easiest parts were pretty much anywhere where he wasn't, because he wasn't moving a bit."

So you're saying there's a chance!

"I hope we play a few games against him this year."

According to Kris Beech, the limited success the behemoth had in our practice session may not even translate to a real NHL game once teams knew what they were up against: "Knowing we were going to play against him, we would take some extra practice and make sure we could hit those holes."

Do you guys have any idea how long it took me to set this up?

In the end, this is a complicated issue but one with a clear answer. There is no chance the NHL would allow a contract to be signed with such an obvious health risk, and though the court case might provide an opening, it wouldn't be a big one given these health concerns. It is also highly unlikely that any team would allow such an embarrassment to the game to take the ice for them.

In addition, not just any fat man would do the trick, as Matt Bradley explained. "If you add maybe three hundred more pounds to that guy, he might be okay. If someone's willing to gain fifteen hundred pounds to go in net, there might be a job for him somewhere." While there have been 1,500-pound men, none have been proportionally built in a way that would fill a hockey goal. In fact, there probably isn't a man in the history of the entire world fat enough to be effective in an NHL game.

That being said, if there was a team that was more concerned with winning than with their reputation, and if they could find a genetic marvel, a man pushing 2,000 pounds who's fatter than anyone the world has ever seen, who could survive making it onto the ice and withstand the pain of frozen hockey pucks being fired off his exposed body, and if that team could then win a legal battle against the NHL, and if the players didn't go on strike over the matter or beat the rotund goalie to death on the ice, that histori-cally obese man could be a cost-efficient and effective goaltender. But what are the chances of that wondrous hog existing, and events unfolding in such a way? Pretty slim.

COULD AN OLYMPIC SWIMMER DOGGIE-PADDLE AND STILL BEAT A REGULAR GUY?

To be a world-class swimmer, you must have flawless technique, endless endurance, astonishing discipline, and freakish God-given ability.

To be a lousy swimmer, you need none of these things.

That was about the extent of my swimming knowledge when I set out to determine whether a world-class swimmer could doggie-paddle and still beat a regular guy. The only other thing I knew for sure was that there was only one place to turn to find my opponent: USA Swimming, which has been the top swimming program in the world for decades. They were willing to accomodate; USA Swimming media coordinator Sara Hunninghake arranged for me to race one of America's greatest swimming legends, three-time Olympic gold medalist Josh Davis.

Davis is a shark in the water, or for a less clichéd analogy, a killer whale . . . or maybe an exceptionally fast sturgeon? Never mind. "He's one of the best swimmers of all time," Sara told me. "I don't know how good of a swimmer you are, but he will not be easy to beat."

As to how good of a swimmer I am, let's put it this way: I wasn't even sure I could swim well enough to qualify as a "regular guy."

The event was to take place at the U.S. National Championships in Irvine, California, and we had two weeks to prepare. While Davis would probably not even think about the event until the day of, I decided that if I was going to defeat this American sports hero, I'd need to pay the price with hard work and train like I'd never trained before.

That is to say, I'd swim in the pool of my building for thirty minutes every day for a week.

The first sign of trouble was that I couldn't complete two laps and could run faster in the water than I could swim. The second sign of trouble was losing to my friend Michelle, who is neither a shark in the water nor a killer whale, but an actress who has asthma and couldn't run a mile if a role in the latest Rob Schneider vehicle depended on it. The third sign of trouble was that I had no fucking clue how to swim properly and looked like I was drowning during my painful attempts to go from one end to the other. Or was that the first sign?

Obviously, just flailing around in the water was getting me nowhere, so back to the drawing board I went. Swimming is unlike, say, running, in that errors in technique with running can be overcome with stamina and will, both of which I have in spades. In swimming, on the other hand, poor technique makes it difficult to achieve even a level of basic competency and leads to a feeling of swimming in cement, or mud, or sadness. To combat this, I resolved to learn the form that won Davis the Olympic gold: freestyle, the fastest and most powerful of all of the strokes.

Thanks to the miracle of modern technology, this would be a cinch. During a weekend trip to Vegas before the event, I pulled up video of Olympic swimmers on the Internet. Every angle imaginable was available—underwater, in slow motion, underwater in slow motion, from the Hubble telescope, you name it. A better training manual could not have been provided. Every day I studied the freestyle technique and then applied it by swimming laps back and forth in the massive wave pool at Mandalay Bay. This, combined with countless cocktails and trips to the buffet, would be my recipe for success.

On Monday, the day of the race, I flew back to Los Angeles. It didn't matter that I was operating on no sleep; my high-tech training regimen, officially dubbed "The Science of Victory," would ensure a win. But as soon as I arrived at the Woollett Aquatics Center in Irvine, I wished I had stayed in Vegas, and no, not just because I was in Irvine. I wasn't intimidated being surrounded by America's greatest swimmers, who were there to compete in the U.S. Nationals; my training made me feel as if I was a peer. No, the big problem was the length of the pool. After dominating the enormous pool at Mandalay Bay, which had waves, no less, I had assumed I'd have no problem with distance.

How very wrong I was. An Olympic-size pool is startlingly long. It's 50 meters, which is roughly three times as long as your standard hotel pool. When I expressed my shock at the distance, Sara Hunninghake, who was there working the event, rolled her eyes and said, "You think that's a long way to go? There's a fifteen-hundred-meter race about to start that I'm sure you'd love. They're swimming for about fifteen consecutive minutes." I neither laughed nor smiled. Sara, I think, took this as her cue to bail me out by offering the use of the 25-yard sprint pool for our race. In what I interpreted as her hoping neither of us would be embarrassed by the race, she said: "There won't be anyone bothering us over there."

Actually, we were going to be bothered. A throng of reporters in attendance to cover the U.S. Nationals got wind of our race and made their way over to where we were setting up. This was fine by me, though. Switching to the smaller pool brought my confidence back to outrageously high levels, and it brought me great joy to think that reporters accustomed to watching the world's best swimmers would now get to see the technique I had worked so hard to perfect. It was like pouring your heart and soul into a low-budget movie and then having Ebert and The Other Guy give it two thumbs up the day after wrap. True, the yellow floaties on my arms weren't playing to great initial reviews, but once I explained they were just a ruse to get Davis to let his guard down, respect was earned/imagined.

When Davis arrived, he seemed the perfect foil: blond, blue eyed, and in top physical condition—just like William Zabka in *Back to School*. Well, he would have been the perfect foil, except he was way too nice. I was hoping he would be mean, arrogant, and snide, and provide further fuel for the engine of rage that propels my swimming. No matter, I wouldn't need this extra motivation. Davis, I learned, was in big trouble.

The past two weeks, while I was making myself better by the day in preparation for the race, Davis had not been sitting around as I had expected. As it turns out, he was also practicing, except, unlike me, he was perfecting getting worse! While I was intensely learning how to swim freestyle like the Olympic hero Davis, he was essentially learning how to swim like me, practicing the doggie-paddle with the extra weight of his kids on his back. This perfection of ruination—elbows locked against his torso, head above water, and kicks kept below the surface—would assure he was doing a true doggie paddle and put him at a huge disadvantage.

Tasting victory, or perhaps it was chlorine, I tossed the floaties aside and performed a mental checklist of the components I had used to perfect Davis's freestyle technique. Davis, wearing goggles and new Speedo swim pants, hopped in the water beside me after going through his stretching routine. As the crowd looked on, we waited for the starter to give us the sign.

Ready . . .

Set . . .

Go!

The wages of sin in Vegas took their toll more than I had imagined. Oh, and I still really sucked at swimming. All of the training I thought was fantastic was total garbage. I was flailing around like an epileptic, and people were laughing at me. At one point Davis, a prince amongst men, actually turned his head around while swimming his doggie-paddle lap and rooted me on. Davis clocked his 50-yard lap at 42.23 seconds, finishing about a quarter lap ahead of me. I did not finish, walking in the final 10 yards.

The laughing crowd called for blood, and a second handicap match was set. Now Davis could swim the freestyle, but he and I started at opposite ends of the sprint pool, the handicap being he had to do 50 yards up and back before I made it 25 yards.

This race proved even more disastrous and humiliating. Fatigue combined with zero talent and hubris added up to a fatal mix of total failure, and I coughed up what was, with 5 yards to go, a certain victory for me.

Any hopes for gleaning analysis from the postmatch talk quickly dissipated as the proceedings turned into a roast at my expense. Phrases like "tried your hardest," "less than ideal," and "absolutely pitiful" were tossed around with cackling laughter. Some observers were overheard saying that the only question was whether Davis would have enough time after finishing his lap to swim over to my lane and rescue me from drowning.

Piling on, Sara said: "It would have been nice to see at least an average swimmer hop in the pool to give Josh a challenge." Please be aware that she considers herself an "average" swimmer even though she competed in high school and on summer league swim teams.

I tried to get the swimming snobs to put Davis's time in perspective

Doggie style.

for me. His 42.23 seconds in the 50-yard doggie-paddle seemed fast to me, but apparently it'd be a very slow time for freestyle. "Even the worst high school girls I've ever coached weren't this slow," said Jim Rusnak, the publications coordinator for USA Swimming. I could only assume that my time was on par with the worst embryos he had ever coached.

But keep in mind, swimming the doggie-paddle is a difficult task. "I was huffing and puffing," Davis told me. He added, "It's so much easier to recover over the water [as in the freestyle]. When everything's gotta stay under the water, all muscles are working. I had to rely on my kick a lot so my legs *and* arms got really tired." Also, this was not the peak of Davis's doggie-stylings. Had I gone faster, he could have cranked it up another notch. Not only did he slow down to turn and yell words of encouragement, but he also took it easy on the turn and was going only "at about ninety,

The science of victory replaced by the art of sadness.

ninety-five percent," he said. "In a race where I was being pushed, I'd have hit the turn really hard and gone after it."

So, sure, I'm not that *strong* a swimmer, and a weekend in Vegas spent eating like a total pig, drinking heavily, and not sleeping didn't help the matter. But really, nothing short of death and reincarnation would have helped. The fact is that a doggie-paddling Davis would beat many competent swimmers. Okay, many swimmers. Okay, no one who has ever swum regularly.

But I found it hard to believe that Davis's time was really as bad as Jim Rusnak had said. To see how the "average" person would do, since no one seemed to think I met that standard, I later took a random sampling of ten friends, neighbors, and people from my gym. The only qualification was that they be in reasonable shape and hadn't swum regularly at any point in their lives. Well, I guess the "average swimmer" isn't even average; the manager of my gym finished at 40 seconds on the money, but no one else beat Davis's time.

Dave Sheets, Duquesne University's swimming coach, told me that Davis's doggie paddle was "very good for most people. You could take a marathon runner and if he doesn't have proper stroke technique, he's not going to go very fast."

Apparently Sara had a different view on the subject and wanted to prove her stuff to Josh Davis: "I think I could take you. If only I had a suit here."

Davis wasn't fooled. "She's all talk! She can get a suit, we're at a swim meet!"

Her bluff called, Sara backed down: "I will not take that chance!" Sadly, I'd be the only person Davis beat on this day.

HOW MANY TOUGH MEN COULD MIKE TYSON DEFEAT IN ONE NIGHT?

Mike Tyson became the undisputed heavyweight champion of the world with a vicious uppercut and a mean streak that terrorized his opponents. Between March 6, 1985, and February 11, 1990, he won thirty-seven consecutive bouts, all but four by KO or TKO. The young Tyson crushed everyone in his path; when challengers like Michael Spinks were touted as legitimate contenders, he would frequently demolish them in the first two rounds. Truly, everything he hit, he destroyed. During this time period he became a national icon and the star of *Mike Tyson's Punchout!!!*, arguably the greatest Nintendo game ever produced. There were no higher places for this modern-day Icarus (of punching) to fly (punch), and so he fell (went batshit insane). Unlike Icarus, who simply fell to earth, Tyson fell past earth and somewhere into outer space/hell/kookooville.

Okay, the metaphor was lost there for sure, but you get the picture.

Since his great run, Tyson went to jail, made a comeback, bit off an opponent's ear, had several run-ins with the law, got a giant tattoo on his face, went back to jail, declared bankruptcy, went to rehab, then hung up his gloves. Now in his forties, he raises pigeons in Arizona, like any lisping ex-felon man-child naturally would, sings "The Monster Mash" with Bobby Brown, and again fields offers to appear in things like jail. Also on his docket of late has been considering a role in a porno with Jenna Jameson (just to be perfectly clear, the "role" entails having sex on camera with Jameson), endorsing online gaming sites, and being a complete freak. It'd be hard to guess who he could defeat in the world of professional boxing, but judging by his most recent loss against journeyman Kevin McBride and the ensuing exhibition "World Tour" that never made it out of Ohio, it's safe to say he's fought his last meaningful fight.

It's hard to imagine now because of the disaster that was Tyson's second act, but he was so dominant early on that he spawned some of the greatest boxing debates of all time. Since no boxer of his era could even come close to matching him, the questions tried to gauge just how good he was: "How much would you have to be paid to get in the ring with Tyson for a round?" Answer: $20 million, and only if I could use a chainsaw. "Is Tyson the best boxer ever?" (no longer applicable). And most interesting of all, the debate that may or may not have inspired the Lou Gossett Jr. epic *Diggstown:* "How many tough men could Tyson beat in one night?" Twenty years later, this was the one question that remained unanswered.

Interestingly, we've seen a fight like this before, and not just in bad movies. On April 26, 1975, George Foreman, in his first match after the humbling "Rumble in the Jungle" loss to Muhammad Ali, fought five professional boxers one after the other in scheduled three-round exhibitions. The spectacle, called Foreman vs. The Five, was the brainchild of Don King and was designed to prove that Foreman deserved a rematch with Ali. The five journeymen fighters were experienced heavyweight professionals; one, Terry Daniels, had gone four rounds in a title fight with Joe Frazier, and another, Alonzo Johnson, had gone ten rounds with Ali. Still, the end result was not pretty for "The Five." They were all knocked out and lasted a total of twelve rounds. It wasn't pretty for Foreman, either: the fight was widely viewed as sad and in no way helped his standing in the boxing world.

Mike Tyson never fought more than one person in a night (unless you want to count the angel and the devil on his shoulders plus Robin Givens as "people"), but if, in his prime, George Foreman could beat five real fighters consecutively, then Lord have mercy what Tyson in his prime would do to amateurs. Where the toughest guy in your hometown gets tough by being in occasional scraps and pushing around people smaller than him, Tyson trained full time and ate, slept, and breathed boxing until he became a killing machine. It's quite certain that no untrained thug would have a chance head to head. The real question is how many ruffians it would take until fatigue and a schmoe with a lucky punch finally defeated him. My initial guess was something really scientific like "infinite," but in the interests of research, and seeing the opening for a great event, I went to the source: Iron Mike himself.

I approached Tyson with a real proposal, not just a hypothetical: He would fight the "10 toughest men in the world" in a pay-per-view event. Each tough would get a round, and any who could knock out Tyson would get a million dollars. Tyson was to get a substantially larger amount for each tough guy he knocked out, with a bonus for KO'ing all of them. Not quite the same as the proposed question, but age did need to be accounted for.

As I laid out the idea, a jovial and somewhat loopy Michael Gerard Tyson grinned from ear to ear as he ran it through his head. Finally, he gave me an answer.

"Ten guys? That's a lot, I'd get tired. Those guys are gonna come out swinging like they think they're gonna make their mark."

While his managers and I worked out particulars of the fight and how money would be distributed (the immediate delivery of a red Ferrari as a "show of good faith" before we even had a contract signed became a sticking point), Iron Mike bowed his head and went silent for a good minute.

Finally he looked up and said, "You want me to hurt people. I don't want to hurt nobody."

When I explained that I simply wanted him to fight for money, just as he had his entire career, Tyson became even more philosophical.

"What if I get hurt? Who's gonna care if I get hurt?"

If that was a concern, I said, we could use larger gloves or headgear. I then asked Mike if he thought he wouldn't be able to beat them.

Tyson laughed maniacally: "No, if I hit 'em, they'd be hurt! Those guys would get killed! I'd give 'em brain damage!"

In retrospect, going to the source would have helped more if I had brought a time machine or an anticrazy serum to inject him with, but there were some nuggets of information in the Tyson conversation that could clue us to the answer. Ultimately, Tyson, even in decline, thought he could get through ten tough guys if the money was right, but with the caveat that stamina issues and wear and tear might eventually cause him to fall to a bouncer from Detroit. Then again, Tyson once famously said, "My power is discombobulatingly devastating. I could feel his muscle tissues collapse under my force. It's ludicrous these mortals even attempt to enter my realm." So maybe he wasn't the greatest judge of his own abilities.

I needed to talk to someone who knew the boxing game and trained top fighters. My quest led me to "Uncle" Al Bonanni, the head talent scout for Don King Productions, who has trained or co-trained nine world champions. I asked him what approach he would take to defeat a top heavyweight if given a group of tough guys.

"Number one, I wouldn't do it."

Fair enough.

"So, I would absolutely not do it. Please put that in there."

Duly noted. Al would not do this.

"And if I was forced to do it for whatever reason—I would absolutely have to be forced to do it; no amount of money in the world would make me want to do it. But let's say in a fictional sense, and not me, I think that that trainer should, number one, have his head examined. After the examination, this fictitious trainer should tell his fighters to basically move around the ring and try to avoid punches for as long as they could. And tell them that once they get hit and get hurt, go down and stay down."

How about the heavyweight? What kind of training would he receive?

"Of course I would tell my heavyweight not to really hurt any of them."

Al, this is no fun.

"Some of the guys could literally be killed. Broken noses, eye injuries, cuts, knocked unconscious, would be minimal. Somebody could die. . . . I don't know any commission that would approve this. It would have to be on a barge or someplace where it's almost like a street fight, or in some country that didn't have an athletic commission. It would be very dangerous, even for the fighter, because the guy could run across the ring and head butt him.

"Again, I would like to stress that I would not do this."

That's it, we need a new trainer.

What about Teddy Atlas? Atlas, who currently spends his time with the Dr. Theodore Atlas Foundation and as a commentator for ESPN, was once a top trainer in the business. He also has a unique perspective on this question because under Cus D'Amato he helped train an up-and-coming Mike Tyson.

It turns out Atlas has had a lot of experience with these "tough guys." When he worked for D'Amato, bruisers would frequently come to the gym wanting to take on one of Cus's fighters. "Just because they may have knocked out a couple of guys on a bar stool and a couple of guys out in the street they thought they could get in the ring with a professional fighter," he said. They were living in a fantasy world, according to Atlas. "Cus usually wouldn't do it because it would be very dangerous for the 'tough' guys."

But when a fight did happen?

"The first thing you find out about these 'tough guys' is they're not so tough. As far as the physical side of it, of course they have no chance. Most of them couldn't even take a professional jab. But the mental and emotional side is even worse."

Teddy went on to say that when they get in the ring against a real boxer, the roughnecks "completely fall apart" and "find themselves in a very, very scary place, and really a place that they can't handle."

Atlas pointed out that street fighting lasts only a moment and is all about anger, adrenaline, and maybe a quick punch or two. And in a street fight, there are all sorts of "outs." If things get bad, someone is always going to jump in and break it up. But boxing is "a discipline" and "there's no way out when they're in that ring." That's why most tough guys, if they ever face a real boxer, say *"No mas"* very quickly. Teddy remembered the time that Renaldo Snipes, who once knocked down Larry Holmes in a heavyweight title fight, went in the ring against a local thug who had knocked out countless street opponents and was known as the "ultimate tough guy." The guy was so spooked he quit after one round, and Snipes hadn't even thrown a punch. This falls right in line with Atlas's take on the proposed fight: "A top heavyweight would not only dismantle any tough guy but he could probably do it without throwing a punch."

But what if a pro fighter had to face a legion of "tough guys"? Wouldn't he have a hard time dealing with fatigue and the mental drain of seeing a completely fresh guy step into the ring as soon as he knocked someone out?

"If you go on and on and on, anything is possible. A guy could deteriorate if anything went on long enough. But I don't know if a good-quality fighter would exert enough to even wear down."

You mean in a given night any top heavyweight could go through as many toughs as he wanted?

"Oh yeah."

So my original guess of "infinite" wasn't that crazy after all. Early in his career, Mike Tyson said, "Without discipline, no matter how good you are, you are nothing! One day . . . you're going to meet a tough guy who takes your best shot. He'll keep coming because he's tough. Don't get discouraged. That's when the discipline comes in." That kind of mental fortitude was obviously lacking from the later stages of Tyson's career, but it would have allowed a young Iron Mike to run through a virtually endless procession of rowdies in a single night.

And if such a spectacle were to take place, by what possible rational justification would it happen? Well, money for one, as my meeting with Tyson showed. Even with an aging, mental, recently incarcerated Kid Dynamite, the event would be a huge draw, as anything with Tyson is still a major event. To quote our favorite former "Baddest Man on the Planet": "I can sell out Madison Square Garden masturbating."

If things keep going in the wrong direction, Mike, it may just come to that yet.

WOULD A MAJOR LEAGUE BATTING CHAMPION DOMINATE IN WIFFLE BALL?

Wiffle ball is like fight club."

Yes, except with Wiffle balls and no fighting, but the point Tom Lynch, a sports marketing consultant who has played in leagues all over the country, is trying to make is that there are some parallels in the underground, word-of-mouth nature of both. There are hundreds of Wiffle ball communities throughout the country, filled with thousands of men who do battle against one another every weekend with plastic bats and plastic balls.

The elite of the Wiffle community is an organization called Fast Plastic. With more than 300 teams, 1,500-plus players, and 18 locations spread across the country, Fast Plastic boasts a level of organization above and beyond anything you could ever possibly imagine for this backyard game, and it's just about the greatest thing ever for someone who loves Wiffle ball. Many of its regions even have minor leagues. The organization's website is so in-depth that it includes player transactions, available free agents, upcoming prospects, and potential draftees. The players range in ability from ex–minor leaguers to guys who can't tie their own shoes, but they all have one thing in common: their baseball days have passed.

Now, let's say a free agent became available in the Fast Plastic league who, instead of spending his time daydreaming about playing Wiffle ball on the weekend, was talented enough to be paid millions of dollars to hit a baseball in front of a nation of adoring fans. And let's say this wasn't just any professional baseball player, but the National League batting champion.

For one day, Freddy Sanchez of the Pittsburgh Pirates, who hit .344 and won the 2006 batting title, was going to face the best of the best that the world of Wiffle ball had to offer.

I headed out to a baseball field in Chandler, Arizona, where I met Jim Balian, who was dressed in his Arizona Vipers uniform. The thirty-one-year-old Balian, when not a senior systems analyst and part-time professor, is one of the best Wiffle ball players in the world—a two-time Wiffle Ball National Champion and MVP. Joining him was teammate and protégé Randy Dalbey, a 6'6", twenty-one-year-old former all-state basketball player; Tom Raven, who played baseball at Azusa Pacific University and has a swing as pretty as Manny Ramirez's; and Kyle Ramsey, one of the best pitchers in all of Wiffle ball. It only took watching them for a minute to see that, unlike many of their major league counterparts, they were real athletes.

Freddy arrived and was about as nice and normal as could be. Instead of spitting on us or demanding no one look him in the eye, he signed autographs for fans and made friendly small talk. It was no way for a professional athlete to act.

We gave Sanchez some warm-ups to get accustomed to the plastic Wiffle ball bat, which isn't the yellow sticklike thing that you grew up using (I really hope you didn't use the big fat red bat). While extremely light, the bats the hard cores use have the dimensions of real baseball bats—perfect for the batting champ. I was becoming concerned that the first inning would never end.

Once we set up the Wiffle ball field in right field, we were ready to start. The rules would be thus: Freddy would get the regulation six innings, three outs an inning, and would play only offense. Since he was an army of one, ghost runners would be used on the base paths as the official rules of Wiffle ball specify. He'd be facing a pitcher throwing from a mound 45 feet away (instead of 60 feet 6 inches, as in major league baseball); three strikes, he'd be out; four balls would be a walk; any fair ball that landed past the infield line would be a single; a double would be when the ball rolled to the fence or hit the fence on the fly but was caught before touching the ground; a triple would be a ball that hit the fence and then the ground; if he hit a ball over the fence, it'd be a homer; and the game would be declared a forfeit if, before the six innings were completed, his mom called him home for dinner.

Play ball.

Balian opened on the mound for the Wifflers.

Holy shit.

As far as Wiffle ball, or any other kind of pitching, is concerned, his pitches were as nasty as nasty gets. Balian has been clocked throwing a Wiffle ball 87 miles per hour, which from 45 feet away is the equivalent of 117 miles per hour in baseball. Using prescuffed balls (which Wiffle ball allows), Jim was throwing pitches that looked like they were done with CGI effects: a drop ball that completely fell off the table, a riser that started an inch off the ground and ended up over the batter's head, and a slider that broke 4 feet.

But he was wild early. Freddy walked to open the game and was fouling off pitches and making Balian work. Sanchez went down with three strikeouts in the first inning but I was sure the levee would break.

By the third inning Freddy was no longer even remotely close to getting a hit. A guy who could pull a 102-mile-per-hour fastball from Joel Zumaya or hit a Pedro curve on a line was missing pitches not by inches but by feet. The foul tips were a thing of the past. Balian's drop ball was untouchable at this point.

Then, the magic happened. After two strikeouts and two walks, Balian left a drop up in the zone and Freddy pounded it to the wall for a double, driving in a ghost runner.

But that was the end of the fun for the batting champ. Balian regained immediate control and polished off the inning with a series of pitches so devastating that two thousand miles away, Chuck Tanner felt a disturbance in the Force.

Break time. Who brought the Sunny-D?

While Freddy licked his wounds, I spoke with Balian about why Sanchez hadn't shown any improvement yet, and why, with the exception of his one hit, he actually seemed to be getting worse.

"I'll analyze the hitter," he said. "If I notice he's even fouling them off better on a certain pitch, I'll stay away from that entirely. You start to develop an understanding of what certain hitters can hit. There's so many pitches you can throw, you need to just stay away from the hitter's strength."

We resumed play with Dalbey on the mound. His stuff was kind of like Balian Light but it was still goodnight nurse for Freddy. K, K, K. The game took on a monotonous air of inevitability at this point. K, K, K. The box score was starting to look like it was done by David Duke.

For the final inning Kyle Ramsey took the mound. Freddy continued taking hard cuts and going after pitches with his trademark intensity, but the results were the same: K, K, K. After an awkward silence, someone said the game was over.

Freddy wins 1–0!

Here's the National League batting champion's box score:

1–19 (.053 average)
18 Ks
4 walks
1 hit by pitch
1 run scored
1 RBI
1 double

For you sabermetric types, that adds up to an Erstadesque VORP of POO.

To understand how Freddy ended up looking like your typical Pittsburgh Pirate, I asked him to compare hitting a Wiffle ball to a baseball.

"This is a lot harder. This is way harder."

How much of the problem was the speed of the pitches and how much was the movement?

"It's a combination, but mainly the movement. I had balls going in, coming away, going up. Eighty-five to ninety percent of it is the movement."

How would the movement compare to, say, a Barry Zito curveball?

"Oh, there's no comparison. I mean, at least with the movement up there [in the majors] you can see it, and you have time to do something with it. With this, I have no time to do anything. The distance isn't that big of a deal; it's just that it's coming in hot and has a lot more movement than what I'm used to."

Well, Freddy does play in the NL Central, so maybe that wasn't as meaningful as it sounded. But later, all-star catcher Paul Lo

Duca confirmed that this is indeed a very difficult adjustment to make, even for a major league hitter in a real division. Lo Duca was the man to talk to because he is a master of both forms; on the back of his rookie card under "Major Accomplishments" he listed making the semifinals in the Wiffle Ball World Series.

Paul wasn't surprised that Sanchez flailed at the Wifflers' offerings. He said it was just like the time he faced softball pitcher Jennie Finch and struck out on four pitches. The real problem was that Finch's pitches moved in ways that major league batters never see—exactly the problem that Freddy had when he was whiffing like Rob Deer. And Freddy had the added challenge of using a bat that was a pound lighter than what he's accustomed to. "Most major leaguers get so used to their stick that they can tell you if it's an ounce off," Paul said. "It took me a year to get used to a wooden bat after coming out of college and using aluminum." If Lo Duca is to be believed, Freddy should have stayed home and tried to calculate pi to the sixty-fifth digit.

But as someone who has hit both a baseball and a Wiffle ball with great success, he says it's all just a matter of adjustment. "We face Randy Johnson and don't strike out every time. . . . I guarantee if you give Freddy a week or a week and a half of swinging that bat, he'd start rocking those guys."

While the idea of Freddy "rocking" Balian and his mates anytime soon might be pushing it, we may see if Lo Duca's prediction was on the money sooner than expected. When I asked Sanchez whether there was anything to be learned from playing Wiffle ball (a question I am quite certain will never be posed to anyone for any reason ever again), he said, "I'd like to get in one of these leagues in the off-season. Once you'd get into the baseball season, the ball would look like a freakin' beachball coming at you. This is definitely good for hand-eye coordination and this is definitely the hardest thing to hit. No doubt about it."

Balian came over and gave Freddy a flyer for the upcoming tournament.

"Awesome. Me, J-Bay, and Grabow are in." (Yes, even Pittsburgh Pirates have cool-guy nicknames; J-Bay is left fielder Jason Bay. Grabow is relief pitcher John Grabow, or G-Bow in Linda Cohn parlance.)

Freddy left, and just as your mother taught you, only after people leave should you start to talk badly about them. But he was such a good guy that there really wasn't anything bad to say besides he stunk at Wiffle ball. Unlike what many people would have done in his shoes, he kept trying hard and didn't make any snide remarks like "The sting of striking out in Wiffle ball is lessened by thoughts of the multimillion-dollar contract I'm preparing to sign." Seeing what a decent guy he was gave me some insight into how he didn't go on a killing spree after starting the season that he led the league in hitting on the bench behind Smilin' Joe Randa.

So the day may have been a tough one for Freddy, but maybe he'll redeem himself if J-Bay and Grabow don't bail on him. But even if he never again enters the den of (Arizona) vipers that is competitive Wiffle ball, he can rest easy knowing that he picked the right ball to be able to hit.

HOW EASY IS IT FOR PRO ATHLETES TO GET LAID? AND HOW EASY IS IT FOR A GROUPIE TO BAG A PRO ATHLETE?

We all grow up with dreams. Some of us want to be astronauts, some want to be doctors or lawyers, some want to be president. And some grow up wanting to bone LeBron James. This was Amanda Mitts's dream, or rather, the one that was assigned to her for a night on the town in Cleveland as we set out to explore the wild world of NBA nightlife.

People with dreams of having sex with pro athletes are called groupies, and they are as much a part of the professional sports landscape as herpes. To find out more about the groupie life, I recruited Amanda Mitts, a twenty-two-year-old student at the University of Toronto, to go undercover and operate as one. Not only would she be trying to screw for sport to see how simple it is for a groupie to bag a pro athlete, but she would also be operating as an investigative journalist to gather as much real information as possible.

Cute, outgoing, and a former model in Los Angeles, Amanda had her own intimate experience with the world of groupiedom, advancing from dating noncelebrities like myself to stars as big as

Andy Spade, brother of *Just Keep Shootin' 'Em*'s David, and international action hero Jean-Claude Van Damme. Essentially, she was like a groupie minor leaguer trying to make her jump to the bigs. Isn't that right, Amanda?

"Who is this LaRon guy again? He plays basketball or something? I'm not really going to have to sleep with one of these guys, right?"

We arrived in Cleveland on a Sunday night for the Tuesday-night game between the Cleveland Cavaliers and the Grizzlies of Memphis. After interviewing cabbies, bartenders, and doormen, it was clear: to nail a pro athlete, Amanda had to think like a pro athlete. So she did the first thing any respectable pro athlete would—she went to a strip club. We hit Christies, the "phattest strip club in Cleveland" (*Fodor's 2006*), pretended we knew what we were doing by ordering a bottle of champagne, and went to work. As I investigated how a lap dance could be worth $400, Amanda asked the girls where to go to get some NBA dongtang.

One of these girls is a groupie.

The responses were as varied as the stretch marks on the harlots' bodies. Ultimately, the consensus was to either go to a nightclub in the Flats that stayed open until 5 A.M., swing by a bar where a party for *Flavor of Love* star "Bootz" was being held, or check out a restaurant that the Cavs and visiting NBA players were known to frequent.

We left and hit all of the spots, but had no luck . . . unless *luck* is defined as almost being raped and killed at the nightclub. (This may not need clarifying, but the "killed" refers to me, the "raped" to her.) The next day it was more of the same—more drinking, more hunting, nothing. The more we searched, the more ridiculous the idea seemed that we were just going to bump into LeBron at some dopey Cleveland club.

But when game day arrived we had renewed hope, since it's common knowledge that groupies use the games as their first contact point in the battle for athletes' sperm. The list of players who have found tramps in the stands during games is extensive and even includes pimp master supreme Matt Bullard. As "One Shining Moment" played in the background, or rather, as I whistled it, Amanda made her way into the arena primed for action, wearing the sluttiest groupie getup imaginable.

"This must be like your Super Bowl," I said. "What are you feeling right now?"

"Discomfort. These pants you made me wear are riding up the crack of my ass. Do you think it's really necessary for me to dress like this?"

Per the game plan, Amanda first went to the front-row seats next to the home bench to make googly eyes. Unfortunately, because our real tickets were next to Uecker and Spuds McKenzie, she kept getting kicked back upstairs. Then, by the tunnels where the players come in and out, she attempted to set up something under the pretense of getting an autograph. Again, security was on to her game, or lack thereof, and tossed her. Frustration was starting to mount, which would have been fine if there was a Cavs player by the name of Antonio Frustration, but in this case we were just about done.

Prepared to give up, after the game we went to the restaurant that had been barren the previous night to at least get a good meal before canvassing the hotel lobbies late at night. The place was packed and was as close to the Century Club as Cleveland was going to get. Just what we were looking for. What was going on, I slyly asked the hostess, Stacey.*

"Everyone comes in here after the games because this is where all the Cavs come."

Victory!

"But what they don't realize is that they have a road game tomorrow so they're already out of town. None of these people would be here if they knew the Cavs weren't coming in."

Defeat.

Amanda and I got a table, wolfed down steaks, and drowned our sorrows. As I was preparing my concession speech, Stacey walked by and asked us how we were doing. Unprompted, she started telling us tales of how wild the bar got on nights the Cavs were there. She said there was such a groupie frenzy that they had to rope off the entire dining area and hire police to keep hussies from sneaking to the other side. One time, a girl literally crawled under the rope just to try to get to one of the players.

Maybe I had ingested too much krunk juice by this point, but I finally opened up and let Stacey in on our mission. After some convincing, and a second look at Amanda's ridiculous getup, she believed us. With the Cavs out of town and no real hope of finding

---

* Some names in this chapter have been changed to protect people's privacy.

LeBron, I let Stacey know that I'd be willing to give $200 to anyone who could at the very least explain how the groupie scene works. She brought over a man by the name of Julius, who didn't want or need the money, but was happy to talk. As one of the top party promoters in Cleveland, Julius had seen everything and hung out with almost every big-name athlete to come through town in the past twenty years.

My first question was whether a player like LeBron could get a girl home just by pulling an "I'm Keith Hernandez."

"Could he? Yeah, but it just doesn't work that way," said Julius. "What you don't understand is the male groupies. The male groupies are as big a part of it as the female groupies. The male groupies are these guys that are willing to lower their self-esteem and do whatever the player says as long as it gets him in with them. They get in all kinds of ways, by laughing way too hard at a joke everyone knows isn't funny, running errands, all kinds of ways. They ain't the same as posse members. They're like lackeys, yes-men for the players. They're the ones going and picking up the girls for the player. They're key to the whole operation, so you need good ones."

This was surprising to me. I was under the impression groupies just chased these guys down. Why would the players need an intermediary?

"I'd say it's about fifty-fifty where the girls are coming up to them and they're approaching the girls. See, something people don't realize is these guys get turned down all the time. All the time. And harsh too. But most of the time the male groupie will go over and tell the girl who they are and invite them over. These dudes are too proud and their egos are too fragile to go up and get turned down like a man. They come to a nice restaurant like this and they'll send their male groupie over to the table and say, 'So and so would like to invite you over for a bottle of champagne.'

"But not all the guys can pull that off at a place like this. A guy like [scrub for the Cavs] won't be able to go to the hot spot and pull any girl. He has to go to different kinds of places. He's gotta go to the second-best strip club in town or a crowded club that the bigger players don't go to because they would get swarmed in and try to do some work."

This was a different dynamic from what Amanda had seen with the pro hockey team in her hometown of Ottawa.

"In Ottawa, just being a Senator is enough. It doesn't matter if you're Daniel Alfredsson or the worst player on the team. It's a small town and girls don't meet a lot of celebs. Their boyfriends are truck drivers or bouncers and all these puck bunnies see screwing a Senator as their ticket to money and a way to impress their friends."

Julius explained that Cleveland, while a shithole, is not the shithole that Ottawa is.

"Right, but you go to a bigger city, and there are more options. Even a city like Cleveland has three sports teams and some celebrities, so your level of fame makes a difference. Just being the twelfth man on the Cavs isn't enough, because the girls have more options."

But even being a scrub on the Cavs makes macking relatively easy compared to how most people have it. "The worst player on the Cavs is still going to get laid any night of the week by something decent. Now, unless they're way on top of the ladder, they ain't always gonna get what they want when they go out, but they're gonna get something. They might not get their number one choice at a club, but they're gonna get something in their top three or four."

Sometimes lower-level players can even use their teammates' star power to get women. And sometimes, that star power is so great it gets the lower-level teammate *and* the lower-level teammate's male groupies laid. "See, the other thing you don't get is that there's levels. The highest level I ever saw was MJ, Rodman, Pippen, and the Bulls. When they'd come into town, there'd be girls packing the lobby of the Ritz-Carlton just to try to get with them. And fine girls. It was like rock stars. My friend [a player on the team] was getting some of that too just from being on the team. So [that friend] sends one of his male groupies down to pick one out, and the male groupie would say, 'Yeah, I'll get you up to be with [a star player], but you gotta do me and [the lower-level player] too.' And the girl'll do it. They'll do anything."

Speaking of a girl who was willing to do anything, I told Julius about Amanda's problems scoring at the game.

Turning to Amanda, he said, "See, if you came to the game with me, that would have been the easiest thing in the world. I've got tickets right behind the Cavs' bench. You'd just stand there and look pretty, make eye contact, and *bam,* it's over. They'd motion to one of their male groupies to come and get your contact info. Happens all the time."

We sat and talked to Julius for two hours, fascinated by the subculture although a little down that we didn't see it firsthand. But as luck would have it, hostess Stacey came over and pointed out a prominent member of the Cleveland Browns (if there is such a thing) at the bar. I instructed Amanda to go over and do her thing. As a girl who had never been in the position of having to approach a guy, she immediately started panicking.

"What do I do? How am I supposed to do this? I'm not going to walk up to him and just tell him 'Let's screw' or something. I don't even want to do this."

Julius calmed her down.

"You're fine so it's gonna be real easy. Just go over there, sit down, and it'll all work itself out. He'll notice you and send one of his boys over."

Amanda took a swig of her drink and made the leap, walking over and having a seat at the bar. Julius and I kept talking. With Amanda gone, he opened up. I asked him more about the actual process.

"It's some caveman shit. It's no class. It's like, 'You know who I am?' The dudes are just looking to get their dick sucked. They're not trying to get girls pregnant or rape suits or any of that shit. . . . They'll leave the bar or club or restaurant, say 'Follow me,' and the girl will drive to their house. They never go to the girl's place because it feels like a setup. So once they get there, it's a little small talk, but if it doesn't happen in like twenty, thirty minutes, then they're just like, 'Is this happening or what?' And if it doesn't, they send the girl packing and go to plan B or C, because the whole time they're talking to the girl at their house, their cell is blowin' up with calls from all sorts of hos or from one of their boys with all kinds of ass lined up."

What some players don't realize, though, is that it comes to a screeching halt the moment they're out of the limelight. "Once these guys retire, they're just like you and me. All of that shit goes away. I'll be playing Madden online with one of my boys who used to be a big deal and now his wife's like, 'You do the laundry yet?' and my boy'll be like 'Sorry, honey, I'll take care of it later.' And I'll laugh and laugh and be like 'Damn, you're like a bitch now!' And my boy'll be like 'Julius, you don't understand, it ain't like how it used to be.' "

Stacey walked by and gave an excited thumbs-up.

Julius beamed ear to ear. "See, didn't I tell you guys this was going to be easy?"

With Amanda making progress, I asked what percentage of athletes Julius had seen who were married or in relationships.

"Pretty much all of them," he said. Later I read that the player Amanda was talking to at the bar was married.

Do the wives and girlfriends know what goes on?

"Yeah. They let it slide as long as it's not in their face. And even if it is, they still let it slide really."

Finally, Amanda came back to the table. Roughly an hour had passed since her departure. A Pulitzer awaits:

"I can't believe you made me do that. Why would any girl lower herself like that?"

Okay, okay, Mother Superior . . . how easy was it?

"I sat down at the bar and a table of black guys sent over some champagne. Then one of them came up and started asking me a million questions, mostly about why I was there and if I was with anyone. I was friendly and eventually I asked what he did. He told me he was a computer programmer, but when I told him where I was from, he said, 'Where's Canada?' So I think that was probably a lie. Most computer programmers have heard of Canada and don't dress like rappers."

Julius laughed. "That's the male groupie. I told you that's exactly the way it would play out, didn't I?"

Amanda continued relaying her brush with fame. "I went to the bathroom and when I came back to the bar I noticed one of the other guys from the table talking to a white guy. They were looking over and obviously talking about me. I looked over and smiled. They both came over. The white guy said, 'He thinks because I own the place I know all the pretty girls.' He said he was the owner, and made a big deal out of letting me know who [the Browns player] was, but almost immediately after the introduction he left. Then [the Browns player] and I started talking. He was standing for the first few minutes, then I invited him to sit down. He was very sweet and very shy. Eventually he asked me for my number and I said I'd take his. He said he was big on text messaging and he asked me to send him a text message right away, which I did. Then the hostess came by and pumped him up some more.

She brought up that he was a big-time football player again since I guess when the owner came over I mentioned I didn't know anything about football. She almost ruined it by bringing that up because he was impressed that I didn't know who he was."

Julius strongly disagreed. "If the girl is playing all coy or isn't impressed by them, typically they'll just move on. They want the easiest thing they can find. They're not lookin' for a challenge. Some of these girls are unbelievable. They know all the stats, everything about the players. And that's what the guys are looking for. He was just playing a role. Trust me, he would have been happier if you knew who he was."

"Well, either way," Amanda went on, "the hostess left and [the Browns player] started putting the pressure on. He said he had to leave because he had to work early the next day and that he'd love it if I came along. I passed. We talked for a few minutes before he left. I noticed he left with that same first guy I had spoken to that was the computer programmer."

From Amanda's description of the events, it appears the "computer programmer" was, as Julius suggested, the male groupie doing the advance work. Once he established who Amanda was (a groupie) and that she was there alone, the restaurant owner brought the player over to make the introduction.

This system has three obvious benefits for the athlete:

1. It spares the player from risking his ego in making an approach.
2. The girl may be impressed by the owner coming over.
3. It confirms the athlete is who he says.

All of which facilitates the player's getting laid. Basically, this restaurant is the most awesome place in the world to go for a womanizing pro athlete. As long as the players get laid at the restaurant, they keep coming back. And as long as they keep coming back, girls keep coming back. And as long as the players and the girls keep coming, the place will always be packed with rich guys who are going to spend money to try to get in on the action. To wit, the hostess and owner were also making introductions for a sketchy guy who had his Rolls parked right out in front of the place and was buying high-priced champagne by the gallon.

I asked Amanda why she hadn't fulfilled her destiny. Certainly a Cleveland Brown would be a step up from the pseudocelebrities she's dated.

"You should just be happy I did this much. That's pretty sad if these girls think it means they're going to be respected from this. How is this fun for girls? What are they hoping to get out of it? I mean, I guess if one of these guys knocked you up, you could squeeze him for money, but to just go around like a cum-dumpster, following guys home and giving them blow jobs? What's the point? Why not just go find some rich banker?"

Ah, a real classy lady. How'd I ever let her go? I disputed her claims of innocence and tested Julius's theory about "levels" by asking what would happen if it wasn't a Cleveland Brown but Michael Jordan who approached her.

"If Jordan came up to me, if he wanted to fly to Vegas, I'd be like 'Hell yeah!' Or if he wanted to go on a date the next day, I might be cool with something like that. Look, I went on 'dates' with you that were us lying around getting drunk and watching *Mr. Show* reruns, so do you really think that if Michael Jordan came up to me and said we were flying to Vegas, I wouldn't go? But if it was like the kind of thing where he just wanted me to go in his limo and blow him, I couldn't see the point in that. You know, when I was in L.A. I'd have famous guys coming up and trying to screw me all the time. But unless I really liked them, I wouldn't even go on a date. I'm not going to sleep with a celebrity just to have a story to tell to my girlfriends."

Julius said that's where Amanda departed from the more dedicated groupies, who aren't just looking for a "rich banker": "These girls are just trying to get with whoever they think is cool to impress their friends. So why not pick a guy who's rich *and* famous? I've been around a lot of pro athletes, celebrities, big business people, you name it. And because the women they run with are star-fuckers to begin with, they all end up preying on each other's girls. I've seen musicians steal girls from businessmen and athletes fuck wives of musicians. The one thing that's consistent is if you're not high up on that ladder and someone who your girl's friends are going to be impressed by is around, you always have to worry."

So the lesson is: life sucks unless you're famous; never get married; and cry yourself to sleep every night at the state of the world. With that uplifting message, we thanked Julius and went on our way. As we were walking out, Amanda checked her phone for text messages. There were five waiting for her from her new friend. Maybe she had finally found true love.

Hey it's was great to meet u, u r a beautiful woman

if I come to Toronto we will have to meet up

Thank u we will hang out again

I'll make sure we meet again

Or u can cum over now ☺

WHAT KIND OF HANDICAP WOULD IT TAKE TO BEAT AN OLYMPIC SPRINTER?

I n one of our first conversations, my editor, Jed Donahue, told me he had a question he'd been waiting ten years to answer. It was an argument he had been carrying on with friends since college, but the idea seemed so ridiculous that they never thought the debate could be settled.

"In the summer of 1996," Jed said, "I was watching the Olympics with my college roommates and we were all amazed by Michael Johnson, the sprinter who wore the gold shoes and dominated in the 200 and 400 meters. So I asked my friends, 'How much of a head start do you think I'd need to beat Johnson?' "

It should probably be noted here that Jed would come in third in a race with a pregnant woman.*

Jed and his roommates couldn't stop arguing about the question. The debate eventually expanded to include their whole circle of friends and evolved: *What if the Olympian wore a parachute on his back? What if he ran in combat boots?* A few years later, on his

---

* Fear not, this is the only time a joke will be borrowed from Tommy Lasorda.

way to catch a flight with some friends, Jed blurted out, "Wait, what if I was allowed to run on an airport moving sidewalk?" From that magical point forward the debate focused on how much the moving sidewalk would affect the length of the head start Jed would need.

Sure, they could have gotten a rough estimate simply by clocking Jed in a sprint and then doing the math to figure out the cushion he'd need. But no one could agree on how the variables of adrenaline, intimidation, and effort would affect the competitors. Some thought these factors would improve Jed's time, others thought they'd hurt his chances, while a third contingent thought he'd simply shit his pants. No, to settle the debate definitively, Jed and his friends needed a real live Olympic sprinter. In other words, the whole scenario had to live in the realm of fantasy.

Until now.

Being the closest thing to the Ricardo Montalban of ridiculous debates about sports, I went to work. With Michael Johnson no longer racing competitively, I came up with a wish list of possible sprinters, and thanks to the help of Jill Geer of USA Track and Field and Emanuel Hudson of HSI Sports Management, I managed to get the #1 name on that list: Maurice Greene. The one-time world record holder in the 100 meters, Greene has won two Olympic gold medals and three World Championships. Respectively, that's one, two, and three more than Donahue.

The next step was to find a moving sidewalk. After scouring malls, casinos, and transit systems all over our great land, I secured permission to stage this freak show—also known as the Battle of the Century—at Los Angeles International Airport. The only time we could get an empty terminal would be at 1 A.M., but Maurice was a trouper and agreed. Everything was coming up Milhouse.

When I called him, Jed couldn't believe it. He immediately e-mailed the good news to the original debaters. Of the wide variety of responses, the best, and most disturbing, came from his friend Brian: "If not for the birth of my son, this would be the most exciting event of my life in the past five years."

Another e-mail came from Jed's friend Mike, who did some hard math to try to figure out, now that this nonsensical debate was becoming a reality, how big of a lead would be appropriate for the 100-meter race. Mike assumed that, given the level of competition, the Olympian wouldn't be running all out and Greene would clock in at about 12 seconds—a far cry from Mo's personal best of 9.79, the former world record. Mike's research (it clearly wasn't a busy day at the office) also revealed that the moving sidewalk would be running at about 2 feet per second, which is not a huge boost. The big variable in this equation was how quickly Jed would be running.

Why was this such a big variable? Because Jed had never run a 100-meter dash in his entire life. "While I know people have referred to you as 'explosive,'" Mike wrote, "I don't think it was in reference to your speed off the mark. And my guess is you will slow down a little toward the end. You may need to stop for a breath. You may need a beer. I'm not sure."

Jed hit the local track over the weekend for "training." His best time came in at 15.76 seconds—*61 percent slower* than Mo's best. Jed had turned the 100 meters from a sprint into a marathon. His practice report was even less encouraging than his time. "The first lesson here is that I am in awful shape. I am so incredibly sore right now it's not even funny. My hamstrings couldn't be any tighter, and I'm hobbling around like an old man." All of this was depressing, for sure, but it did help fill in the calculations in this absurd equation. Ultimately, the consortium of debaters decided that, if a cartoon jet pack couldn't be provided, 35 meters should be the head start.

On the day of the battle, Jed hopped on a flight to L.A. and met

We all just got along.

me at the airport. We discussed strategy (read: me asking Jed to be careful not to die), and just before 1 A.M., Maurice Greene strutted into LAX, looking like a champ—in top physical condition and adorned head to toe in sponsored track gear. Mo seemed a little apprehensive, as if this were an elaborate prank . . . which was understandable, given that Jed was not in a Lycra running suit but a Schaefer Beer T-shirt. After exchanging pleasantries with us, Mo curiously looked Jed up and down, paused for a second, and said, "So, you work out every day?"

Once Mo warmed up and Jed got a feel for running on and off the moving sidewalk—a transition that proved surprisingly smooth; there would be no limb severings for the local paper on this day—we were ready to settle this once and for all. Only one hitch: Jed's 35-meter head start was nixed by the great Greene. After some unexpectedly intense negotiations with Mo, it was agreed that Jed would have to make do with a mere 31-meter head start. Of the 69 meters Jed would be running, about half—35 meters—would be on the moving sidewalk.

An airport security guard was there to officiate the start. Jed and Maurice got into their stances. A sense of excitement was in the air. It was just like the sprinting events at the Olympics, except a white man had a chance to win.

And then they were off.

Jed was flying (in the same way an Air Congo plane "can" fly), and when he landed perfectly on the moving sidewalk, Maurice was so far behind that my first thought was a panicky, "Man, we gave Jed way too big of an edge. He's going to win easily." But then Mo began closing that huge gap very, very quickly. Even with the moving walkway, there was such a difference in their speeds that it looked a bit like Herman Munster being chased down by the Flash.

In the last 10 meters the Kansas City Comet (not Jed) made up ground at a remarkable pace, and the two competitors reached the tape at what appeared to be the exact same moment. A photo finish! After several reviews of the video footage, we determined that, to sanity's horror, Jed had defeated Olympic gold medalist Maurice Greene, by a nose.

As I was trying to figure out how to make sure the seventh seal didn't open, a wheezing Donahue broke the silence by asking a frustrated-looking Greene a simple question: "Rematch?"

Mo laughed and said, "Yeah, let's go, one more." But from the look in his eye it appeared he was thinking, *And this time, I'm going to destroy this fucker.*

Three things were notable about the rematch:

1. Greene was clearly going all-out. Although the distance wasn't official (I'm pretty sure my wobbly measurement was longer than 100 meters), Mo's winning time in the second race was 10.7 sec-

onds, or about .9 seconds slower than his personal best, the former world record, and significantly faster than the Donahue camp had anticipated him running. That time is pretty amazing given that he was running on carpet, without spikes or starting blocks, and not exactly against stellar competition.

2. Mo blew by Jed right near the finish line, and as he crossed the tape, he shouted a triumphant "Yes!" at the top of his lungs. This was in an exhibition, against an out-of-shape book editor, at 1 A.M., with almost no one watching but an airport cleaning crew. That's the kind of competitiveness it takes to become a world-class athlete. See question 43, "Are Athletes Insane?"

3. Just before the finish line Jed began to stumble, stayed up for a few awkward steps like a punch-drunk boxer, and then did a face plant on the airport carpet. Finally, someone else knew what it was like to humiliate himself against the world's best athletes— it had been a pretty lonely club for me and Rex Grossman.

At this point Mo and Jed were both spent, and it was about two in the morning. A rubber match wasn't meant to be. So the Battle of the Century was . . . a tie.

In the postmatch interview, a winded Greene analyzed the battle.

"I had figured it out. If I was going to make it happen [i.e., catch Jed], I have to get it from the start. I have to close the distance down before he reaches the little walkway because he gets extra help there. So I have to close the distance down *fast,* . . . which will allow me to catch him at the end. The first time I miscalculated it and it was a little closer than I thought it was going to be. For the second one I knew I'd have to put a little bit more into the beginning."

After hearing Mo's analysis, I realized what had happened. Be-

The Battle of the Century.

fore the race, I couldn't figure out why Greene haggled so long over the size of the head start. Why the hell would this legendary runner care so much about 1 or 2 meters? But now I understood: Mo had sized Jed up simply from watching him jog around and run on and off the moving sidewalk. Just from that evaluation he had known almost exactly what it would take to win. In the second race Mo was definitely running as hard as he could, and his haggling over the head start turned out to be Rain Man–esque: his projection was dead-on. Mo Greene knew right away what Donahue and his friends had been trying to figure out for a decade.

How did Jed's friends react as news of the race filtered in from L.A.? Riots in the streets. They were thrilled that he'd won the first race, although I'm pretty sure Jed didn't mention that he was given a head start. One of his friends, Steve, who was there that night in 1996 for the beginning of the debate, summed up the reaction when he wrote, "It's just amazing that something we talked about as a goof some ten years ago—something that had little to no chance of ever happening—has actually happened. Amazing. Life is amazing."

WOULD SUMO WRESTLERS MAKE GREAT NFL LINEMEN?

Talk to most NFL fans about sumo wrestlers and you'll quickly find that their knowledge of the practitioners of this sacred and ancient sport is confined to three specific areas:

1. They're fat.
2. Their names are unpronounceable.
3. There was once one who was the WWF champion.

In reality, sumo wrestlers are not that different from these fans' sporting heroes, the gritty men who wage war in the trenches: NFL linemen. Linemen, like sumos, make kick-ass professional wrestlers (Stone Cold Steve Austin and the Rock being two examples) and have unpronounceable names (Maake Kemoeatu, Babatunde Oshinowo, and Rob Smith). And, of course, both sumos and linemen are massive, though many sumos aren't quite the heifers you probably think they are. Yes, some are the kinds of guys who'll need to be buried in piano boxes, but many of the best ones are actually slightly lighter than the average NFL lineman, who tips the scales at 311 pounds. Chiyonofuji Mitsugu, one of the most dominant sumos of the modern era, weighed in at only 280 pounds. There's a height differential, too: sumos rarely are taller than 6'4", while linemen routinely top 6'5" (eighty linemen now stand 6'6" or taller).

Beyond the superficial similarities, both sumo wrestlers and NFL linemen must have tremendous physical strength and agile feet to be successful, and they must be able to pivot and accelerate on command. The techniques are also comparable. Sumos and linemen both start from a dead standstill with a hand on the ground, take an incredibly quick first step off of a signal, and try to physically dominate their opponents by pushing them back within a confined space.

With all these similarities, and with NFL teams already finding top talent on basketball courts (tight ends Antonio Gates and Tony Gonzalez), on Australian rules football fields (punters Ben Graham and Darren Bennett), and on the moon (Clinton Portis and Chad Johnson), maybe NFL scouts should start looking at the girthy athletes of the Far East.*

But before we assume that NFL teams will be asking sumos to ditch their silk thongs for the heavy pads of the NFL, we should look at how some real-life sumo-to-football transitions have gone.

In 2005 the 6'3", 306-pound Masakazu Goda went from being a low-ranked sumo to playing in NFL Europe as a center. Although Goda didn't make much of an impact on the field, he felt the top sumos could do quite well in the NFL if given some coaching and time. "The initial hit that sumo wrestlers make is more powerful than a football player's," he told Henry Hodgson of NFLEurope .com, "and their pushing—equivalent to drive blocking—is way be-

---

* Maybe some sumo trainers should start looking on football fields for talent, too. Chad Rowan (Akebono), Salevaa Atisanoe (Konishiki), and Fiamalu Penitani (Musashimaru) are all Hawaiians with high school football backgrounds who rose to the highest ranks of sumo. If these guys could swing it, it seems fair to conclude that some NFL players could do well in the sumo world with training.

yond anything that a football player could achieve in terms of power."

Unfortunately, his own play didn't do much to actually show that sumos could pancake opposing linemen in the NFL; Goda didn't even start for his NFL Europe team. Like any good professional athlete, though, he had an excuse for his failures. He blamed his struggles on his difficulties understanding English: "The one thing holding me back now is the language barrier." This struck me as odd because his English was already much better than Sean Salisbury's, and he understood football better than him as well. Still, a Berlitz course could have gotten Goda at least up to the speed of Neil Smith. The larger issue was a lack of talent.

Of course, Goda was a pretty bad sumo, too (poor Goda), so it really couldn't be expected that he would waltz right into the Colts' starting lineup, although the Raiders' may be another story. The lesson to be learned here is that you can't stink at sumo and become an instant NFL player.

You also can't be old, as we learned in the case of Masaru Hanada, a sumo who was actually impressive on the football field. Hanada is one of only sixty-seven men to ever become a *yokozuna* (no WWF fans, not *the* Yokozuna; the term refers to the highest rank of sumo). He retired from sumo at the age of thirty and decided to follow his dream of playing professional football. In a possible case of translator fraud he instead tried out for the Arizona Rattlers of the Arena Football League in 2001. Warren Anderson of the sports performance center Rehab Plus in Phoenix, Arizona, who has trained fifty first-round NFL draft picks over the past twenty years, trained Hanada and said he had no football experience but still displayed a great deal of talent and skill.

At about 5'11", 275 pounds, Hanada "was a little undersized" for a defensive lineman, Anderson told me, but his athleticism gave him a better shot than the larger, 500-pound-type sumos.

"Some of these really overweight guys have no chance," Anderson said. "They're gonna get sealed off, get their legs cut out." Hanada "was a very good athlete and maybe had the best balance of anyone we've ever seen. He obviously understood leverage and all of those things." At his Rattlers tryout Hanada "really manhandled" a college prospect he went one-on-one against.

But as great a sumo as he was, and as well as he did at his tryout, there was a problem; he didn't even try football until he was thirty, an age when a lot of linemen have already retired, physically deteriorated, or been incarcerated for brandishing illegal firearms (applicable to Bears linemen only). By the time Hanada learned the nuances of the game and got up to speed, it would probably be too late for an NFL team to take a real interest.

So after scratching "old" and "bad" off my list of sumo targets, I went looking for just the right guys to take American football by storm.

The more research I did, though, the more I realized it wouldn't be so easy to lure the non-old, non-bad guys over to the States. Goda explained the problem of motivating the best sumos to leave their country and try a sport that is about as popular in Japan as Kabuki is here. "The top echelon of sumo wrestlers are extremely well paid, and have a huge following in Japan, so I think it is unlikely that any of them would make the change to football."

Also, there's the issue of culture shock, or to put a finer point on it, dealing with a major downgrade in lifestyle. Warren Anderson described what Hanada experienced when he went to the Arizona Rattlers tryout and had to get dressed by himself in a trailer. "Hanada was used to literally having servants, twelve people dressing him in Japan. I'm serious, man. These sumos are like royalty, especially the *yokozunas*."

Andrew Freund, the founder of the California Sumo Association and the U.S. Sumo Open, told me that the high-ranking sumos in

Japan "are treated like gods." "What's the incentive for a guy that has spent his whole life in this culture and has finally reached the top of his profession and has ten lower-ranked sumos waiting on him hand and foot to make the switch?" Fair enough. If I had a maid and people were nice to me, I wouldn't even leave Shitsburgh for the pounding of the NFL.

But not all Japanese sumos are living the life. In fact, for every Masaru Hanada (the good one), there are a dozen Masakazu Godas (the bad one). As Freund put it, "Out of nine hundred top sumo guys, all but the top seventy are just living on room and board. It's bizarre to an American mindset but those guys are living the hardest life. It's like being in the military . . . they have no freedom all year round, they're basically slaves."

This doesn't sound like an environment where you can bring a PlayStation and your favorite bong. Such indoctrination could cause rifts with teammates when these disciplined warriors get to the States. *Pac-Man-San, you have made it rain for the last time. You shall bring shame and dishonor to the name of the Titans of Tennessee no more.*

Fortunately for our purposes, the Japanese don't have a monopoly on good sumo wrestlers. Although Japan is home to the pro sumo ranks, almost one in three wrestlers in the top division are not Japanese, with Mongolians leading the way. In fact, the only active *yokozuna* as of 2007 was a Mongolian, Asashoryu Akinori. And as dominant in the Japanese sumo ranks as Akinori is, the president of the Mongolian sumo federation told Freund, "We have guys who are much better than him. Much better." Freund says these elite sumos are kept out because Japan's pro sumo league puts restrictions on foreign competition, allowing "no more than one foreigner per stable" of wrestlers. "If pro sumo in Japan opened their doors to anyone, there'd be a thousand Mongolians in there in a second." He figured that "ten of the top twenty sumos in the world aren't even in the league." It's just like what is happening in America with the AND-1 players in basketball, except the AND-1 guys have no restriction on them and are not actually good.

The Mongolians finally give us some possibilities. In terms of them making the transition to football, Freund believes their amateur champions will have none of the restrictions or hang-ups of the Japanese professionals. They are younger (even the champions), more athletic, and better sumos. "For better or for worse, they're not attached to the tradition," Freund said. "If they have an opportunity, they'll go for it." Also, even factoring in the exchange rate, they don't make a whole lot of money. With Mongolia's per-capita GDP at about $2,000, which, for perspective, is less than the nightly expenditures associated with going to Scores; a

Formerly a proud tradition.

contract for the NFL minimum salary would make any of them the Warren Buffett of Ulaanbaatar.

The only remaining obstacle to pulling off this East-meets-West experiment was getting visas for my Mongolian Monsters of the Midway—a huge problem, since the Mongolian government has a real concern that these national heroes would prefer to be anywhere but Mongolia. But Andrew was coordinating the sumo scenes for the film *Ocean's 13* and was able to secure visas for two wrestlers to come to Los Angeles for the shoot. The test cases would be the 6'1", 340-pound Byambajav "Byamba" Ulambayar and the 6'2", 300-pound Bayanbat "Bayanaa" Davaadalai. While I feared that after meeting Celine Dion on the set they'd flee the country and head back to their yurts, I put together a tryout for the two with Gene Miranda, a veteran Arena League coach currently with the Los Angeles Avengers.

These guys were exactly who we were looking for: they were young, athletic, and talented sumos. Byamba was only twenty-one and had won the world sumo championship a week before the tryout. A former pro sumo in Japan, he was the highest-ranked sumo in his stable before quitting at the age of eighteen because of problems with the lifestyle. This was a real talent, and considering that before the tryout he was learning American dance moves from spectators and hitting on every girl in sight, he seemed to have the whole package for the NFL.

Bayanaa was twenty-seven and an outstanding sumo as well, but not near the level of Byamba. What was encouraging, though, was that he was a multisport athlete, and one of the sports he excelled in was football. Through an interpreter, he explained to me that he was a dominant football player on the university level as a student in Japan.

Freund mentioned another advantage the two sumos had: their

work ethic. "We know they're going to be willing to put the work in. They'd train four or five hours a day, no break, seven days a week. Basically wake up at four or five in the morning, train all morning with no food, and have their first meal around noon." This was just like Pro Bowl defensive tackle Sam Adams's regimen, except for all of that stupid stuff about waking up early, exercising, and not eating.

On a beautiful, sunny day we met at the field at West Los Angeles College. Gene ran the guys through all of the standard drills: forty, shuttle runs, one-man sled, and a variety of agility drills. Their speed was just decent, but everything else was top-notch. They showed some very quick feet in the shuttle runs and agility drills. Their flexibility was uncanny; both men were able to do full splits. And when it came time to hit, they were animals. Most important, they were coachable, showing great improvement even as quickly as from one rep to the next. Although Byamba, the world champ, was incredibly strong and powerful in a confined space, Bayanaa was the star of the show. That might sound surprising considering that he is a much lesser sumo and not as physically gifted, but it goes to show the value of even a little football experience. It's also an indication of how good Bayanaa and other top sumos could be with some instruction and practice.

Gene, for one, was impressed. When I asked him whether his team would give these guys a shot, he said, "We would take a look. They have the ability to play the game. These guys are as strong as anyone. If you can punch and knock a guy back, you're doing something. You can see the aggression."

He went on: "The size and the strength and the athleticism in a big man, that's hard to find. You get these guys that are three hundred forty pounds and they can't move. Athletically, movement wise, fast twitch muscles, they're right there with our guys. Their training is probably very different than what we do, but if they could implement our training techniques, they could do it." (The Arena League has training techniques? I thought they just pulled fans out of the stands who were holding the winning tickets.)

Gene's comments were encouraging, but the real test would be the NFL, so I sent a tape of the workout to Karl Dunbar, the line coach for the Minnesota Vikings. He was also impressed. Maybe more so. Dunbar said they have "very good measurables and look like players in this league. . . . I think their sumo training makes them better (more explosive) than half of the OL/DL in the league right now.

"If these kids were coming out of high school, it would be better for them to learn the raw skills you need to be a football player. Some small college or JC would be great. With them the im-

The Mongolian Monsters of the Midway.

provement would be tremendous because they don't have any bad habits. . . . It doesn't take long to learn if they are willing and have good teachers."

This plan was working out a lot better than my scheme to introduce Americans to yak's milk. I decided to get one more opinion, this time from someone responsible for NFL player evaluation. I went to John Idzik, the vice president of football administration for the Seattle Seahawks, and asked him if I was wrong to think lots of athletes around the world could be outstanding in the NFL with some training.

"There's no doubt you're right. I mean, just by sheer numbers. There's premium athletes wherever you go. I went overseas to Scotland to coach in an international league one year. We got a lot of rugby players and a lot of soccer players who were certainly athletic enough."

So why don't scouts go after these guys? They must be really lazy and stupid 'n' stuff because I found these beasts and don't even do this for a living.

"The competition is so fierce just in the States alone. Just by tapping in to the normal avenues of player acquisition, colleges, D-I, D-I-AA, all the way down to D-III, these are kids that have been recruited, that have been schooled. There is a vast array of selection just within the standard groups. Now, to go outside of that group and have a guy who may be ahead in some innate-type abilities but will be so far behind in other areas, how much are you going to invest? I think the opportunity cost in spending time in finding the diamond in the rough in a sumo league somewhere versus the well-schooled football environment is too great."

This is a fair and intelligent point. However, while some might call it a shrewd cost-benefit analysis, it can also be viewed as complacency. Very few men have the measurables of truly elite NFL linemen, and given the way scouting has evolved, the NFL is aware of virtually all of the ones in the United States. With literally billions of men in the world, there must be some with the size and speed of Casey Hampton. Since the position can be learned fairly easily, a year on the practice squad would seem to be a worthwhile investment if a team found one of these manimals.

Whatever the case, NFL teams aren't pursuing the talent in the Far East right now, and there's no way that highly respected sumos are going to start leaving their stables in droves for the glory that can be had in NFL Europe. But all it takes is a breakthrough and, just as we saw with Antonio Gates and basketball-playing tight ends, NFL teams will be scrambling for the next one ("one" refers to sumo wrestlers, not Orientals, you racist), no matter how silly the idea seemed not long ago. Just as Mongolian wrestlers identified Japanese sumo as ripe for the picking, perhaps more athletes from the East will come to see that their skills can easily translate to football. We'd see a new wave of linemen shaking up the football world and causing NFL fans across America to exclaim with joy, "That large man from the country I cannot identify on a map, whose name I dare not even attempt to pronounce, is doing a rather fine job for the team representing the town in which I live!"

ARE DART PROFESSIONALS GREAT BEER PONG PLAYERS?

The popularity of many games is closely tied to the participant's ability to get drunk while playing (quarters, Golden Tee, cow tipping), but none have as devoted a following as darts and beer pong.

Darts, which originated around the turn of the twentieth century in England, is played in bars and pubs across the world and enjoys a certain respectability. Befitting the more mature participants, dart players pretend that drinking beer is secondary to the game itself. In fact, there are rumors that in some games of darts, no beer is drunk at all.

No one knows beer pong's origins, which, when you think about it, makes sense. Beer pong (also known as Beirut) is an up-and-coming game played by young participants in basements, living rooms, frat houses, and anytime the 'rents aren't home. It drops many of the pretenses of darts, as drinking is actually an essential part of the game.

In beer pong, teams of two stand at opposite ends of a long table in front of a triangle of plastic cups partially filled with beer. Players take turns attempting to throw a Ping-Pong ball into the other team's cups. When a player sinks a ball, the other team must chug the beer in the made cup and remove that cup from the table. A team wins by landing balls in all of the opponent's cups. You got that, broham?

Though there are many variations of each game, both darts and beer pong have a lot in common beyond providing a way for young and old to get sloshed. Both require the competitors to remain stationary (apart from the occasional swaying) and throw an instrument at a fixed target roughly 8 feet away: dart players throw from a distance of 7 feet 9.25 inches, while beer pong is usually played on tables at least 8 feet long. The throwing technique is similar in both games, as the projectile is held between the pointer finger and thumb, with the motion an abbreviated toss that starts around eye level. Both require no real athleticism, but place a premium on dead-on accuracy. Also, Beer Pong had an assistant named Darts, and Darts had an assistant named Beer Pong.

The difference is that in darts there is a level above and beyond just getting drunk with friends. For real dart enthusiasts, there's a pot of beer at the end of the rainbow—a professional circuit, where purses for events can go up to a million dollars. A handful of pro dart players can make hundreds of thousands of dollars in prize money and sponsorships in a given year, and because of the ability to make a living, they can justify to themselves and others practicing for hours on end.

But that may all be changing now that beer pong is starting to make its way out of the frat house. In 2006, Las Vegas hosted the first annual World Series of Beer Pong. The top prize of $10,000 doubled to $20,000 in 2007, and Billy Gaines, one of the World Series cofounders, along with Duncan Carroll, says he hopes to have that number around $100,000 soon enough. "If there's a hundred grand on the line," Gaines told me, "you're going to see guys lining up cups and going into serious training."

That's why, although Billy's greatest fear would undoubtedly have to be "no beer," not far behind is that pro dart players will take the game from, in his words, "the college students, white-collar professionals, and Iraq war veterans" who wage battle on those hallowed and puke-stained tables. "I'm worried these guys are going to come in and dominate the game," he said. "My guess is if you find a dart player who also has great natural depth perception, you might have someone who is unbeatable."

Not being much of a beer-pong traditionalist, I moved forward. The essence of the matchup would be seeing how well professionals who train regularly to sharpen a specific skill set, dart players, can do in a recreational game they've never played where that skill set translates directly, beer pong.

To find a dartsman up for the challenge of playing the best beer pong players the University of Southern California fraternity system had to offer, I asked around, and the experts seemed to agree: Paul Lim was our man. Lim, born in Singapore, is the only man to throw a perfect nine-dart game of 501 at the World Championships, a feat rarer than throwing a perfect game in baseball, and an accomplishment that netted him an $88,000 bonus. He's been ranked #1 six times by the American Darts Organization (ADO) and had won his seventh national championship the weekend before we played. Basically, Lim is as good as it gets.

Which is even better than I had imagined. While we were setting up, Paul found the frat's dartboard and tossed three consecutive bull's-eyes. And then another three. And another three. At this point he grabbed a beer. He seemed surprised that everyone in the entire room was staring, jaws agape. "Ah, that's nothing. My record is fifty-two bull's-eyes in a row."

As we prepared to play, I asked him whether he had any experience with beer pong. His answer was a testament to the greatness of the home entertainment center.

"When I was a chef in Papua New Guinea, there aren't many activities there so all I'd do was play darts. There were times when I'd practice with a bucket eight feet away and would sit down with another bucket of pebbles next to me—about the same distance as what you're setting up there—and just pitch them in. I did that for about three years."

The beer pong game started with Paul and me versus the frat's reigning champs. Right off the bat there was good news and bad news for Mr. Lim. The good news was that like a good shooter in basketball, when Paul missed, it was long or short, not to the left or right, meaning he just needed to get the depth down. The bad news was that throwing the ball on a dead line with no arc left him somewhere north of fucking terrible.

Paul missed his first eight shots and was becoming frustrated.

I hope they didn't roofie Paul. He's my ride home.

"I need a higher arc. This isn't working." The USC boys sensed weakness. Catchphrases and bad beer jokes were flying; clearly, commercials had been watched.

But we were still in the hunt because as Paul was ricocheting balls off the front and back of the cups, I was dominating. I hadn't played more than three games of beer pong in the past ten years, but as a high school senior I played almost daily in a makeshift league with a travel schedule that was based largely around whose parents got home late or were out of town. However, Paul's inexperience was too big of a burden to overcome, and we lost the first game by one cup. Come on, Lim, get your shit together.

Game two added some new wrinkles to the contest. For one, Paul was completely hammered. But shockingly, so were the USC boys, one of whom required a sub. The other wrinkle was that Paul, in spite, or perhaps because, of his impairment, suddenly got it down, and we combined like Voltron to form a devastating tandem. My beautiful, high-arcing shots were effective early in the match when the cups were close together and less skill was required, and Paul was a deadly weapon when it became imperative to aim at one cup.

We had them on the ropes. The frat's best player was wearing down and the beer part of beer pong was playing a factor. "I'm hurting," he said. "These two games are going way too fast. Usually we play against people who don't play that well and I can pace myself. You guys are giving us quite a game, I can tell by my sobriety level." Who had these guys been playing, the Tri-Lams?

But the frat's sober sub was on a mission, sniping cup after cup and taking the game down to one apiece. Two turns of misses were traded until Paul, with beer in his veins, dropped the game winner. To celebrate, a tickertape parade was held in my imagination, and Paul and I shared an awkward high five. Each team had won a game, and the match was declared a victory for us since I'm the one doing the writing. Others called it a tie.

The nerds finally get their long-awaited revenge.

What did we learn? The easy answer, of course, would be nothing. But it was obvious to everyone that Paul's ability to consistently put the ball on a straight line separated him from your
run-of-the-mill beer pong player. He improved dramatically from
game one to game two, going from the worst player on the table to
the best, and it was pretty easy to see that his jump from game two
to game forty would be enormous.

Part of what makes pros great at their sport is their level of dedication and willingness to practice. If Paul was given a month and
he had any kind of incentive, instead of watching TV, lounging
around, or coming up with excuses not to practice like you or I
would, you can be damn sure he'd be throwing a Ping-Pong ball
into a cup until his fingers bled and then he would fill another cup
with his own blood and aim for that one, just for good measure.
Combine that discipline with an unparalleled ability to deliver an

object on a straight line and you've got potentially the world's greatest beer pong player.

Billy Gaines's fear of dart players taking over if money was on the line went from a funny joke to becoming very real. Paul loved the game and was planning on preaching the gospel of beer pong, but with a twist that might further push the balance of power to the old guys.

"I'm going to introduce this to Asia now. And we're going to play with scotch or sake."

God bless you always, Paul Lim.

CAN BASKETBALL PLAYERS REALLY "MAKE CHANGE" OFF THE TOP OF THE BACKBOARD?

E arl "The Goat" Manigault is widely regarded as one of the greatest playground basketball players of all time. Although he never played in the NBA and only briefly played in college, the legend of Manigault has spread far and wide and led to his play being glorified in magazines, books, and even a movie starring Don Cheadle called *Rebound: The Legend of Earl "The Goat" Manigault*. There are a number of tales regarding Manigault's prowess, but the central story that propelled his legend was that he had such extraordinary leaping ability he could pull dollar bills off the top of the backboard and leave change. What made this even more amazing was that Manigault was, depending on who you talk to, somewhere between 5′11″ and 6′1″. Considering that the top of the backboard is at thirteen feet and the average six-foot-tall man can only touch about eight feet high standing flat-footed, Manigault would have had to jump at least sixty inches to even come close. That would mean the Goat's "making change" was a feat on par with Michael Jordan's game-winning dunk from half court in the film *Space Jam*. In other words, pure fiction.

The legend of touching the top of the backboard has gone on for years, and it has been excitedly attributed to so many different players that it's commonly assumed any number of guys in the NBA can do it. But in a sport where any individual achievement is promoted ad nauseam, we've never seen any proof of it actually being done.

I went to the epicenter of basketball talent (no, not Greece) to talk to the U.S. national team. Certainly, if it could be done, one of America's basketball stars would be able to do it.

While Coach Mike Krzyzewski had the players practicing cheers to boost team spirit instead of learning how to beat a zone defense or defend a pick and roll, I asked then–general manager of the Denver Nuggets Kiki Vandeweghe, a former all-star, whether he'd ever seen anyone reach the mountaintop.

"No, I've never seen it. That's a long way up there. I don't think it can be done."

What about Kiki's former teammate David Thompson? Presumably the 6'4" guard with what people claimed was a 44-inch vertical could grab a quarter off the top of the backboard.

Kiki shook his head solemnly.

"You hear a lot of stories."

He looked up at the top of the backboard.

"No, I don't think he could do that."

When Coach K was finally done passing out Amex applications, I talked to Amare Stoudamire, who is 6'10" and was one of the best leapers in the NBA before a major knee injury.

"I've never touched the top of the backboard and I've never seen it done," he said. "Myself, I came close, maybe three or four inches from the top. If you're lookin' for a guy who can do it, talk to LeBron James."

So off to LeBron I went. When asked, he shook his head no as well.

"Everyone says I can, but I can't do it. I've tried. I can get up

The Myth of the 44-Inch Vertical Leap

Next time Dick Vitale starts screaming that some diaper dandy has a 44-inch vertical, keep in mind this comment from Bill Foran, the Miami Heat's strength and conditioning coach: "I hear people talking about vertical jumps above 40 inches, but those are not true vertical jumps. Most NBA players have vertical jumps in the 28–34 inch range. The highest I have ever tested is 36½ inches. Ironically, it was not a basketball player, but an Olympic triple jumper from Greece."

Foran explained that a true vertical jump measures "the jump reach minus the standing reach." The jump reach is how high you can touch when you "jump straight up without taking a step"; the standing reach is "how high you can extend one arm above your head while keeping both feet together and flat on the floor."

So basically, anytime you hear someone talk about how high a player's vertical jump is, they're just making up a number.

for sure but that's a long way. Dwight's the only man in the world who could do something like that, you gotta talk to him."

"Dwight" was Dwight Howard, the first pick in the 2004 draft, who stands 6'11" and is an absolute physical freak. Do a search online and you'll see extensive video of Dwight's leaping exploits. His team, the Orlando Magic, has documented some of his more amazing stunts, most famously him literally kissing the rim. In the 2007 Slam Dunk contest, he dunked a ball while slapping a sticker shockingly high on the backboard.

Hornets point guard Chris Paul told me, "I think Dwight can. I asked him before practice today and he said he can but I've never seen him do it."

I asked Chris if he could get Dwight to try.

"I don't know. Depends on how he feels. I want to see it, too."

Have you ever seen anyone do it?

"Uh uh."

So that's total crap when people say Earl Manigault could do it, since he was like 6 feet tall?

"I believe it, though. You ain't never seen the movie *Rebound*?"

You mean the one with Don Cheadle?

"Yeah."

You know that's not a documentary, right?

When Chris and I approached Dwight and asked him, he beamed ear to ear.

"I can. I've never heard of anyone else that can do it but I can get up there. I did it in high school when I was seventeen for the first time. Now, I can't grab stuff off of it but I can get up there."

When we asked to see it, Dwight politely begged off but said he'd do it for me later. He told me to set it up with the Magic. So, a week later, I called the team and they said my trip would be unnecessary; they had all kinds of great video with Howard leaping, including Dwight touching the top of the backboard. For the first time in the history of basketball we were going to have documentation.

Well, the footage ended up being bunk. On the video Dwight ended up touching somewhere just north of the square on the backboard a couple of times. Because Howard seemed like a nice guy and I wanted to take him at his word, I asked the Magic's VP of communications, Joel Glass, when we could coordinate the jump per the original plans Dwight and I discussed. Joel stated that no matter what Dwight told me, he would not be allowed to jump, citing injury concerns.

I pointed out that jumping in the air one time would be less dangerous than most of the things Dwight did in a typical NBA game and I added that I had never heard of anyone, ever, in the history of basketball getting hurt this way. So Joel started giving a variety of other reasons, all bordering on the insane.

Next I contacted Dwight's agency, Goodwin Sports, to let them know that I would be willing to spend my own time and money having someone come to Orlando to document the leap. They said that it sounded good and that they'd check with Dwight and get back to me. The official response came from Mary Ford, Howard's publicist at Goodwin, who said he could do it but it was too time consuming. When I explained that it would literally be one jump after practice, the total time of which would be somewhere in the neighborhood of ten seconds, the agency took two weeks to say no. And this time she hedged. "Well, he can do it but he can't *always* do it."

You can look at this a couple of different ways:

1. Dwight can't touch the top of the backboard and the Magic and his agency were covering for him. Alarm bells go off since they have footage of different kinds of leaping stunts but not the most-talked-about one in basketball history. Twice in the 2007 season Dwight tried to impress with his leaping ability, once at the Slam Dunk contest and again when his teammates doubted he could still reach a piece of tape high on the backboard that he had touched when he was a rookie. However, both the sticker and the piece of tape were 12'6" high, which left him a full six inches short of our milestone. Combine this with him not trying to touch the top when the players of the U.S. national team asked, all the different excuses his organization and agency gave, and the historically murky nature of the claims, and there are certainly doubts.

2. Dwight really can touch the top of the backboard but the people surrounding him are awful.

It's a tough call. Dwight is astounding athletically and by all accounts is a nice and honest guy, but pro athletes, even ones with the best intentions, are notoriously bad about overestimating their own abilities. It's very easy for someone to think they're touching the top when really they're 4 or 5 inches below. After years of bullshit, I needed proof.

My next lead was Shawn Marion, who was rumored to be able to pull it off. A call to the Suns led to some internal research followed by them telling me he "used" to be able to do it. The team could produce no documentation, though, and no one who could even vouch for the claim.

But but but . . . there was hope! And the hope was in the person of James "Flight" White, a 6'7" string bean rookie for the San Antonio Spurs.

Dunking, in a way, is an art (in the same way that Boone's Farm is a wine, but I digress), and in that respect it's often a matter of taste and preference as to who the "best" is. But while at the University of Cincinnati, White performed a variety of dunks so improbable that they had never been attempted in competition, let alone completed, before he flushed them down. To give an idea of White's leaping ability, it was mind-blowing when Dr. J took off from the foul line and dunked in 1976; it was jaw dropping the way Michael Jordan took off from the foul line and dunked in 1987; but in 2001 James White took off from the foul line and dunked *while putting the ball between his legs!*

There is no one—and I stress, no one—in the history of professional basketball who can even come close to doing this. Vince Carter, Kobe Bryant, Michael Jordan, Dr. J, Kenny "Sky" Walker, Dee Brown, Spud Webb, Terence Stansbury, Dominique Wilkins, the entire cast of *Slamball*—none of these guys could pull off this dunk. Isaiah Rider won a dunk contest in 1994 just by virtue of the fact that he could go between his legs and dunk at all, and as mentioned, Jordan and Dr. J won dunk contests by being able to dunk from the foul line. It's questionable whether David Thompson or Earl Manigault could do either. James White combined the two.

So when I came across an interview from the *Indianapolis Star* with White that read:

Q: Can you touch the top of the backboard?

A: Yeah.

I immediately called his agent, Bill McCandless, to set up something.

Bill had his concerns, but was intrigued.

"That's really the biggest old wives' tale out there. If you're around basketball, you grow up hearing all the time about guys being able to do that and it's always nonsense.

"I'll tell you this, though, James does not bullshit about this kind of stuff. I don't know if you're aware of this but he had thought about becoming a decathlete. The guy has Olympic leaping ability. Jumping off of one leg, he's like no other."

McCandless said that even without training White qualified for the Olympic trials in the high jump by leaping 7'4" and the long jump with a distance of 25'7".

This sounded promising. He called James and quickly got back to me.

"James said he's for sure done it. Now, he might only be able to do it one out of one hundred times, but he said he'd give it a shot if you want to send a camera crew."

White arrived at the court at the University of Cincinnati ready to fly, but first he wanted to clarify something about his top-of-the-backboard exploits.

"I've never actually done it, per se. But doing the vertical test at the University of Cincinnati, I've touched as high as the top of the backboard."

Imagine how high he could have jumped if his nut wasn't busted.

78

How fitting for this topic. Thinking back to his "Yeah" response to the *Indianapolis Star* interview, I started to wonder whether NBA players saying they've touched the top of the backboard was like kids in junior high saying they've "gone all the way."

But James wanted to show his stuff. Since he jumps off of one foot, we put a yardstick off of the side of the top of the backboard. Not exactly the same thing as touching the top of the backboard, but one step at a time. If he couldn't get the yardstick, then there'd be no reason to go further.

There was no reason to go further.

James was close. Damn close. But his best jump left him more than 2 inches from the yardstick.

Okay, maybe I was being pessimistic when I said there was no reason to go further. There had been rumors of a "busted nut" (is that part of the knee or something?) that took place an hour before the jump, slowing James down, so a month later we tried again, this time after practice with the Spurs in San Antonio.

Again, close but not quite.

As to whether White can do it or not, you can draw your own conclusions. My money says that he can. He was only a few inches off, and I don't think James would have taken the time to jump for us twice, or offered to try again before we ran into a book deadline, if it was something he couldn't do.

But whether James White can or can't reach the top is secondary in this discussion. The point is, if a 6'7" Olympic-caliber high jumper who can do dunks that Vince Carter and Michael Jordan dare not attempt is struggling to reach a yardstick off of the side of the hoop, there is no player in history who has ever touched the top of the backboard. And certainly no one who has ever "made change."

And no, Don Cheadle jumping off of a trampoline doesn't count.

HOW WOULD A PSYCHIC DO IN A ROCK, PAPER, SCISSORS TOURNAMENT?

I n the world of one-handed anaerobic sports, there are few events more anticipated than the annual World Rock Paper Scissors Championship. In it, the game of Rock, Paper, Scissors (RPS) is a highly contested five-hundred-person battle with only one winner, or depending on how you look at it, no winners.

Competitive RPS, much like the amateur version, relies on the ability to predict what your opponent will throw so you can counter with the victorious symbol. Some people claim to be good at this due to their dedication to "advanced" RPS strategies. They would advise beginner players to read books on strategy, study film of an opponent's tendencies, and spend countless hours compiling statistics on trends in the hopes of gaining even a slight edge. But isn't there an easier way to win?

If you were a *psychic,* you would know by now that there certainly is!

Since these mutants haven't yet been banned from the sport, I decided to enter one in the World Rock Paper Scissors Championship in Toronto. To ensure we had the real deal and not some cheap carny imposter, I conducted a long and arduous recruitment process, the principal component of which was a Google search for "Psychic + Toronto." This exhaustive manhunt led me to JoAnne Iacobaccio, also known as Wistaria, who has been an "International Psychic Reader" since 1986. I felt like Albert Brooks in *The Scout,* ready to make my mark by unveiling an amazingly talented athlete in what had the makings of a bad movie.

JoAnne arrived at the brewery in which this prestigious athletic event was being held ready to win the $7,000 first-place prize. She would be going against competitors from every location imaginable, including Australia, Sweden, England, Germany, and Jail. Our own Amanda Mitts, groupie to the stars (see Question 5), was on hand to follow the proceedings and found a confident Iacobaccio.

AMANDA: So, how are you going to do?

WISTARIA: I'm going to win, of course. I'm psychic.

A: What's your edge?

W: I hear voices that tell me which way to go. I'm clairaudient so I hear voices and clairvoyant so I see what's going on before it takes place.

A: Is it a child's voice or an adult's voice?

W: It's a big godly voice.

A: So have you ever used your psychic powers to win a contest or prizes?

W: They know me at the casino as well. The slot machines. I've got a sense of where to go and I go straight for it.

The interview continues in this vein for pages. Please look for it in its entirety in the upcoming Three Rivers Press book *I Can't Believe This Was a Real Conversation.*

The first round was upon us and we were already in business. As JoAnne watched the match before hers, she accurately predicted the victorious party. What are the odds!?!

Even more incredibly, Bob Cooper, the man who JoAnne predicted would win said match, revealed that he was in attendance due to an experience with the mystical. A twenty-eight-year-old sales manager from north London, Cooper flew to the RPS Championship on the recommendation of a psychic who told him he would win.

"I would have been nervous if I wasn't so sure I was going to win," Cooper said. "Now that I have two psychics backing me, it's a pretty good sign."

Even with this certainty, Bob prepared for the event by spending two hours each day playing friends and engaging in "hard work, training, and lots of research into tactics, body language, and basic psychology. I went through extensive training, read *The Official Rock Paper Scissors Strategy Guide,* and studied the twenty-seven possible RPS Gambits before competing."

Frankly, this sounded like twenty-seven kinds of retarded. The World RPS Society website defines a "Gambit" as "a series of three successive moves made with strategic intention" and calls the use of Gambits "one of the greatest and most enduring breakthroughs in RPS strategy." Supposedly, "selecting throws in advance helps prevent unconscious patterns from forming and can sometimes reduce the subconscious signals that give away the next throw, often called 'tells.' "

My feeling was that having a strategy in RPS was on par with having a strategy for winning a coin toss. History supported my belief. All kinds of buffoons have won the World RPS Championship, including a guy who took a Zen approach and cleared his mind before each throw so he wouldn't be predictable.

But Graham Walker, coauthor of *The Official Rock Paper Scissors Strategy Guide,* who along with his brother Douglas puts on the Championship, told me that it is possible to have strategy in such a seemingly random game. According to Graham, the game is not random and the percentage of throws never comes close to even thirds.

"Rock way overindexes and is by far the most common throw, especially amongst amateurs and more specifically with men," he explained. So logically, Graham said, the best throw against amateur players is paper. "Paper actually underindexes against the expected averages and is the least common throw." The RPS site has it at 29.6 percent.

Also, he said that "people have a tendency to throw the symbol that would have won the previous hand." Meaning, if they lost the previous hand to paper, they will typically throw scissors next.*

So the game isn't all random luck?

"Humans actually can't play randomly. No matter how small, no matter how subtle, they fall into patterns. When people try to approximate randomness, it can actually become quite predictable. For instance, a lot of people wouldn't think you could play a hand three times in a row because that would be predictable, but in reality runs of three throws in a row happen all of the time if you're really randomizing it."

Okay, this is all well and good, Graham, but then why do we not see any real levels of consistency for players in the past championships? Why have dominant players not emerged through the years, and how do people who have never played before, some of whom are clearly mental defectives, do so well?

"It's about gaining the smallest advantage over a period of time. What it boils down to is the person who gets that micro edge will really have a better chance of winning than anyone else. If you can consciously identify a trend that's taking over at a tournament, you

---

* Remember all this and you can win a lot of money from your friends! All right, maybe some money. Well, maybe you'll get to ride shotgun once or twice from it, assuming Graham didn't just make all of that up.

have an edge. It may only play out over ten thousand throws and that doesn't mean you can't get busted out at any time."

A slight edge over ten thousand throws wasn't going to cut it for me. As far as I was concerned, the only surefire way to victory was to know what your opponent was about to throw by reading his or her mind. Thankfully, we had this covered with JoAnne.

Game time was here and it was JoAnne 's time to shine. We were going to be in for a long one. With five hundred competitors, we were going to have to wait for JoAnne to advance through nine rounds before she could claim the first-place prize. The fear was that with all the time between the opening rounds and the finals, the normals would begin realizing that they had no chance to win and would demand entry-fee refunds from the organizers. What if before we could claim victory, the organizers caved to the riotous mob and decided that JoAnne's devil's magik was an unfair advantage? I was in the middle of giving Amanda explicit instructions that if any kind of discriminatory actions were taking place to immediately contact . . . when I heard from the other end someone screaming in the background: "The psychic is out!"

What? What? What?

JoAnne was done. She lost her first round 9 to 1. Maybe she should have read up on the Gambits instead of listening to those goddamn voices. When I expressed my concerns to Amanda, she suggested I clear my chakras and calm down.

"No, Todd, you don't understand, the guy she was playing was really into it so JoAnne let him win. He was really nervous and afterward he told me he was practicing for like weeks. But she still did really well. I think he was a pro or something."

Oh, well then! What an amazing success! Not only had JoAnne shown that she could use her mystical abilities to take one hand from a high-level RPS professional, but she had also had the compassion to give an emotionally fragile man a chance.*

"Yes," JoAnne explained, "speaking with him before the competition, just randomly somebody I picked out of the crowd, I started talking to him and got to know him. . . . He was such a nice guy and he wanted it so bad there was no way I could take it away from him. You could see it in the handshake in the beginning. He's got some confidence-building going on right now, I can see it. Nothing happens by coincidence."

Her competitor agreed that his victory was no coincidence. He explained that he had specifically lined up to play JoAnne because "that [psychic] stuff is all bullshit. I wanted to play her just so I could prove it."

Speaking of coincidences—excuse me, cosmic happenings—Bob Cooper, the competitor from England, won the entire tournament. What carried Bob to victory? Was it his in-depth studying of the game? The confidence from the two psychics? His practicing two hours a day? His enormous beard and BluBlocker sunglasses?

We found out when ol' Bob opined on his mastery of the game with the BBC. "I prefer not to discuss my strategy because I plan to defend my title at next year's World Championships."

JoAnne, not surprisingly, had been on top of the Bob situation in advance. "Ah, yes, I could see that coming. You can see a person's energy shift when they are a winner versus a loser." Geez, it sure would have been nice if she had let the rest of us know so we didn't have to wait around for her to lose.

---

* Many at the RPS Championships claimed to be "professional" players. This is like winning $1,000 in the lottery and claiming to be a "lottery professional." No one on the "pro circuit" wins consistently enough to earn a living. When I asked Graham about the "pros," he had this to say, which, to me, summed it up perfectly: "If there were enough events and the money were big enough, you could certainly make money as a professional."

Why not just win the whole thing yourself, JoAnne?

"You have to always keep the greater good in mind. I'm a good sport. And I wanted to go get some drinks."

Like Biff Tannen in *Back to the Future II,* JoAnne had the ability to see into the future. But unlike the power-hungry Biff, instead of using her power to enslave mankind for her own personal gain, she chose the high road. Thank you, JoAnne. Thank you from us all.

ARE THERE PRO ATHLETES WHO HAVE TO PINCH PENNIES?*

The glamour! The prestige! The studio apartment in a low-rent part of Pittsburgh!

Some professional athletes are paid well immediately, continue to be paid well through their careers, and then retire and manage their money correctly. These guys take what may be an absurd skill (throwing a ball hard and making it spin funny) and turn it into a lifestyle that hasn't been seen since Ted DiBiase ruled the land.

But that's not the reality for the majority of pro athletes. In fact, many have the same concerns as the average twenty-something.

A pretty typical professional athlete is Jonah Bayliss, a twenty-six-year-old relief pitcher for the Pittsburgh Pirates. He pitched in eleven games for the Kansas City Royals in 2005 and was called to the majors by the Pirates three days before our discussion on the high-flying life of a pro baseball player.

"I'm looking for the cheapest apartment I can find," he told me. "A little studio apartment with a three- or a four-month lease somewhere."

As unappealing as living in the cheapest studio apartment in Pittsburgh sounds, including to the homeless in warm climates,

---

* This question was submitted by Neil Hamburger, comedian.

Bayliss's living situation was actually pretty good compared to out-fielder Mike Cameron's when he first came into the league.

"When I first came up I stayed with my mom. Until my third year I stayed with her." He neither confirmed nor denied whether she also packed his lunch and tied his shoes for him before he went to the park.

Granted, Cameron has made more than $37 million in his major league career, but like most established big leaguers, it took him a while to get "I just pissed on your new rug for fun! Here's some cash!" kind of money. From when Cameron came up in 1995 to when he got his first seven-figure deal in 2000, he made only $909,000 in the majors. Sure, that sounds like pretty good money; his rookie salary of $109,000 was comparable to that of a first-year lawyer. But unlike a young lawyer, if Cameron blew out his knee, he had no idea where his next paycheck would come from. Additionally, his skill set doesn't translate into any other part of the workplace, unless your company softball team is desperate for a former all-star center fielder with a torn ACL.

Said Cameron, "You don't know how long you're gonna be around. You're coming from literally nothing. Money management is a big part of what you're doing out here." A hard thing to do when you now have enough money coming in to buy everything you've ever dreamed of.

Which brings us back to Jonah.

Bayliss was a seventh-round pick, which is pretty high in base-ball. For his signing bonus he was paid $100,000. It helped him get through the tough times of minor league baseball, where salaries range anywhere from $1,050 to $2,150 a month—roughly what a high school janitor makes.

"I have a lot of good friends in the minors and they're scrap-ing," Bayliss said. "They've got to get jobs in the off-season. Minor league baseball is tough. It'll stick it to you."

But Bayliss was in the majors, and with the current major league minimum salary at $327,000 he was doing very well. However, this didn't mean he was going to be living it up quite yet. "Even the minimum is good money but it's not 'set for life' money," he said. "I could break my leg tomorrow. I treat myself where I can, but me treating myself isn't like how some guys do. I have an Infiniti SUV but it's not like a huge extravagance. I watch my money. It's more like the way a lot of fans live. There's certainly nothing else I'd rather be doing, but at the same time a lot of people do have the misconception that everyone in baseball does whatever they want and goes wherever they please. It's not like that."

He may not be living like Roger Dorn, but there're gotta be a lot of freebies and some good perks. Right?

"Eh, not really. I mean it depends on the team. If you're the twenty-fifth man on the Red Sox, maybe. I think it's something you earn. Being able to get reservations at a real nice restaurant, if Jonah Bayliss calls up, they're going to be like 'who?' "

But what about the groupies? Pro ball must be pretty nice for that, huh?

"Not that I've found. If there are, point me in the direction."

Of course, Bayliss had been with the Pirates only a few days by this point, so to get a better sense of life in the bigs, I checked in with him a couple months later and hit him with Twenty Questions: Money, Power, and Bitches edition.

"Money is no different. It's still an issue. When we had talked, I got sent down ten days later and just got called back up about a month ago. I'm still saving pennies."

How much have you made?

"Fifty something."

Do you invest? Any mutual funds, stocks?

"I'm going to look into it now. I mean, I still don't really have a financial chunk to play around with. Now I'm still kind of just taking what I have and throwing it in a savings account."

Any change on getting freebies as a local celebrity? I hear they really roll out the red carpet at Arby's for Matt Capps.

"Ah, I won't say never. But in terms of free meals and bigger stuff, no, unfortunately."

So what are your off-season plans? Lying on a yacht somewhere?

"This year I'm going down to Venezuela to play winter ball. It's not bad. Ten grand a month. And I'm a bottom-of-the-barrel guy. If you're an established player, it can be at least twenty. That's pretty much my off-season. I'm going to play, go back home before the holidays, and then it's off to spring training."

Did you find a place to live yet?

"No, I've just been living in a hotel."

Does the team pay for it?

"No, they give you seven free nights; you pay for the rest. It's a hundred bucks a night. It's not bad at all. The Marriott Spring Hill. Can't beat the location. [The Marriott is literally right across the street from the park.] I roll out of bed and walk over here. You can't beat that. It's got a fridge."

Wow, a fridge! I've seen those on *Cribs*! But how about your adoring public? Do people recognize you at Pittsburgh bars?

"I'd say they do now."

Does this new recognition help with the groupie scene?

Big smile from Jonah. "I'm sure you can find them if you're looking for them."

But you never would look for them.

"Never."

All in all, Jonah Bayliss is living basically the same life as many people his age; he just has to play for the Pirates to do so. He has perks like a fridge and a car, but if his hand falls off tomorrow, that high life could be gone in a flash.

CAN FANS HIT AS WELL AS PITCHERS?

"These pitchers suck at hitting. Certainly I could at least hit .100!"

—Mike V., Chicago, Illinois

This statement was submitted to me while I was doing interviews for ESPN.com. It was apropos of nothing but for some reason Mike thought I was the man to validate his belief. Mike was in his mid-thirties and had no experience playing baseball beyond Little League, yet he insisted that major league pitchers were so bad that almost any moderately coordinated athlete could do better than some of them. One of his gems: "Just watch these guys try to get a bunt down even. They can't even do that. Some of them don't even hold the bat right."

Five years later, I wanted to give Mike his time to shine. I dug up his e-mail address from a laptop that hadn't been used in four years and proposed that he take on a major league pitcher specifically to address the question he had asked. With typical dickery, Mike said he'd be there and "show me what the fuck was up."

ESPN baseball writer Rob Neyer had a similar experience—not in being a dick, but in dealing with fans who thought they could hit as well as a pitcher. "Not only could a fan not hit a pitcher well, he couldn't hit one at all," Neyer told me. "A major league curveball is eighty miles per hour and most people couldn't even hit an eighty-mile-per-hour fastball. Most people, if they went and faced a major league pitcher, would literally not even see the ball coming towards them. My experience is not with an actual pitcher, but I went up against a pitching machine that was replicating a ninety-mile-per-hour slider from Randy Johnson and all I saw was a blur. The machine wasn't calibrated properly and it missed my shin by about two and a half inches. It was so fast, I didn't even have time to be scared. I had almost no chance of hitting it."

American League MVP Justin Morneau said guys like Mike are crazy to mock big-league pitchers for the way they hit. "It's a lot different when you're actually in there. I can tell you that much." Perfect. Mike was done.

To give Mike his comeuppance, I lined up Paul Abbott, a veteran pitcher who won seventeen games for the Mariners in 2001. After turning down some invitations to spring training, Paul was sitting out the year to coach his son at Fullerton College. He had told me he wasn't in top shape, but still, a major league pitcher only a year removed from the big leagues is in good enough shape to be by far the best pitcher you've ever seen. He would murder Mike, figuratively and possibly literally if he had control problems or got stuck talking to him.

Twisted visions danced in my head of Mike trying to hit Paul: beer belly, sweatpants, and totally unathletic, ducking at curveballs that ended up being strikes, swinging and missing at balls that bounced 3 feet in front of home plate or were already in the catcher's mitt. I wanted Mike to look like all the Bad News Bears rolled up into one middle-aged doofus. Minus Tatum O'Neal and Kelly Leak. Even Engelberg was probably too talented a hitter for my fantasy.

But alas, three days before the big matchup, Mike e-mailed me and made up some lame excuse about his kid having a game and having "better things to do than waste my time showing up" Abbott.

This was fine, because I harbored delusions of grandeur myself. Unlike Mike, I had a baseball background, playing through high school and American Legion (which is a step up from high school ball) before retiring to pursue a career playing "Tony LaRussa Baseball" on Sega Genesis and screaming at the Pirates on the television.

I feared the ten-year layoff would be too much to overcome, but batting against the professional Wiffle ball guys two weeks before the event (see Question 4)* helped prepare me for the speed and movement on Abbott's pitches. On my third at-bat I managed to slap a single up the middle on a high fastball. In seven at-bats, I put the ball in play three times and had what appeared to be one hit, maybe two hits if we're talking about high-school-level fielders. By the end of the hitting session, I was pretty confident that I could make contact against major league pitching, and if I got a fastball in an area I liked or an off-speed pitch that hung, I might even be able to hit it hard. This, however, is not the same as hitting .100 in the majors. Here's why:

The speed of the fastball I could certainly handle. Paul was probably throwing in the mid-eighties, which is slow by major league standards (yet much faster than the ninety-mile-per-hour "Very Fast" at your local batting cage). Even if the fastball was cranked up to the mid-nineties, I think I would still have been able to get around on it . . . assuming I was told it was coming down the middle. Paul's ability to control pitches with such speed and movement made me look worse than Gary Carter's perm. He located pitches in places where I could do nothing with them— spotting fastballs on the outside corner, or snapping a slider under my hands for a strike three that I just assumed would be a ball.

Really, anytime he got his off-speed stuff over the plate was

* I scored two runs in four innings against Balian and his buddies. Deez nutz.

better for him than it was for me. I looked really dumb trying to hit his curve, and his best pitch, his changeup, he wasn't even able to locate. His off-speed pitches were so much faster than what I'd been used to seeing, and were thrown with so much more deception and movement, that it was hard to identify them before it was too late. I checked my swing more times in seven at-bats than I had in my entire life.

Also, for many fans, including myself, hitting against major league fielders would require a different approach entirely. Just laying the bat on the ball and making contact can get you a lot of hits against subpar fielders, but to consistently get hits past a major league infield using a wooden bat takes some power. One of the balls I hit was a grounder between first and second that would have been a hit on any level I've ever played, but would be a routine put-out for any major league second baseman. Even my "single" up the middle might have been turned into an out by a diving Jose Reyes. Throw in that these fielders have arms stronger than

Multiple choice: Is this batter on steroids, HGH, or Butterfingers?

most college pitchers, and that most fans aren't running with unique speed, and what you remember being a hit in high school is not the same as a hit in the majors.

Paul's overall evaluation? Steve Jeltz without the power. "You can hit a little, but it's different in the majors. I'd put you around .080."

Reasonable as that was, I wasn't willing to accept that in a world where David Eckstein could be World Series MVP and Neifi Perez once hit .298, this was the peak of my abilities. I asked Paul the classic insane fan question: "Okay, but what would I hit if I trained?"

"Well, there's a really easy way to do it: look at what you did in high school, take what some pitchers in the majors did in high school, and then take your comps and see how they do in the majors."

(For the record, Paul Abbott hit .475 with power in a tough high school conference and then hit .250 in the majors. He took some BP after my display, and you could immediately see the difference. He looked like Albert Pujols compared to everyone I had ever played with.)

I looked at the worst-hitting pitchers with at least a hundred at-bats in the major leagues. Research showed a wide range of results. In 154 career at-bats, Tim Hudson had hit .117. In 2006, he hit .095, which is roughly what Paul thought I would hit. But it's only against the best of the best that Tim looks awkward and incompetent. As bad as Hudson may look to a casual fan watching at home, he is, by the standard of your average high school baseball player, an outstanding hitter. In batting practice, he shows a quick and powerful swing, hitting to all fields well and with some pop. This stands to reason: Tim was an All-SEC outfielder at Auburn and hit .396 with 18 home runs and 95 RBI. I could only assume in high school he hit 1.000 with a home run every at-bat.

As it turned out, my guess wasn't far off: Hudson's junior and senior years of high school combined he hit .589 with 18 home runs, 11 doubles, and 7 triples.

Hudson was clearly out of my league, and therefore not a good comp, so I started doing research on some of the other feebs.

Brian Moehler, a career .050 hitter in the majors, hit .353 with one homer, 25 runs, and 22 ribbies in 119 at-bats for his American Legion team. His high school coach told me, "That was a good team in a good league, so he could hit a little to do that."

Matt Clement, .095 in 348 major league at-bats, attended Butler High School in Pennsylvania and played third base his junior and senior years. His senior year, he had the highest batting average on the team with .429, but he didn't have much power.

I also came across pitchers who outright sucked. Mark Redman has the second lowest average in the majors among pitchers with 100 at-bats at .062. In high school he wasn't much better. His senior season at Escondido High in California he hit .133.

Ben Sheets clocked in at .078 in the majors and in high school was such a sped that they had to DH for him when he pitched. I asked his high school coach, Bob Lemons, how Sheets was even able to hit .078 in the majors. "He might have overcome his fear, because in high school he didn't want to get hit. I've seen him a couple times at the plate [in the majors] and he looks like a pitcher hitting, but he does take his hacks. Some pitchers want to work the count or make the guy work, but Ben's up there swinging."

Based on these findings, it's hard to say how good I could get against major league pitching. I have no power but I also never hit under .350 in any season I played, so using Abbott's method of evaluation, Moehler and Clement seemed like they were within range. Ben Sheets and Mark Redman sounded like total spazzes, so I'd have to think I'm at least as "good" a hitter as them as well.

But to think that an All-SEC outfielder was among the worst-hitting pitchers was not exactly encouraging, since I couldn't even *make* the college team he dominated on.

Abbott started really piling on: "Let's say you came right out of high school and went into the minors, stayed at it, had some pro training, and got used to seeing those kinds of pitches: maybe like .100 to .150. That's probably around what the worst-hitting pitchers do."

"And really," Paul added, "you're a much better hitter than the 'average fan.' So that number is going to be much lower for most people. You've got enough ability and bat control that every once in a while you're going to get a fastball down the pipe and hit it on a line or bloop it in somewhere. But if you show you can hit a little, now they're going to start buzzing you inside, figuring out the holes in your swing, and treating you like a real hitter. That's going to make it a lot harder."

My ego, and Mom, say that with hard work anything is possible, and it's hard to fathom that if Randy Johnson can be a career .127 hitter in the majors, a reasonably coordinated fan, with a lifetime dedicated to the game and high-level training, couldn't eventually get to the .200 mark. But that's a long-off, optimistic, borderline-crazy hypothetical. The here and now is that fans certainly do not hit as well as major league pitchers, and the large majority don't even have the potential to hit as well as the very worst ones with extensive training. So the next time you see one of these seemingly awkward creatures going down on strikes, don't think you could finish your hot dog and come out of the stands and do better. To put a finer point on it, unless you were a pretty good hitter in high school or college and have been training *daily* for years with professional instruction, hitting .100 in the major leagues is not a realistic proposition.

Now, where does all of this leave ol' Mike? Well, hopefully not composing another e-mail to me. White Sox fan Ted Kwitkowski once said, "If it's got tits or wheels, it ain't nothing but trouble," but I'm not sure that's applicable here. However, Hall of Fame general manager Branch Rickey had a nugget that did fit: "Never surrender opportunity for security." By not taking a chance, Mike gave up the opportunity to be embarrassed publicly for the safety of false bravado and private self-loathing. . . . Wait, maybe he had it right to begin with.

DO PRO ATHLETES REALLY PLAY HIGH?

An NBA player's umpteenth look-away pass on a fast break flies out of bounds, and your buddy sarcastically says, "What the hell is that guy smoking?" Courtesy laughs all around, and no one really pays the comment a second thought. But the tired joke may have a basis in reality more often than you'd think. Or if you're a Trailblazers fan, the following may not surprise you at all.

Grizzled former NBA power forward/car wash magnate Charles Oakley, calling the league's drug policy "a joke," told the *New York Post*, "You got guys out there playing high every night. You got 60 percent of your league on marijuana." Other estimates of the number of NBA ballers who *play* under the influence range from as low as 10 percent to as high as 75 percent. Whatever the actual number, one thing's for sure: with marijuana not tested for by the league, NBA action is fannnntastically drug addled.

But while the NBA is most notorious for players toking doobie bongs, it isn't the only sport where hep cats are tuning in and dropping out.

Skier Bode Miller famously said on *60 Minutes* that he had competed drunk on more than one occasion. The late Stu Ungar, the only three-time winner of the World Series of Poker, was found passed out in his hotel room from a drug overdose during the 1990 WSOP—but he had already racked up so many chips that he still finished ninth, even after the dealers kept picking up his blinds. LPGA golfer Laura Baugh, formerly a raging alcoholic, arrived drunk at tournaments and hid minibottles of champagne in her golf bag. After getting plastered during a rain delay of a tournament and birdieing her last five holes, Baugh had this to say: "One of the beguiling things about drinking is that it can help you play better."

You got that, kids?

It's not just fringe athletes that are getting twisted, either.

The violent nature of the NFL wouldn't seem to allow for much in-game recreational use, but in reality the sidelines can be wilder than the Vikings' party boat. Former All Pro linebacker Thomas "Hollywood" Henderson has admitted to sniffing liquefied cocaine during games including Super Bowl XIII. Lawrence Taylor, notorious for his drug and alcohol use, claimed in his 2003 book, *LT: Over the Edge* (later made into the poorly received children's film *LT: Over the Hedge*), that "I never played when I was high." But he did admit, "Many times I'd be out all night, and then have to take a lot of that over-the-counter speed [that] truck drivers take to stay up." Former teammate Butch Woolfolk said LT "drank so much liquor it would come out of his pores." And a former college teammate, Donnell Thompson, said that he once took Taylor out to bars all afternoon before a Giants' preseason night game and "got him wasted." Remember, though, LT didn't play high.

Many football players will ingest just about anything to endure the physical pain of playing. The list of players who have had painkiller addictions is extensive, including quarterback Brett Favre and, most extremely, defensive end Jason Peter, who had an eighty-Vicodin-a-day habit. Said Peter: "You do what you gotta do to be on the field." Somebody tell that to Fred Taylor.

While football players may need all sorts of pain-relieving remedies for their hard-knock lives, baseball players basically exercise only about ten minutes a game. Despite this, or perhaps because of it, their drug choices are both plentiful and varied. (Note to Red Sox fans: Please keep in mind that I'm focusing solely on players, so neither Butch Hobson nor Grady Little qualifies.)

In his classic inside-the-locker-room account *Ball Four,* pitcher Jim Bouton became one of the first to speak publicly about players' reliance on pregame "greenies," also known as speed or amphetamines, which are used more as a performance enhancer than for anything recreational. In a *Playboy* interview in 1979, baseball role model Pete Rose admitted using amphetamines, and in October of 2006 he made a similar confession to David Letterman. But sandwiched between those two interviews was testimony he gave under oath in the case of a doctor accused of illegally prescribing greenies to the Phillies, in which he gave a different response: "What's a greenie?" This Pete Rose character does not sound very trustworthy!

Major League Baseball finally banned amphetamines before the 2006 season, when Larry "Chipper" Jones and many other players were saying that use of greenies was still prevalent. When Arizona Diamondbacks relief pitcher Jason Grimsley was busted later that year, he told federal authorities that major leaguers took greenies "like aspirin."

It's not as common as greenies, but big leaguers have been known to step on the field liquored up. In his autobiography, pitcher David Wells said he was "half drunk" during his 1998 perfect game. It's one more trait that Wells has in common with his idol Babe Ruth, who, legend has it, was often bombed on the field. Other Yankees known for playing shit-faced are Hall of Famers Mickey Mantle and Whitey Ford, after whom the Betty Ford Clinic was named.

Almost every current major leaguer I spoke to knew of players who had stepped on the field under the influence. When asked what the signs were, the players typically responded the way Giant Ryan Klesko and Padre Jake Peavy did: "I just knew." Interestingly, another Padre, center fielder Mike Cameron, had a more intimate experience with game-day tipsiness:

"Shit, I've played drunk."

When?

"New York City."

What were the circumstances?

"I went four for four with two jacks and eight ribbies. I'm not saying that's the only day I played drunk, but that was the best one."

Further evidence that vodka tonics may replace anabolic steroids as the new performance enhancer of choice.

Moving up the party ladder to hard drugs, there have been a number of cocaine scandals in baseball, the most prominent involving former AL MVP Vida Blue and NL MVP Dave Parker. Another NL MVP, Keith Hernandez, didn't mind doing a little coke as a pick-me-up before a game. And according to writer Alan Schwarz, all-star Tim "Rock" Raines described during the Pittsburgh drug trials "how he kept a gram of cocaine in his uniform and snorted during games."

Perhaps the pinnacle of illegal drug use in any sport was Pirates pitcher Dock Ellis's 1970 no-hitter against the San Diego Padres. His first-person account of the game sounds a bit like that of a Cubs fan at Wrigley Field who's been out in the sun too long. Of course, it makes perfect sense . . . once you know he says he was on LSD at the time. "I can only remember bits and pieces of the game. I was psyched. I had a feeling of euphoria. . . . The ball was small sometimes, the ball was large sometimes, sometimes I saw the catcher, sometimes I didn't. . . . I chewed my gum until it turned to powder."

Dock Ellis, bringing together America's mainstream and counterculture national pastimes with startling brilliance. Shine on, you crazy diamond.

HOW BIG IS THE GAP BETWEEN MALE AND FEMALE ATHLETES?

Artie Lange is a comedian, actor, and regular on Howard Stern's radio show. He's thirty-nine years old, stands 5'9", and weighs in at "somewhere between 200 and 300 pounds depending on how much he's eaten or thrown up that day," according to ArtieLangeDeathWatch.com. Referring to that website—which ran for years but was discontinued because "while this started out as a goof, as Artie's life falls apart, it becomes less funny"—Lange said, "They're making a couple of very good points." Artie has a major, major drinking problem. He has been in and out of rehab for abusing coke and speed, and is famed for saying, "I snorted heroin once by accident. It was amazing. But kids, don't snort heroin. It's too good." Artie was once called a "soul mate" by none other than Courtney Love. He is, by all accounts, a fat and drunken mess.

Artie Lange also came within one basket of beating a professional women's basketball player in a game of one-on-one. Lange took on Marissa Graby, the twenty-four-year-old, 6'2" former captain of a Penn State Final Four team and a WABA and WEBA all-star, during an episode of *The Howard Stern Show* on April 23, 2003. The game came about after Lange claimed he could beat a sixth man on a WNBA team even though he hadn't even played in high school and hadn't picked up a basketball (or possibly even exercised) in a year. His comment drew laughter and ridicule, and

Stern and sidekick Robin Quivers placed bets that the degenerate comedian wouldn't even score 4 points in a game to 15.

To everyone's surprise, the game was a battle. Lange, between drinking spectators' beers, sank threes from all over the court while Graby went inside against the smaller and slothful radio host. A heavily winded Lange took a 14–10 lead and had game point before finally running out of steam (or whiskey—whatever it is he runs on) and losing to the much taller and more fit professional.

The bets and arguments that Artie Lange inspired on the Stern show were nothing unusual. The "Battle of the Sexes" debate is without question the most frequently and heatedly argued of all of the questions on the sporting landscape. With this controversial subject, even more than with racial issues and Joe Dumars's Hall of Fame candidacy, rational argument is frequently ignored. Do a quick Internet search for "Men versus Women, sports" and be prepared for countless hours of laughter-filled reading (the laughing "at," not laughing "with" variety).

At one extreme you have the out-of-shape Al Bundys, or in more drastic cases, Ted Bundys, who believe that practically *any* man could beat even the best female athletes in any given sport. This is just ridiculous—the recent Clay Aiken/Laila Ali bloodbath being a prime example.

At the other extreme you have a much larger segment of fans— women and men—who claim that the top men and women are not far off athletically. Many of them contend that the only reason women aren't in men's professional sports is that they aren't "allowed." One person commented in a blog post: "The same arguments were used when they used to segregate sports by race. If they hadn't integrated sports, great athletes like Michael Jordan would have never gotten the recognition that they deserve. . . . Once all sports are integrated, the great women athletes will get the recognition that they deserve." You may not need to be told this, but that is also ridiculous.

The truth of the matter is that the gap between pro female athletes and their male counterparts is much wider than the general public understands and considerably more severe than the sports media has ever presented. Not surprisingly, the gap is largest in sports where size, strength, and speed are essential. Somewhat more surprisingly, there's also a significant gap separating men and women in the games that are almost exclusively skill based.

Speed, Endurance, and Strength

In 1988, in Seoul, South Korea, sprinter Florence Griffith Joyner blew away the competition in the 100 meters with a time so startlingly fast that it still holds as the Olympic record today.

Also in 1988, Curtis Johnson in Palmetto, Florida, set a less heralded record that also stands to this day: fastest 100 meters by a fourteen-year-old boy in the United States.

Their times were virtually identical, with Flo-Jo doing her 100 in 10.62 seconds and Cur-Jo running a 10.64.

That was no exception. Let's take a look at some Olympic records compared with boys' U.S. high school records for the ages of fourteen and fifteen:

Speed/Endurance Record Times				
Distance	U.S. Boys' 14	Women's Olympic	U.S. Boys' 15	Men's Olympic
100M	10.64	10.62	10.42	9.84
200M	21.49	21.34	20.97	19.32
400M	47.16	48.25	46.55	43.49
800M	1:55.9	1:53.43	1:51.03	1:42.58
1,500M	4:04.1	3:53.96	3:51.5	3:32.07
5,000M	15:46.8	14:40.79	14:32.8	13:05.59
10,000M	32:48.0	30:17.49	31:43.2	27:05.10

Leaping Records (in meters)

Distance	U.S. Boys' 14	Women's Olympic	U.S. Boys' 15	Men's Olympic
High Jump	2.04	2.06	2.18	2.39
Long Jump	7.21	7.40	7.49	8.90
Pole Vault	4.72	4.91	5.33	5.95
Triple Jump	14.74	15.33	14.98	18.09

The most obvious gap is in the area of strength, which can be seen clearly in Olympic weightlifting records. While men's and women's weightlifting have different weight classes, they do overlap in the 69-kilogram class. Here are the records for that weight class (high school stats unavailable):

Weightlifting Records (in kilograms)

Event	Women's	Men's
Snatch	122.5	165.0
Clean and jerk	152.5	195.0

What's amazing is how often the women's records are slightly better than the boys 14s' but slightly worse than the boys 15s'. Based on this data, it's clear that puberty is an enormous factor in separating male and female athletes. (It seems obvious that any serious discussion of *why* there is a gap between men and women athletes should begin and possibly end here.)

If women are at such a disadvantage in terms of strength, speed, leaping ability, and endurance, it stands to reason that they may struggle in sports where these are major components of performance.

Basketball

The sport that generates the most questions and passion about male vs. female athletic competition is basketball. There's so much debate in part because many NBA fans feel that the league's subsidization of the WNBA forces them to sit through invasive cross-promotions that give the WNBA far more attention than its fan base would warrant.

Artie Lange wasn't alone when he said he thought he could beat a WNBA player; he was just one of the only guys to say it on national radio. Part of this might be attributed to the runaway box office hit *Juwanna Mann,* but there are men of varying shapes, sizes, and athletic abilities across the United States who insist they'd tear it up in the WNBA. Certainly, not all of these men are correct; many of the guys who say this would make Artie Lange look like LeBron James.

I asked Mike Thibault, the head coach for the WNBA's Connecticut Sun and a former coach for the NBA's Milwaukee Bucks, why some men who can't even make a layup think they could play in the WNBA. "The reality is it's very easy to say that from the view from the couch," he remarked. Having spent days at a time on the couch, I decided to see if the historic Lange vs. Graby showdown was a fluky near-upset along the lines of Princeton almost beating Georgetown in 1989. I arranged a one-on-one battle against a current pro and former honorable mention All Pac-10 point guard for UCLA; it turned out to be a Kaufmanesque romp: 21–14.*

---

* When I began writing this chapter I put out an open call looking for a game against a female pro, and to her credit, Natalie Nakase was the only player who contacted me with an interest in playing a real game. We were both point guards and there was not an enormous spread in skill, but the fact that I was 9 inches taller and 60 pounds heavier made for a total mismatch. This physical advantage allowed me to block almost any shot she took, grab every rebound, and shoot over

I spoke to basketball Hall of Famer Nancy Lieberman about the Lange match and the phenomenon of guys who get out of breath going to the kitchen for a beer giving a game to professional women's players. "Yeah," she said, "maybe some of these guys could win a game of one-on-one, but I'd like to see them try to get up and down the court." I feel comfortable speaking for both myself and Artie in saying we will not be taking her up on that challenge.

However, there are a number of examples of direct, full-court, five-on-five competition between men and women. On the college level, many Division I women's teams scrimmage against men's intramural players to improve the quality of women's play. And what kind of players help the women improve their play? Well, to say the least, a mixed bag. "We don't cut anyone, so it's a wide range," said Dean Lockwood, assistant coach for the powerhouse University of Tennessee Lady Vols. "We like to have a core group that you can keep around for two or three years. There are two guys who could have played small D-I, a couple guys who maybe could have played D-II or D-III, and then some guys who probably couldn't start for a high school team."

Sonny Vaccaro, the longtime shoe company executive who knows the world of amateur basketball inside and out, told me that the male intramural players "are very competitive against" the women's teams. When asked whether those guys were Division I–caliber players, he laughed. "No, they're not. That's for sure."

I asked Sonny how he thought women's basketball measured up

---

her from the three-point line at will, and probably tells you all you need to know about the differences in the men's and women's games. As a comparison, I would have a hard time even dribbling the ball and getting a shot off against the *worst* scholarship player on UCLA's men's team.

to the men's game. He replied, "If they [the WNBA] had an all-star team that practiced, I think they could be competitive on a low Division I level." But that would only be if they played with the women's ball, because the men's ball "is bigger and harder to shoot with."

Vaccaro, who virtually created the world of competitive high school summer basketball, said that the nation's best male fourteen- or fifteen-year-old players could also beat a low-level D-I men's team. So I asked if maybe by proxy these young teenagers could defeat a WNBA team.

"Yes," he said, "by proxy, they could."

The gold medal–winning U.S. women's Olympic squad, featuring Lisa Leslie, has also played against men, specifically, against the goofs of the NBA Entertainment League, who wouldn't beat a good high school JV team (league leading scorer: Brian McKnight). According to Shane Duffy, the league's "commissioner," the entertainers almost beat the women's team, getting down ten quickly and then playing them even for the rest of the game.

A good way to understand this issue is if Artie Lange is on par with the sixth man on a women's Final Four team, it stands to reason that Michael Rapaport may be the equivalent of a WNBA starter.

Champions of the women's game are quick to say that although the ladies may play below the rim, they play a more fundamentally sound brand of basketball. Anybody who has watched Josh Smith in action knows that fundamentals and teamwork aren't always at a premium in the NBA, but the truth is that they are just as bad in the women's game. WNBA games are littered with turnovers (WNBA: 0.77 turnovers per minute; NBA: 0.56 turnovers per minute). Also, WNBA players hit free throws at the same clip as their male counterparts (74 percent) even though they have the significant advantage of shooting with a smaller ball.

And statistics don't bear out the idea that teamwork is a hallmark of the WNBA game: 58 percent of hoops are assisted on for the women compared with 57 percent for the men. By my calculations, the women players are only 1 percent more unselfish than NBA players, which is something you never want anyone saying about you.

Tennis

Mention "Battle of the Sexes," and most people will immediately think of the 1973 match between Billie Jean King and Bobby Riggs, which King won in straight sets, 6–4, 6–3, 6–3. It was hailed as a major victory for the women's athletic movement, but really, it wasn't that far off from Lange vs. Graby. King, at the age of twenty-nine, was in her athletic prime, while Riggs, in his youth a great player, was fifty-five years old and out of shape . . . although that hadn't prevented him from beating the #1 female player in the world, Margaret Court, four months earlier.

Another view on the subject can be provided by the 1992 pay-per-view match between Jimmy Connors and Martina Navratilova. The forty-year-old Connors moved to the Senior Tour that year, while Navratilova, thirty-five, was ranked #5 in the world on the real women's tour. Connors won handily, 7–5, 6–2, even though he only got one serve and Martina was allowed to use half of each doubles alley.

But the best gauge is a little-known match held on a side court at the Australian Open in 1998. At the time, Serena and Venus Williams, already forces on the WTA, were making a lot of noise about how they could compete on the men's tour. One man took up the challenge, the 203rd-ranked male player in the world: a fun-loving, chain-smoking, German junkballer named Karsten Braasch.

It was an interesting matchup because the general perception, fueled through the years by the Williams sisters and promoted by the media, was that while these two probably weren't capable of being the *best* players on the men's tour, they could certainly beat many male pros.

Serena was trounced, 6–1, and Venus fell 6–2. By all accounts, Braasch went easy on them. Watching the match, Serena's coach Nick Bollettieri said, "He's being kind to her." Braasch himself said, "I took at least fifty percent off my serve. I came out with a few hard ones, but not too much because then it's not fun anymore and it was supposed to be fun."

Serena was, for once, humbled: "I didn't know it would be that hard. I hit shots that would have been winners on the women's tour and he got to them easily."

After the match, Braasch commented on how wide the gap between the top women professionals and men really was. "Against anyone in the top five hundred, [they would have] no chance, because I was playing like six hundred today."

John McEnroe took it a step further: "Any good college male player could beat the Williams sisters, and so could any man on the Senior Tour."

Soccer

For anyone who lived through the nineties, when the subject of "Girl Power" comes up, the mind immediately goes to the Spice Girls and the U.S. women's national soccer team. The national squad—which came into the public's consciousness with Brandi Chastain's made penalty kick/striptease in the 1999 World Cup—is the premier team in the world, having won two of the four World Cups.

At the suggestion of the team's publicist, Aaron Heifetz, I attended a scrimmage they were having against a boys 15 club team from Southern California. It was a tightly contested match that the women won 2–0. The boys were a midlevel Southern California club team, which makes them better than your average high school soccer team but obviously not the nation's best for their age range. The boys looked marginally quicker, the women looked marginally more skilled and more disciplined, but all in all it was pretty even.

After the match, I called Aaron, who has worked in women's soccer for years, to see whether the game was representative of a typical performance.

"We scrimmage against boys' teams all of the time," he said. "The boys thirteens we can handle pretty consistently, but when the boys start really developing at fourteen, and especially fifteen, that's when you start to see real separation and they pass up even the best women's players. They're just bigger, stronger, and faster. What're you going to do? Our younger girls from the youth program can compete pretty well with the younger boys. The fifteen-and-under girls can even play with some of the boy twelves."

Aaron went on: "Skill-wise, when we have our top eleven players out there, it's as good as or sometimes better than the boys fifteens. It's just that when they get to puberty, they're too fast for us. Eventually they might get a breakaway, or jump on a set play. That's how it usually happens. We're hanging in there, we have a lot of possession, then they get a breakaway or jump over someone for a header. That's how they usually get their goals. Now, if we're going to play seventeen-year-old boys, we are defending eighty percent of the game and they're just packing us in."

But Aaron provided a reality check for the out-of-shape guys with no soccer experience who probably think, "Hey, I've gotta be better than some fifteen-year-old kid, so I'm sure I could take the women's Olympic players."

"Well, most guys definitely could not compete at this level. In fact, most wouldn't be able to last five minutes in a game like this."

Golf

For all the talk of Michelle Wie eventually moving to the men's tour and surpassing Jack Nicklaus's majors record, no woman has made the cut on the PGA Tour since Babe Didrikson Zaharias at the 1945 Tucson Open. The teenaged Wie, despite having had success on the LPGA, as of this writing has painfully tried and failed several times to make it to the weekend at a PGA men's tournament.

Annika Sörenstam, the most dominant female golfer of her generation, played in a PGA event in 2003 at the Colonial. The short course played to her strengths, placing a premium on accuracy rather than driving distance. She still missed the cut, shooting 5 over par, which tied her for ninety-sixth out of 111. Sörenstam was not impressed by her own performance: "It was a great week but I've got to go back to my tour, where I belong. I'm glad I did it, but this is way over my head."

Her play garnered her respect from some of her male competitors, however, Rocco Mediate for one. "She's great," Mediate told me. "Her swing is so good it makes a different sound when she hits the ball."

What about low-level club players who think they could take her?

"Are you kidding me? How many guys in the world do you think can even go out and break par from the white tees?"

Hockey

The U.S. women's ice hockey team, who landed on a Wheaties box after winning the gold medal at the 1998 Winter Olympics, has had some fierce contests with their archrival the Canadian women's national team. But they've actually faced tougher competition than their Canuck counterparts: boys' high school hockey teams.

On January 5, 2006, the U.S. women's team lost to the Warroad (Minnesota) High School boys' team, 2–1. Later that month they took on three Connecticut high school teams, losing all three games. All of the defeats came in games played without checking, which would have been a huge advantage for the bigger and stronger boys' teams. The boys' teams also mixed in JV players.

These outcomes weren't aberrations; the women's Canadian national team, which won the Olympic gold medal in 2006, regularly plays and loses to Midget AAA men's teams (sixteen- to eighteen-year-olds).

Manon Rhéaume was the goaltender for the Canadian team at the 1992 and 1994 Women's World Championships, winning a gold medal both times. After leaving the national team she gained (some) fame and (no) fortune when the Tampa Bay Lightning stuck her in net as a publicity stunt and she became the first woman ever to play in an NHL exhibition game. With this precedent set, Rhéaume played a total of fifteen games for seven minor league professional hockey teams in the span of four years, finishing with a Goals Against Average of 4.47, about double that of a solid pro goalie.

Baseball

From 1994 to 1997 the Colorado Silver Bullets, an all-women traveling baseball team, played against semipro and amateur men's teams throughout the country. The original plan was to play the teams of the Northern League, an independent professional league that's the equivalent of A ball, but after they lost their first game, 19–0, that was scrapped. Said Hall of Fame pitcher Phil Niekro, the team's manager, "At this time, I feel that we cannot compete at their level." The team went on to play and lose against beer league teams, military teams, and under-eighteen squads before folding from financial losses.

Ila Borders, the Manon Rhéaume of baseball, played professionally from 1997 to 2000. Her three-year totals included a 2–4 record and an ERA of 6.73 in the Northern League. However, Yankee centerfielder Johnny Damon's throwing motion leads many experts to believe that the door might be open for women to play the national pastime. Tom Whaley, executive vice president for the St. Paul Saints, told me that Borders had impressed him when she pitched for them during the 1997 season. "She was good. She was so smart on the mound. She really had a unique feel for pitching."

Whaley added, "I don't think there's any question that she'd strike out anyone who just grabbed a bat and came out of the stands."

Tom makes a good point, but actually, Borders did face an average fan: none other than Artie Lange. With $10,000 going in her pocket if she struck out Lange, he walked and singled off of her. Lange was a good high school baseball player but at the time of the confrontation was best at being a blubbery mess.

Pool

Washington Post columnist Fred Bowen has written, "I figure that the women can compete with men at any game where physical strength and raw speed are not essential." No, Artie Lange didn't beat Bowen in a writing competition to prove him wrong. In fact, while Bowen is overstating the case, the gap between men and women does indeed shrink in sports where size, strength, and speed play less of a role.

Billiards is a good example of a game where the difference becomes less extreme. Hall of Famer Jean Balukas actually competed on the men's tour in 1979 and finished in the middle of the pack in some events. Currently, top-ranked players Allison Fisher and Karen Corr are both capable of winning matches against male professional players.

But while the gap shrinks, it doesn't disappear entirely. Bowen wrote that pool is one of the games that "should be no problem" for women, and he added, "So why are there separate leagues or tournaments for women?" Doing a little research may have helped Fred solve this mystery. Even the great female billiards players haven't been able to consistently compete with male pros over an extended period of time. In 1998, the #1–ranked Fisher played a gimmick 9-ball series against 55-year-old Grady Mathews; Mathews won, 11 games to 10. Corr, meanwhile, has been a middling player when competing in lower-level, regional men's events.

The most famous women's pool player, former World #1 Jeanette "The Black Widow" Lee, told me, "You would not believe how many men, in my world, can wax me."

But she was talking about the top players in the world, not just any guy in a bar.

"I hear guys who aren't even good pool players all the time telling me they can beat me. It's a joke. They wouldn't have a prayer."

Darts

"Darts has nothing to do with strength, speed, height, or weight. By all rights it should be the same. But it's not even close."

That was Paul Lim, the top darts player of the United States, commenting on the fact that men consistently outperform women in darts.

He continued: "I've heard a lot of people talk about how women and men should be the same even though they aren't in golf, but in golf there is power involved. Same with bowling. In darts I just can't figure out why there would be a difference."

I suggested that the difference might be attributable to fewer women playing, but he blew that idea out of the water.

"In Japan we did a survey," he said. "There are roughly a million people in Japan playing darts right now and it's a fifty/fifty male/female split."

Lim has played against some of the best women in darts. "I recently did an exhibition in Japan for Sega where they invited the top female steel-tip player in the world, Trina Gulliver. She's a good player, but out of a hundred games I'd beat her eighty-five times."

Paul wasn't bragging. He was genuinely puzzled by the gap between male and female players. "Why, though? I can't figure it out."

The numbers bear out Lim's case. "The top women have about a 110-point 3-dart average," he pointed out. "The top men are in the 125 to 135 range." Also, according to the British Darts Organisation, the highest fifty tournament averages among men at the World Professional Darts Championships range from 31.56 down to 29.42; the women's highest fifty averages range from 27.93 down to 20.03. That's a significant difference.

Troubled as he was by the disparity, Lim couldn't avoid the obvious conclusion: "There are just so many good male dart players. The top women may not be in the top thousand players in the world."

The Gap

So when all of the data are laid down, just how big a difference is there between the top male and female athletes? Well, when you consider that women's Olympic records in track and field are on par with the records for American fourteen- and fifteen-year-old boys, that Olympic gold medal–winning women's teams frequently lose to high-school-age boys' teams, that top women's tennis players are absolutely annihilated by low-ranked male pros and well-past-their-prime greats, and that even in skill games like darts and billiards the top women aren't competitive, the conclusion seems inescapable: while the gap varies from sport to sport and individual to individual, overall it is enormous—and certainly much larger than is ever suggested in the media or is understood by the general public.

It's important to remember, though, that this refers very specifically to the differences between the world's elite male athletes and the world's elite female athletes. Not *every* guy sitting at home in front of the TV could, just by virtue of being a man, beat the top female athletes in their chosen sport, just as most couldn't defeat the elite teen males. In fact, in skill-based sports like pool or darts, it's a foregone conclusion that the armchair warriors would lose. In other words, if you saw Jeanette Lee at your local pool hall, Stacy Bromberg throwing darts at your local tavern, or Martina Hingis playing on your local tennis court, you would most likely come away impressed by their ability. This is where the bashers of women's sports go most horribly wrong.

The best female players are real athletes and need to be given athletic respect. As to how that fits into the sporting landscape for viewers who pay to watch the best of the best is a separate debate. But there does at least need to be a baseline of understanding that even though the very top female pros are not in the same universe as the male pros, they truly can play much better than a lot of guys who say otherwise. Probably even that loudmouth at the bar in the Zubaz pants who keeps telling you he'd kill Sheryl Swoopes.

ARE THERE GREAT PLAYERS WHO NEVER GOT A SHOT AT THE PROS?

"There's this bagger at my local supermarket who keeps telling me he could have played in the NBA. Is there even a 1% chance this is true?"

—Brian M., mortgage broker

Chances are you've heard this kind of thing before. Even if your local bagger isn't bending your ear about how he owned Chauncey Billups back in AAU, you've probably read about a bunch of players who'd supposedly be dominating in the NBA if only they had gotten a shot. This is a recurring theme in magazines like *Slam!* and *Dime*, which exist primarily as vehicles to sell overpriced new shoes and ruin the world.

Take the man *Dime* described as "arguably this generation's best playground player who never made it to the NBA." Ed "Booger" Smith built his reputation on the blacktops of Brooklyn, becoming so legendary that *Sports Illustrated* put him on its cover and dubbed him "King of the Streets." The storyline has always been that the only thing keeping Smith out of the NBA was an opportunity.

Well, while it's widely known that he never got a chance in the NBA, a little known fact is that in 1999 he did get a shot with the

Brooklyn Kings of the United States Basketball League (USBL). This minor league is the basketball equivalent of Double A baseball and a great proving ground for players with NBA aspirations. Many NBA teams send scouts to USBL games, and a number of NBA players, including Anthony Mason and Darrell Armstrong, got their start in the league.

Booger's first game was a total shambles and it didn't get much better from there. He was both small (5'9", 140) and slow, with no outside shot and very limited real skills. As a coach in the USBL at the time, I was on the opposing bench at that first game and saw all of the glory that was Booger. So did Mark Argenziano, USBL talent evaluator, who summed up the playground legend's performance perfectly: "Jarrod West [a 5'10" second-tier USBL point guard] turned him inside out."

In an effort to entertain the home crowd, Booger tried the full-court passes and flashy ballhandling that had helped his legend grow. Some of these attempts brought the crowd to their feet, but most resulted in turnovers. This is an acceptable excitement vs. success ratio in a pickup basketball game where everyone is a 4-F, but not in a professional league. For a point guard in a real game, launching behind-the-back passes into the third row gets your ass on the bench. And that's exactly where Booger went in the second half. Soon he was sent back home . . . which was to Brooklyn . . . which was not very far at all.

Booger Smith isn't the only playground legend whose talent hasn't matched his press clippings, as Argenziano pointed out. "*Slam!* magazine did a feature on the fifty greatest streetball players ever. Six of them were on that Brooklyn Kings team and they didn't even make the playoffs."

No matter how much these magazines want you (or more appropriately, your thirteen-year-old brother) to believe the best basketball players are the ones you'll only hear about through reading their articles, the reality is that most of what they write about playground legends is ridiculously misplaced hype.

But the funny part is, when you dig beyond this fantasy world and do real scouting, you discover that plenty of players *could* compete in the NBA if given a chance . . . just not always the guys getting the press. One candidate was on the floor the day Booger Smith made my eyes bleed. While Booger was busy throwing the ball into the stands, another player from Brooklyn who made his name on the blacktops, William "Junie" Sanders, was virtually unstoppable, scoring 44 points and carrying the Kings to victory. Junie had played professionally in leagues all around the world, and he never averaged fewer than 17 points per game in any of them. Having heard so much about Booger, and much less about Junie, seeing the difference between the two was remarkable.

Of course, just being able to score 44 in a USBL game doesn't mean someone could play in the NBA. While it's entirely possible Sanders had the talent to be a legitimate NBA player if things broke right for him, one of the difficulties for a little known player to even get a chance, and what minimizes his value to an NBA team, can be duplicate skills. Being able to score in bunches, which was Junie's calling card, is a difficult skill to get recognized for when almost every NBA team has top-notch scorers who take the majority of the shots.

When it comes to high-caliber pro basketball players like Junie, the evaluation process becomes tricky. Typically, when dipping outside of the traditional player talent pools (i.e., Division I college and European players taken in the first round of the NBA draft), pro teams are looking for role players who have a specific skill (shooting, rebounding, defense) and can work within a team framework, take care of the ball, and not cause problems. Not exactly the profile of most street legends. In other words, in a pickup game among NBA players, a casual fan might think specialists like Trenton Hassell, Reggie Evans, and Jason Kapono are the worst players on the floor, but in a structured NBA game where the "stars" are taking the majority of the shots, they have much more value than gunners who are going to get their 20 points on twenty-four shots and don't bring anything else to the table.

Argenziano cited one of the best examples of a player of this ilk. "Damon Jones couldn't get off the bench for the [USBL's] Jacksonville Barracudas in 1998, but has had a very good NBA career because he's such a good standstill shooter." Argenziano mentioned two other USBL point guards, one who reached the NBA and one who didn't. "Curt Smith was the MVP of the league and an excellent minor league guy, but he just didn't have that pro game. He didn't have that real extra gear or three-point range you need as a point guard in the NBA for catch-and-shoot situations. Now, Curt didn't go to the NBA, but his backup Moochie Norris did. Curt was probably a better overall player than Moochie, but Moochie can do the things you need to be in the NBA." Actually, Moochie cannot do the things you need to be in the NBA, but Mark's point is understood.

Beyond skill-set, politics also play a factor in determining why some players make it to the league and others don't. It's not unheard of for a player to get drafted as a favor to the team's star, if the player's college coach has ties to the organization, if the player has name recognition from college, if the player is from a foreign market the team is trying to break into, or if the team is trying to appease the fan base by taking a local kid. Sometimes a team will simply be comfortable working with a certain agent, or will agree to bring in one of an agent's players in order to get a chance to sign another of his clients.

And there are even more considerations, said Argenziano: "Having a bad attitude, 'right place wrong time,' an injury, not playing hard, not having your talents utilized or the right kind of talents—all of these things contribute to not being in the league."

With all of this in mind, I asked Portland Trailblazers coach Nate McMillan how many guys he thought could be in the NBA who aren't. Nate looked at me like it was the craziest question he'd ever heard.

"If you're good enough, you'll make it," he said flatly.

Well, aren't there a lot of really good guys who almost didn't get a chance?

"Name someone."

Darrell Armstrong.

"Yeah, but he made it. Gimme someone else."

Junie Sanders.

"Never heard of him. Gimme someone else."

D'Or Fisher (who played center for West Virginia University).

"Never heard of him."

Well, maybe there's a position for me in the front office of the Trailblazers then.

Cold stare. "There's thirty teams. If you're good enough, you'll make it."

But there are a lot of things that go into making an NBA team. Just because you're not currently on one doesn't mean—

"If you're good enough, you'll make it."

McMillan's attitudes largely explain why there are so many talented players banging on the door of the NBA who can't get in. But on the other hand you have guys like Cleveland Cavaliers general manager Danny Ferry and former Nuggets GM Kiki Vandeweghe who get that almost nothing in life is a pure meritocracy, let alone the NBA.

I hit Kiki with my friend's question about the grocery bagger. "If it's your bagger, you never know," he said, "but there's certainly a number of guys who could be in the NBA and aren't. A lot of it is circumstance. Sometimes you just don't get on the right track and then you never get back on the radar."

Ferry also didn't see making the league as some kind of divine justice. He cited many of the considerations Argenziano did, plus many others. A big factor, Ferry said, is guaranteed contracts. Even if first-round draft picks never develop, or if veterans locked in to long-term deals drop off in performance, teams will stick with them because they can't get rid of the contracts. Actually, we can take Ferry's point a step further: Even if a first-rounder's original team gives up on him (which takes a lot, because this is admitting they made a mistake drafting him in the first place), often other teams will be willing to take a chance on him—and give him another guaranteed deal—because of that first-round pedigree. By the time everyone realizes the player isn't good, he's already been in the league five or six years. And by that point he might be a veteran leader or a good influence in the locker room, so he sticks around for another five or six years even though he was never good enough to play in the league to begin with. You know, like Danny Ferry.

Blowing a huge hole in Nate McMillan's argument, Ferry added, "The line between the bottom third of the league and the next 150 people is very, very thin. The contract situation, the team situation, and so on, means guys don't always get the same opportunity. I'm probably exaggerating a little; it's probably more like the last 150 to 200 people where there's a lot of guys who could fill those spots."

For a closer perspective on what it's like to be on the outside looking in, I approached Bruce Bowen, a man who for years couldn't find a home on an NBA roster, going from the CBA to Europe to being waived by NBA teams before finding a role as a defensive pest on the San Antonio Spurs.

"Why you tryin' to ask that kinda stuff? This ain't no rags-to-riches story!"

Well, maybe NBA players aren't the best athletes to talk to about this subject. Besides, it's not like baggers trying to be NBA point guards are the only potential Cinderella stories; player personnel decisions in all sports can be a total crapshoot. There are countless baseball players who tore up the minor leagues but never made it because they were considered too small or otherwise didn't look the part, or because, like Junie Sanders with the NBA, they didn't fill a specific need. (Think about those left-handed relievers who always have jobs because major league teams need lefty specialists.) One player who almost got overlooked was Bryan Harvey, who was playing for his company's softball team and on a stroke of luck got signed by the Angels after pitching one time in a weekend semipro tournament; he became a two-time all-star closer.

Then there are football players like two-time MVP Kurt Warner, who really did work in a grocery store before making the NFL, and Hall of Fame quarterback Warren Moon, who had so much trouble getting a tryout that he finally went to play in Canada to start his career. Pro Bowl linebacker Ronald McKinnon *literally* had his name picked out of a hat by the Arizona Cardinals coaching staff when they were deciding between cast-off players for an extra body for training camp.

The patron saint of the overlooked is, of course, Vince Papale. Papale, whose story was given the Hollywood treatment in the Mark Wahlberg movie *Invincible,* barely played football in high school and didn't play at all in college. But while working as a bartender and substitute teacher, he caught on in the World Football League. After the WFL, he got a private tryout with Coach Dick Vermeil of the Philadelphia Eagles and made the team as a wide receiver and special teams player. At the age of thirty, he became the oldest rookie nonkicker to play in the NFL.

Papale told me that other guys like him could play in the NFL but aren't given the opportunity. "The scouts just assume they have it all figured out," he said. "They've got an ego about them where it's like, 'Hey, there's no way we missed anybody.' . . . I had a football aptitude but I didn't have a football *pedigree*. I didn't have a college experience; I didn't have a high school experience; the only experience I had was playing in bar leagues. That's the main thing working against you if you're not coming through the system. They just assume because you don't have a pedigree that you can't play the game."

Although there's no movie about him, there's a modern-day Papale playing for the San Diego Chargers by the name of Clinton Hart. Hart passed up opportunities to play college football in order to stay close to home to care for his family and pursue a baseball career. When baseball didn't work out, he walked into a tryout for Arena2—the minor league for Arena Football—and made the team. He worked his way up to the Arena Football League and NFL Europe before finally making the Philadelphia Eagles.

Hart agreed that NFL teams miss some good players by focusing on pedigree. "There's NFL guys with big names that if no one knew who they were, they couldn't make an Arena2 team. They come to the [NFL] and it's overwhelming to them. Can't handle the pressure, can't handle the books, can't learn and adjust. But there's guys who weren't that big of a name in college who are playing in Arena and better than these guys but never got the opportunity. I was in the right place at the right time, but that's not the case for everyone. [NFL teams] overlook a lot of people because they weren't the big name in college or it can be something as simple as a bad 40 time. And once all of the teams pass on a guy, no one wants to take a chance ever again. I don't understand it, but it is what it is."

Now, for every Vince Papale or Clinton Hart there are a hundred Booger Smiths whose game doesn't match their hype. And chances are that, no matter how many times they tell you otherwise, the bagger at your local supermarket couldn't have played point guard for the Pistons and your uncle Rico couldn't have starred in the NFL. But all of the Nate McMillans of the world can't change the simple truth that professional scouting isn't perfect, and sometimes deserving players end up putting cartons of eggs into paper bags instead of basketballs into hoops.

HOW WOULD A PRO BOWLER DO AT SKEE-BALL?

P-D-W.

If you know what those initials stand for, there's a good chance you already have a smile on your face. If you don't, allow me to bring a little more joy into your life.

PDW stands for Pete David Weber, and it's what the pro bowling star yells into the camera to express his excitement after a big roll in a match . . . sometimes punctuating it by making the "suck it" *V* gesture toward his crotch and yelling "Get it right there!" Weber, always seen in televised matches wearing his trademark sunglasses, is the bad boy of bowling (having been suspended for "conduct unbecoming a professional") and is one of the most entertaining personalities in all of sports.

Weber's moves, influenced by the WWE, are a godsend, but beyond his colorful stage persona, he's also one of the best bowlers of all time. The son of legend Dick Weber, Pete made the Hall of Fame in 2002, and through 2006 had won thirty-two events, seven major titles, and three Bowler of the Year awards. Some say he single-handedly rescued the Pro Bowlers Association (PBA) from the verge of bankruptcy and made it a viable business. Now I was going to see if he could help me win a shitload of tickets at skee-ball.

Skee-ball, for those who grew up in communist Russia, is a game played at family fun centers where a player rolls a tennis-sized ball up a ramp nine times, attempting to get it to enter one of five different holes, each marked with a different point value ranging from 10 to 50. Newer machines also have two 100-point holes. It's just like bowling except the track is inclined, there are no gutters, and you can win a Chinese finger torture toy or super bouncy ball if you do well.

I met up with Pete and his wife, Tracy, at the Par-Tee Center in their hometown just outside of St. Louis, Missouri. It would go down like this: Pete and I would play five games apiece to see how many tickets we could win from the skee-ball machine. The more tickets, the more chintzy prizes we could get at the counter. I was curious to see what kind of crap a guy like Pete could win if he wanted to hang around amusement centers all day.

We put the quarters in the game, the balls rolled down, and PDW held the skee-ball up like he was looking at the Hope Diamond. "This'll work."

Rolling for trinkets.

We were both rolling well, combining for 670 points through the first two games. Strategically, Pete and I weren't trying to bank the balls off the rail as some heathens do but instead were firing them straight in, going for the 40s and 50s. (Pete, playing on a newer-model machine, would occasionally go for a 100.)

I was hot in the third game, nailing 40 after 40 and ending up with 260 points. When I looked over to gloat, Pete, appropriately, had put up a 300 game. (Asked how many 300 games he had in bowling, Pete said, "Ah, I don't even know, who cares." But when Tracy said "Ninety-four," Pete chimed in, "Yeah, and that's at [the age of] thirty-nine.") After the fourth game we were still scorching: Pete had a 270 and I put up a 240.

We had one more game to play, and what would a day with PDW be without a little competition to make things interesting? I challenged Pete to a bet. One game of skee-ball, winner take all. All = tickets for worthless trinkets.

Pete immediately went for the jugular and began nailing everything. I fell behind and started desperately going for 50s, but it was too late. I lost to the Hall of Famer 270 to 170.

"That's right, I won," Pete said. "PDW is definitely in the house. Now I'm taking all the tickets!"

Weber grabbed his tickets and mine.

"I think I've got enough to get a stick of gum now."

As Pete studied his prize options, I asked the proprietor of the establishment what the all-time skee-ball record was.

"What's the record here? Well, we don't officially have a record but the most I've really seen is about 290."

This guy just put up a 300 game, I said.

"Well yeah, but he's PDW."

I asked Pete how he would do if he got to play every day.

"Nine 40s would be 360 so my strategy would be to get more balls in the 40 than you got. I pretty much go for the 40s. It's got a little bigger hole on it, the ball hits a little easier. . . . 50s got a small little hole, it's a little further up there to get, so 40 is probably a good one. If you keep doing it every day, it's like any sport, eventually your eye-hand coordination is going to take over and you're gonna figure out how to get the 50s too."

Grinning ear to ear, PDW took the tickets and bought Tracy a sour apple lollipop, saying: "A sour apple for the sour apple." The rest of his tickets he used to get more junk for his kids. Compared to hardcore skee-ball players, our scores weren't great, but all in all, we won thirty-nine tickets in a span of about twenty minutes, spending a total of five dollars. Had we played for an hour or so, we could have had some totally tubular prizes like a clock radio or plastic jewelry. A day with PDW at Dave & Busters could have netted almost anything in the joint. But my inane daydream fantasies of busting out Chuck E. Cheese's were sadly interrupted when the owner of the rec center asked Pete to autograph a skee-ball. Goodbyes were said, and Pete and his wife were off into the cold St. Louis morning with worlds to conquer, lollipops to eat, and people to be told to "Suck it."

Weber	*Gallagher*
200	150
130	190
300	260
270	240
270	170
——	——
1,170	1,010

HOW MANY TAMPA BAY DEVIL RAYS CAN THE AVERAGE MAJOR LEAGUER NAME?

Countless baseball fans can tell you every player on every major league team. This level of knowledge garners them no financial reward, no greater social status, and no additional respect from their peers. In fact, this pursuit of worthless knowledge may detract from all three. But many of these fans assume that if they can recite rosters for pure enjoyment, the people who are paid to play baseball for a living must know this information as well.

I asked Detroit Tiger Chris Shelton, while he intently watched a Reds-Marlins battle in the team's locker room before a game, what the difference was between perception and reality when it came to baseball players' knowledge of their coworkers.

"The idea that we know all of the guys in the league is definitely not the case," he said. "I keep up with baseball in general. I was a huge fan growing up, but it's a lot harder to watch games now since we're playing when a lot of the other games are going on. Defensively, you have to know the hitters you play, and obviously the pitchers too, but most guys don't know every player on every team."

Major League Baseball is obviously not one big happy family, but how far from sitting at the grown-up table are some of the fringe players? There was only one way to test major leaguers' knowledge: a pop quiz. I asked players how many guys they could name from the most obscure team in baseball, the Tampa Bay Devil Rays.

All told, I quizzed thirty-seven major leaguers, and on average they named only six active Devil Rays—a little less than a quarter of Tampa Bay's twenty-five-man roster. And really, the average major leaguer probably couldn't identify nearly that many, since a lot of players who would have done poorly elected not to participate in the quiz at all. A representative response came from Mariners center fielder Jeremy Reed: "I'm not getting involved in that." When told what the average was, he replied, "Oh, I couldn't name that many."

There was a noticeable difference in the knowledge level of pitchers and hitters, with pitchers naming more Rays. AL players also tended to do a lot better than NL players. For instance, the Tigers, who had just faced mighty Tampa, scored best with an average of eight. The Dodgers, in the NL, fared the worst with an average of four (despite having four ex-Rays on their squad).

Not counting ex–Devil Rays Julio Lugo, Toby Hall, Mark Hendrickson, and Joe Beimel (who has played with both the Devil Rays *and* the NL equivalent Pirates), White Sox slugger Craig Wilson correctly named the most D-Rays. After telling me, "I know most of the guys in the league," he quickly named the entire Devil Rays starting lineup, including a player the Devil Rays incorrectly identified as their starting first baseman, Travis Lee. All told, Wilson finished with a grand total of eighteen, and this was off the top of his head. (Can we get Wilson, who is as funny as he is knowledgeable, in the announcer's booth somewhere during the playoffs? There's a possibility that Tim McCarver doesn't even know the Devil Rays exist.)

Most players couldn't come close to eighteen. Seattle Mariners all-star second basemen José López got a goose egg, and Padres ace Jake Peavy could come up with only one name. "I know Carl Crawford and that's about it," he said.* "The American League in general I don't pay much attention to." He must be in an NL-only fantasy league.

So despite what some fans might think, pro baseball players aren't sitting around discussing how Johnny Gomes's rehab assignment is going or if Edwin Jackson is ever going to turn it around. For that matter, I'm pretty sure a pop quiz asking players to name all of *their own* teammates wouldn't have come back with all A-pluses—if you could even get someone to take the quiz. In reality, while the number of players the average major leaguer can name would certainly put him in the "knowledgeable fan" category, the pros just aren't as familiar with MLB rosters as hardcore fantasy nerds. For instance, I highly doubt any major leaguers wasted three months trying to figure out who the D-Rays closer was going to be . . . unlike myself. The Rays coaches may not have spent as much time thinking about this issue as I did.

Beyond a lack of general interest, why is it so hard for players to keep track of their fellow major leaguers? Well, although your coworkers aren't on television every night (unless you work for a company whose executive management is perpetually under indictment), take a look around your own company. You may know everyone in Accounting, but over in Human Resources you can barely keep up with the new hires. A similar thing happens in the MLB. Journeyman catcher Todd Pratt put it succinctly: "With all the player transaction, if you don't play a team, you're not gonna know a lot of guys on them. Unless they've been around for a

---

* Crawford was the one guy everyone could name—everyone except for Lopez, that is. Pitcher Scott Kazmir came in a distant second in terms of mentions.

while or you played with them, it's hard to keep track with all of the player movement now."

Of course, it's even harder to keep track of the poor D-Rays, who lose ninety to a hundred games every year. Pitcher Mark Hendrickson, who played two and a half seasons in Tampa Bay, explained it best: "When you're not winning, no one wants to pay attention to you."

Not even your opponents.

HOW GOOD ARE PRO GOLFERS AT MINIATURE GOLF?

We've all played miniature golf and had a blast. Through the windmill, into the trapdoor, over the drawbridge, we whacked our brightly colored ball with our junky plastic putter and hoped for the best.

But how would a PGA pro do under these circumstances? Yes, they putt for millions of dollars, but would men who need absolute quiet to hit a shot be able to deal with putting through a waterfall? To find out, I went to Statler's miniature golf course in Greensburg, Pennsylvania, and played the town's finest: PGA Tour veteran Rocco Mediate.

One of the best iron players in all of golf, Rocco has had a career that puts him in fast company: he is forty-seventh on the all-time earnings list with more than $12 million in winnings, has five career tournament wins, and has been ranked in the top twenty in the world. Maybe more important for our purposes, Rocco is a pro's pro. He's the kind of guy you could stick on any course, anywhere in the world, and he'd put up a good number. He fits the mental profile of someone who can handle putting a red ball up a fake anthill without the help of a caddy, a plumb bob, and a sports psychologist. Said Tiger Woods about the easygoing Mediate: "Rocco is very loose. No matter whether he's shooting eighty or sixty, he's still the same."

Before our match, though, Rocco was pessimistic about his chances. "I'm not a good Putt-Putter," he said. It's true that as far as PGA Tour pros go, Rocco is not the greatest of putters, and back problems have led him to switch between a long and conventional stick, which has further hindered him on the greens. That being said, Rocco is still a better putter than almost anyone on the planet.

We started and as it turned out, Rocco's evaluation of his Putt-Putt game was pretty much on the money. His ball was caroming every which way over the first eight holes, with a variety of poor approaches and missed 5-footers. "I'm a bogey golfer," Rocco said with a hint of disgust. "I'm a bogey Putt-Putt golfer." I, on the other hand, was shooting a sizzling even par and jumped out to a 5-stroke lead. "I'm a beastly golfer," I said. "I'm a beastly Putt-Putt golfer."

It was only going from bad to worse for Roc Live when on a particularly brutal hole he had to fish his ball out of the water. Making a double bogey 4, he could only laugh: "This is ridiculous!"

As Tiger indicated, it can be tough to read the laid-back Mediate, but I got the sense on the front 9 that Rocco wasn't exactly treating our no-stakes grudge match like it was a playoff at the U.S. Open. When he came storming back, I couldn't tell if he was getting a feel for the Statler's course, if his competitive instincts kicked in, or if it was just that he finally finished his mochaccino but the game was on. After thirteen holes he was 6 over par, only 3 strokes behind.

We successfully navigated the waterfall for dueling pars, but by the time he drained an ace on the sixteenth hole, he had shaved my once-insurmountable lead to just 1 stroke.

This was getting Normanesque. While Rocco easily parred out, I bogeyed 17 and found myself on 18 looking at a 3-foot putt to save par, a tie in the match, and possibly the world.

Shitballs!

Victory for the PGA champ, although a ruling from the cashier on the ball Rocco dumped in the water is still pending.

For as bad of a putter as I am and as good as Rocco is on the "big course," this was about the best I could have hoped for. But it would be a stretch to say that our pro was actually good at miniature golf. What kept him in check?

Rocco, always with a smile, blamed his rather ordinary performance on the conditions: "I don't have my own equipment. The ball's not perfect. Nothing's perfect. The balls aren't even white. No [courtesy] cars, no free stuff to take home. What was I supposed to do out here?"

Using the dulcet tones of Jim Nantz to bring a sense of seriousness to my question, I asked Rocco how the greens compared speed-wise with those on the PGA Tour. "These greens are pretty fast—they'd be like an eleven or twelve," he said, referring to what greens measure on the Stimpmeter. That was quick, even for the tour, but not so fast that Rocco couldn't handle them. The bigger problem was that the outdoor carpet at Statler's wasn't kept in as good a shape as the bikini-wax greens at Augusta, to say the least. The slickness, combined with the fact that the ball could hit an uneven patch and literally jump 3 inches to either side, made it a tough surface even for a PGA Tour pro to putt on.

Still, after a shaky front 9, when Rocco had a clean look at the cup, he'd invariably hit it in. His stroke also enabled him to consistently hit his target when trying to bounce a shot off of a rail or a rock. However, according to Rocco, hitting his intended target was not always a good thing: "When you play a Putt-Putt course for the first time, you don't know the angles so it's hard. And there's a lot of things we saw that even if you hit the ball where you're aiming it can turn out in bad ways."

These times when the correct target could even be identified were few and far between. More often Rocco's "strategy" came down to hitting a fluky putt that got him in the general area and then knocking in a gimme. In that respect, much of what went on in our match involved dumb luck. Having a good stroke doesn't make as much of a difference when you don't know the angle to play or can't see your target or the hole. Course knowledge is a key factor.

Professional mini golfers—and yes, there are professionals (see sidebar)—say that experience and course knowledge are so important that they can actually trump even the best PGA putter's skill. Top MGer Danny McCaslin tried to prove that in 2005 when he took on Ben Crane, the PGA's #1-ranked putter that year, in a televised mini golf exhibition. This matchup interested me because it pitted the very best against the very best: McCaslin is a great deal better at mini golf than I am (which is not saying much), and Crane is a better putter than Mediate is (which is saying something). Also, the event was televised, meaning that unlike Rocco, Crane had something on the line. McCaslin stayed neck and neck with the PGA player until losing on the final hole. Though he actually went on to win the second round, McCaslin expressed his frustration about not winning the first one: "I should be able to take care of business. He's probably got a better stroke than I do, but you've got to know how to practice. He doesn't know how to practice Putt-Putt." Never have truer words been spoken.

Danny's brother Matt, another professional MGer, has boasted, "If I got on a course with Tiger Woods, and he didn't practice, I'd beat him." As ridiculous as that sounds, Matt might be right. Basically, these guys are like video game players who have all the cheat codes. (Up, Up, Down, Down, Left, Right, Left, Right, B, A, START does not get you a hole in one, however.)

That's what dawned on me as Rocco and I talked after our match. He was describing the differences between a PGA Tour pro and the best guy at your club, but he could just as easily have been talking about the rough-and-tumble world of mini golf.

"If I take on the best player at your local club, he could beat me if he's a scratch player and I've never seen the golf course. Because he knows the course, he knows he's going to shoot sixty-five, sixty-six, sixty-seven. Well, if I've never seen the place, I'm going to be hitting a lot of blind shots and have to really play well to shoot that. Now, out of ten tries, he might still only beat me once, but it could happen. But let's go across the street where no one's seen the golf course. Then I've got him.

"That's the definition of a touring pro. We can take our game anywhere and play well, whereas a club player may only be able to perform at their home course."

Rocco looked back at a course filled with waterfalls and draw-bridges and laughed. "Well, hopefully we can take our game anywhere and play well, but as you saw today, it doesn't happen all the time."

Are There Really Pro Miniature Golfers?

Rarely have any of us, the normal people of the world, given a second thought to our score in miniature golf beyond "Ha ha, I beat you!" or "Is 8 the highest score you can have on a hole?" That is where you and I diverge from another segment of the population: the members of the United States ProMiniGolf Association, or USPMGA for "short." For even more brevity you can call them professional mini-golfers, or just "different." Bob Detwiler of the USPMGA: "Our tour is the PGA of miniature golf. You have to have the same skill level as a Tiger Woods or a Phil Mickelson to be successful on our tour." Yes, Bob! Rad!

These "different" people don't see the game the way you and I do. Their strategy extends past picking their favorite color ball; they bring their own putters to the course, arrive at tournaments days before to learn where to hit every shot, use a dimpleless ball (some bring twenty different balls, sometimes switching between holes to one that may better suit the terrain), and laugh out of derision, not absurdity, at the drawbridge. Some mini golfers even play in the Professional Putters Association and consider it below their athletic dignity to play on a course with a windmill or a clown's mouth. These proud warriors play on "Putt-Putt" courses, which have wooden rails and are much more boring than what you'd find at your local children's amusement center.

This may seem rather obsessive or a waste of time, but they're very good at what they do. There are pro miniature golfers who have shot perfect 18s in competition on a Putt-Putt course, meaning a hole in one on every hole. They can regularly break par (par being a 2 on each hole) on the "adventure courses" that you and I (or Rocco) sometimes lose a ball on. The "sport" even has a following of sorts in Europe, with purses going up to five figures and government subsidies paying for team psychologists and trainers. This, along with a semblance of national pride and having better things to do, may help explain why there are no American men ranked in the top two hundred in the world.

COULD ANY CELEBRITIES PLAY IN THE PROS?*

N o. No, they couldn't.
There are always stories floating around about how athletically talented certain celebrities are. The theme of these stories is invariably that the celeb in question could compete with pro athletes if they so chose but their passion for music/acting/rehab led them to a different career path.

A perfect example of how this phenomenon reaches absurd proportions came in the fall of 1999 when rap mogul Percy "Master P" Miller got a stunt tryout with the NBA's Toronto Raptors. To get an idea of the epidemic, the number of stories that ran about Master P's basketball prowess actually surpassed the number of Jar-Jar Binks jokes made that year. If you believed everything you were told, or even some of what you read, you'd think this guy was about to take over the NBA, when in reality, the Master had just found another stage to shit on.

No, you don't understand, Master P can really hoop! He almost made the Raptors!

A more telling evaluation came from Raptors guard Tracy McGrady, who in talking about Master P's game could have been

---

* This question was submitted by Chris Jackson, founder of H.O.P.E.

describing any ten-year-old's: "He's got a good jump shot from fifteen feet that he's going to knock down if he's not guarded."

Appropriately, P shot 28 percent from the field during his pre-season run before being cut. Even more disappointing for the Master was when he found out he owed the Raptors $50 million per the contract his agency negotiated for him.

Publicists, and sometimes celebrities themselves, spin these tales all the time, and they get traction with the public because trash entertainment sources like E!, *Access Hollywood, Extra,* and *ESPN the Magazine* eat up the garbage. Sadly, many writers and TV producers are willing to outright lie and do the publicists' bidding in the interest of gaining more access to their celebrity clients.

In what seems like another life, a young, slumming writer by the name of Todd Gallagher interviewed rap star Christopher "Ludacris" Bridges for ESPN.com. It seemed like an odd fit for a sports site, but his publicist assured me that he was a huge baseball fan and actually pursued a pro baseball career before getting into music.

An unedited excerpt:

> LUDA: Baseball was my main sport. That was my thing. I had all kinds
> of trophies and was a big baseball fan growing up. I played
> shortstop, was fast, could do it all. But I kind of got tired of it . . .

Wait for it, wait for it . . .

> LUDA: . . . and quit when I was about twelve.

Well, at least he was a big fan, right?

> TG: Would you rather be able to hit with the power of Mark McGwire,
> run like Rickey Henderson, field like Ozzie Smith, or hit for average
> like Ichiro?

LUDA: Who's the one that hit home runs?

TG: McGwire.

LUDA: Oh yeah, that one. Then that's who I'll pick. Hit for power like McGwire. You don't have to be fast if you can hit homers—and your average isn't important either. He's a home run hitter, and that's what I'm looking to do every time—hit a home run.

Luda isn't the only player in the game trying to hit fake home runs every time. This same sad, desperate writer we'll just call TG interviewed Frankie Muniz of *Agent Cody Banks 2: Destination London* fame. Muniz was very impressed with his own basketball skills; in a hoops scene for *Malcolm in the Middle,* he told me, the show's producers yelled at him to "tone it down" on the dribbling.

"Really?" I asked. "It wasn't believable?"

"No, because I was like—I was too good."

This was not temporary insanity stemming from eating too much candy before we spoke. An interviewer from PBS's *In My Life* once asked Muniz, "Would you consider playing basketball professionally?" His response: "In a second. Me and Li'l Bow Wow were just talking about it because he wants to be in the NBA too. We always play in the charity games together and against each other. He said, 'Dude, I'd do anything to get into the NBA.' I said, 'Dude, I'd do anything to get into any professional basketball league. Not even just the NBA.' "

Bow Wow (formerly Li'l Bow Wow) is twenty years old, stands 5'7", and has never played organized basketball on *any* level, let alone professionally. Muniz is 5'6", twenty-one years old, and a mediocre player in the NBA Entertainment League, where the level of competition is lower than high school ball. To give you an idea of where Frankie's abilities fall, he's better than Coolio but not as good as Roger Lodge. It's telling that PBS would ask Muniz whether he would "consider" playing basketball professionally; it's equally telling that the actor didn't immediately reply, "Are you utterly bat-shit insane?"

In Frankie's case, this bizarre personality defect probably stems from being a child actor and never being around anyone who introduced him to reality. For others, though, like Ludacris, the motivation goes far beyond immature vanity. Sports movies have become so popular that actors all want roles in these films. And to get a role as an athlete in a sports movie, it helps to be thought of as someone who has actually played sports somewhere other than on PlayStation.

Agents and managers try to convince film producers that their client could have played pro basketball or was a star center fielder in high school before choosing the theater. Part of this process is having the star's publicist flood the press with wild exaggerations of their client's abilities, knowing it can help get an audition or role that may have been previously unthinkable. If the client is deluded enough to already believe it or sees the value in carrying out the lie, all the better.

To get a more complete picture of celebrities' athletic ability, I talked to Mark Ellis, who as a sports coordinator for more than twenty-five films, including *Invincible, The Longest Yard, Miracle,* and *Summer Catch,* is the first guy the studios turn to when they need to make actors look like athletes.

"There's a reason some people are drawn to the athletic field and some people are drawn to drama class," Mark said. "It doesn't mean you can't do both, but it's rare.

"I tell all my athletes in all my movies when I bring these actors into training camp, 'Guys, these fellas can do things that you cannot do. They're very good at their skill set; you guys can't cry on cue, you guys can't pull off a dramatic scene, you guys aren't trained in this capacity. Now, they can't run a comeback, they can't rush the passer, they can't hit a line drive in the gap, they can't turn two.' "

Wait, Freddie Prinze Jr. can't turn two?

I asked Mark how many actors who are in sports movies could even play high school sports. I thought this would be an interesting gauge because Mark's expertise and knowledge of the celebrity talent pool means the actors he auditions are ones who realistically have a chance at getting the role of a pro athlete. In other words, not Frankie Muniz or Ludacris.

"Out of ten actors we audition for football films," he said, "maybe four or five could make a good high school team." Not too good, fake celeb athletes, considering that saying someone could *make* a high school team is about on par with "That guy can really hold a water bottle."

I asked Mark a few more specific questions, like whether he had to tell Oliver Stone that NFL coaches typically aren't 5'4" and don't yell "Hoo-ha!" after every play, but he chose to be very professional and discreet, which was unfortunate.

The fact of the matter is that almost none of these guys can play. From Snoop Dogg to Garth Brooks to Nelly, the celebs who are supposedly very talented athletes would have a hard time making a decent high school team in their sport of choice. Yes, there are a few who might be able to not embarrass themselves, like singer Brian McKnight, or perhaps even the Master of P, but just being average and getting a stunt tryout with a pro team turns the legend into "He's good enough to play in the pros!"

So when ESPN.com relaunches Page 3 with an article on how James Van Der Beek is thinking about playing for the Dodgers, or on how much ability Kevin Federline is showing as the QB in the remake of *We Are Marshall,* just know that it's always 100 percent bullshit.

And pray for me that I'm not the one writing the article.

Oh, These Guys Suck, Too

Let's further dismantle the hype machine and dispel some other myths about how good athletes are outside of their primary area of expertise: They all stink. From Michael Jordan's crappy golf game to Bronson Arroyo's terrible music career, none of these guys can do anything other than their sport nearly as well as we have to hear about.

Coincidentally, the one area where athletes seem to do okay is acting. Mike Ditka, Jesse Ventura, Ray Allen, Lyle Alzado, OJ, "Rowdy" Roddy Piper, Alex Karras, Dennis Rodman, Hulk Hogan, Brian Bosworth, Rick Fox, Shaquille O'Neal, Penny Hardaway, Howie Long, and even the great Michael Jordan are just some of the countless athletes who have tried their hand at memorizing and repeating lines. Granted, athletes turned actors have had varying degrees of success (Good: Dwayne "The Rock" Johnson; Bad: Brett Favre; Ugly: Shawn Bradley [Rimshot, please! My arms are tired from flying here!]), but while being a supporting actor in a movie that grosses $100 million is well respected and high paying, a number of athletes have pulled it off. Conversely, there are no actors remotely capable of making the switch to being even a backup catcher on the D-Rays. Conclusion: playing a sport may be harder than acting.

Outside of acting, by all accounts the most talented performer off the court is former NBA power forward Wayman Tisdale, who has reportedly released a number of albums with basketball-themed titles like *Power Forward* and *In the Zone*. Pick one up, if really boring jazz performed by a former NBA player is your thing. If so, may I also recommend *Out to Lunch* by Mel Turpin, *A Love Supreme* by Shawn Kemp, and Blue Edwards's *Kind of Blue*.

PLAYING ONE-HANDED, COULD A PRO BILLIARDS PLAYER BEAT AN AMATEUR?

In the popular documentary *The Color of Money*, Tom Cruise used the powers of Scientology to sink billiard balls one-handed. The film was a huge success, but Cruise's mind-bending artistry led many to question just how *real* this documentary was and if his one-handed shot-making was nothing more than a David Copperfield–esque trick pulled in editing.

To find a pool player as talented as the great Cruise, I called Hard Times Billiards in Bellflower, California, and asked for Dave Hemmah, the head pro, who knows the best of the best. Dave named the top one-handed players he had ever seen (that is, guys he had seen play very well using one hand by choice, not guys with hooks for one of their hands): the mercurial and temperamental Jose Parica, a living legend; Tang Hoa, a master at the pool game known as one pocket; and a man by the name of Morro, who I had never heard of.

I spent about a week attempting to hunt down Parica, but I might as well have teamed up with Bruce Willis and tried to find bin Laden. Next on my wish list was Tang Hoa, but he was traveling and unavailable for an extended period of time. I called back

Hemmah to see if he really thought Morro was that good. Dave said he was and convinced me to at least give him a call.

As it turned out, "Morro" was the nickname of Ismael Paez, a player I had most certainly heard of. In fact, I'd seen Paez play many times on TV, including his run to the World Championship finals. This was one of the greatest players in the world. He was a guy who could run out a table (*running out* means to break and then make all of the balls without missing) like it was his job, which it sort of was. In fact, with $5,000 on the line, he once spotted Kiefer Sutherland eight games in a race to nine, then ran nine racks in a row to win the match. When I first arrived, I saw Paez effortlessly run both the solids *and* stripes before sinking the 8-ball.

But even if Paez turned out to be better than the great Cruise, I believed that this was a matchup I should finally win. Let's put aside the false modesty for a minute. I am a very good pool player. Not exactly the world's greatest pickup line, but the truth nonetheless. The highlight of my pool "career" came in a bar in Kona, Hawaii, when I ran out three consecutive tables for a hundred bucks a game before leaving under the threat of physical violence. Hi, my name's Todd and I'm a total degenerate.

In fact, I thought my background in pool would make for such a lopsided matchup that I considered finding a replacement opponent for Paez. My confidence level was so high I actually felt bad for Paez because of the destruction he was about to be subjected to.

Then I saw him warm up one-handed.

He was sinking shot after shot. Apparently, big-money games of one-handed pool used to be very popular. Was it too late to go back to pretending to be too good and finding a replacement?

Meanwhile, as primarily a bar player and not being nearly as good as Paez, I was having a hard time adapting to the professional-sized table, which is both longer and wider than one you'd find at your local watering hole. Pro tables also have tighter, narrower pockets, making any kind of shot-making more difficult.

I won the coin toss (my first win to date versus a professional) and had the right to break. I snapped a decent one and made a solid. Then I took my first shot and made another one. And another, and another, and a sister and a brother. I was locked in. All told I ran six balls and left Paez staring at a lot of his own to make.

Which was a bit of a problem . . . for me. With my solids out of his way, Paez had all the room in the world to operate. Playing with barely any hesitation, to the point that it didn't even look like he was lining up his shots, Paez cleared the table with ease before just missing on the 8-ball in the corner pocket on a shot I didn't realize was even possible to attempt.

Showoff.

This left me with a long and difficult shot off the rail at the 6-ball. A make and I'd shoot back down table for an easy tap-in on the 8-ball for the win. A miss and the 8 would be Paez's.

Nailed it.

Gallagher: 1

Paez: 0

My shame at being proud of winning a game against a man playing one-handed was through the roof, but there was no time for confused emotions. The next three games were a battle. I was still playing out of my mind, but Paez was making shots with one hand I couldn't make with two. It became clear that the hardest part of playing one-handed for him was when the ball was in the middle of the table and he had to reach for it or when there was congestion and he had to "jack up," or elevate, the cue over a ball. If the table was open, or if he could lay the cue against the rail, I might as well have been watching on TV.

We traded wins, so it all came down to the fifth and final game. Paez had the break and was heating up; he had just run the table and I was worried I'd lose the match without even getting another shot. That became a realistic concern as Paez broke and again ran every ball until scratching on his final make before the 8-ball. This gave me an open table and ball in hand, a situation pros run out on 999 times out of 1,000. Of course, I'm not a pro, and I screwed it up, leaving one of my stripes on the table and the 8. Going for the win, Paez kicked my ball in on his attempt at the 8. This left me with my own attempt at the 8-ball on a long cut shot down the rail. I missed, but thankfully Paez was left with no shot. Oh, I meant it would be no shot for me. Paez banked it in easily—to refresh, playing with one hand—and took the match. Piss.

What a brave fight I gave him, though! The match may not have been won, but *respect* certainly was!

Eh, not quite. In the postgame conversation, I found Paez was left a little unsatisfied. "See," he told me, "to people who don't play, they see your game and think you are an excellent player. But to a pro you're nothing. I have not shot one-handed in a very long time. Give me a month, two months, you come back and it would not be so good for you."

So all that nonsense about how good I am and how well I played is to say this: These guys are freakishly good. I played just about as well as I could and not only did I lose, but if we had played more games and if Paez had gotten more practice, it probably wouldn't have even been that close. Unless you can run out table after table, or are the best pool player you have ever met, this is probably a case where the Professionals have the best of the Joefessionals.

I'll give the final word to the lovely Jamie Greenberg, who has accompanied me to many of my low-level money games through the bars of Los Angeles and lost a side bet on my Paez match to one of the camera guys.

"You played great. That's about the best I've seen out of you. Maybe if you practice really hard and make him play with his feet next time, you can even win."

ARE THOSE GUYS REALLY ATHLETES?

L et's consider two potential athletes, Billy Mitchell and Jeff Gordon. Mitchell gets to his machine, and in a grueling test of endurance, spends hours at the controls until victory is his. Gordon does the same. They both must withstand a nonstop barrage of reflex-testing hazards while remaining laser-focused for an extended length of time. They are both at the mercy of their machines, since one malfunction will mean the end of their competition.

The difference between these two men is that Jeff Gordon is a championship-level NASCAR driver, while Billy Mitchell is a marathon video-game player who holds the world record for Pac-Man.

For all their similarities, Billy Mitchell is not considered an athlete by any means but Jeff Gordon in some circles unequivocally is. Sure, Mitchell doesn't have to deal with 200-mile-per-hour turns, G-forces, or Junior comin' up his tail pipe, but then again, Gordon doesn't have to deal with Blinky, Inky, Pinky, or Clyde. They both rely on machines to do most of the hard work, and many of their raw skills (reflexes, long-term endurance, putting quarters in a slot) are similar.

The debate about what makes someone an athlete rages on in bars and living rooms across the country among people who are almost without exception not athletic themselves. By definition, an athlete is "a person who is trained or skilled in exercises, sports, or games requiring physical strength, agility, or stamina." Based on this definition, a good rule of thumb is that you shouldn't be able to look at the person performing the sport and say, "I could beat that guy in a race" or "I'm bigger and stronger than him" or "Hot damn, that lard-ass looks like he's going to keel over and die!" If you wouldn't take the guy on your team for a pickup game of football or basketball, then you're probably talking about a nonathlete.

Are you thinking what I'm thinking? Exactly. Now that we've eliminated NASCAR drivers and video-game players from the conversation, let's look at some other competitors. While the legendary warriors who have advanced to the top ranks of games such as darts, pool, and bowling are universally regarded as something less than real athletes—and most rational people seem to understand that anyone who engages in one-dimensional activities and endurance tests like eating a bunch of food in a sitting, riding around on a bicycle, or jogging thirty miles is not a real athlete—what about the professionals stuck in that middle ground of coolness where a guy on the street might legitimately think he could kick their asses? I'm referring, of course, to the lonesome football kickers, slovenly baseball relief pitchers, and white-bread pro golfers.

The Kicker

Mocked by fans and teammates alike, kickers are barely even considered a part of the team even though they can win or lose a game. "During practice," said Joe Conlin, who played football at the University of Pittsburgh, "I wouldn't even call them by their first name, just 'Kicker.' We're beating our heads in during two-a-days and they're holding the sticks and spotting the ball. You're a two-hundred-sixty-pound lineman who just went through a full practice and they're in the ice tub before you with a sore leg."

The kicker is usually thought of as a frail, effeminate, foreign man with boundless energy and a funny name—Balki Bartokomous with a helmet and shoulder pads.

There are two defining moments for the view of kicker as nonathlete:

1. The Arizona Cardinals' Bill Gramatica blowing out his ACL while celebrating a routine first-quarter field goal against the New York Giants in 2001. After making the kick, Gramatica collapsed to the ground in the midst of his incredibly embarrassing celebration, which involved a series of fist pumps followed by a jump in the air with an uppercut. Quarterback Brett Favre said, "If our kicker ever hurt himself like that, I'd go over and boot him right in the ass." Rarr! Show 'em how a real man plays a game, Brett!

2. The Miami Dolphins' Garo Yepremian's pass in Super Bowl VII, which made Lamar Latrell's limp-wristed javelin toss in *Revenge of the Nerds* look masculine by comparison. When asked about the play, a blocked kick that resulted in Yepremian's infamous backward pass/fumble and the Washington Redskins' only points of the game, the kicker replied, "Many big people were chasing me. I didn't know what to do. So I thought I would surprise them and throw it."*

---

* Yepremian, voted kicker of the decade for the 1970s by the Pro Football Hall of Fame, barely missed having both of the defining kicker-as-weirdo moments. The story, possibly apocryphal, goes that in his rookie year, after kicking an extra point in a game his team was badly losing, he ran off the field with his arms raised, yelling, "I keek a touchdown!" The quote would serve as the title for his autobiography. Yepremian followed up that lighthearted book with *In the Face! I Keek a Da Touchdown Again!*, *In My Country the Touchdown Keek You!*, and the deeply personal *I No Keek a Da Touchdown*, about his family's struggles escaping the brutal genocide in his native Armenia.

But are kickers really so hopeless? A quick look around the league shows different breeds. On one hand, you've got Sebastian Janikowski, who was a top junior soccer player, and Mike Vanderjagt, who started his college career as a quarterback for Michigan State.

On the other hand, you've got Bill Gramatica and his equally ridiculous brother Martin; Cole Ford, who attempted to kill Siegfried and Roy for, in the words of psychiatrist Norton Roitman, "the illusionists' treatment, dominance, and unhealthy intimacy he saw them having with their animals"; and Ray Finkel, who assumed the identity of a Miami police lieutenant and kidnapped the Dolphins' mascot as well as their star quarterback, Dan Marino, before the Super Bowl.

Pros: In terms of athleticism, kicking a ball at the NFL level is a feat at least on par with being Tony Siragusa . . . kickers are required to run and occasionally make tackles . . . they sometimes work out with the team and typically are in pretty good shape . . . most kickers have some kind of successful athletic background, usually in soccer . . . they'd probably rip up your backyard football game . . . bonus points for Mark Schlereth hating them.

Cons: The embarrassments and indignities of kickers know no bounds . . . the Gramaticas come off like yoga instructors . . . it's so easy that Tony Danza became good enough to be an NFL kicker just by kicking the hydraulic lever of his garbage truck . . . Jeff Reed sent around pictures of his shaved privates . . . *Lonesome Kicker* . . . Seabass Janikowski's gut . . . Gary Anderson.

Verdict: These guys are in pretty rough shape. About the only way they could get out of the athletic ghetto is if we included their partners in kicking, the punters. People frequently lump punters and kickers together, not entirely unfairly, but when it comes to athletic backgrounds, punters do separate themselves.

Brian Moorman was an all-state sprinter in high school, Darren Bennett and Ben Graham were successful Australian rules football players before jumping to the NFL, and Todd Sauerbrun does steroids, makes jarring tackles on special teams, and is basically John Daly minus the golden mullet and the propensity to shake uncontrollably when engaged in his sport. Also, on the whole, punters aren't knee deep in weirdness like their smaller and frailer brothers—although the late, great Reggie Roby used to wear a wristwatch on the field of play, and Jaguars punter Chris Hanson missed an entire season after cutting his leg with an axe placed in the locker room as a motivational tool and, in a separate incident, burned himself severely while making fondue at his home with Jaguars kicker Jarret Holmes.

The Relief Pitcher

The relief pitcher is widely considered the laziest and fattest part of a lazy and fat sport that was built by and for the lazy and the fat. This reputation was sadly reinforced by two separate incidents in 2005 when the portly Antonio Alfonseca of the Florida Marlins had to be forcibly restrained by teammates from eating his own extra fingers during a rain delay, and the Indians' corpulent closer Bob Wickman took the mound in an important divisional game against the Tigers wearing a beer helmet.

Relief pitchers have a long and storied history of nonathleticism in a sport where for years even positional players have been called into question. John Kruk, before ruining *Baseball Tonight*, ruined the reputation of baseball players everywhere when he said what everyone had been thinking all along about the porcine first baseman: "I'm not an athlete. I'm a professional baseball player." The blubbery Babe Ruth supposedly once ate twelve hot dogs and drank eight bottles of soda between games of a doubleheader, and Tony Gwynn's mom needed to make him a special double-XL uniform so he could play with the Padres.

So to stand out as out-of-shape and nonathletic in a sport filled with the out-of-shape and nonathletic takes some work. But still, relievers have done it. In addition to Wickman and Alfonseca, we've recently been treated to chubbers like Bobby Jenks, Rick White, Ray King, Francisco Cordero, and Armando Benitez. Before that there was the recently departed Rod "Shooter" Beck, who during a minor league stint, crushed beers after games with fans in the stadium parking lot. (He did this, of course, in the motor home that he lived in.) The enormous and beloved Rich Garces, also known as "El Guapo" ate himself out of the league. Charlie Kerfeld, who was caught eating a plate of ribs in the bullpen, asked for—and received—thirty-seven boxes of Jell-O in his contract. And Terry Forster, who was once called "a fat tub of goo" by David Letterman on national television, opined, "A waist is a terrible thing to mind."

To be fair, relief pitchers aren't that much porkier than their starting brethren. Major league pitching staffs in 2007 included some total hogs who are very successful at their craft— C. C. Sabathia, David Wells, Bartolo Colon, Livan Hernandez, and Sidney Ponson*—as well as a number of young, up-and-coming butterballs, led by Runelvys Hernandez, who began 2006 on the disabled list for the Royals with "weight problems." They're just part of the long list of fat fatties, from Mickey Lolich to Rick Reuschel to Fernando Valenzuela, who through the years have done very well as starters. Like a lot of relievers, these men were poorly conditioned, but at least they had the stamina to pitch more than one inning in a given day.

---

* Ponson is not, in fact, successful at his craft.

Pros: Being able to pitch on the major league level is, in many ways, a gift, and one is either blessed with the talent to do it or not. To be a baseball pitcher, you also typically have to be pretty tall and reasonably strong. It's near the top of the food chain in terms of athletic respect; kids all across the world grow up wanting to be a baseball player. Most pitchers were the best positional baseball player on their high school team and can hit way better than a guy off the street (see Question 12).

Cons: Relievers are out of shape and don't have to run or jump. Just look at some of those slobs.

Verdict: Overall, these are athletes, but barely.

The Golfer

Golf requires a massive amount of skill, composure, and dedication. Athleticism? Not so much. The game involves hitting a ball with a stick and walking to where you hit it so you can hit it again. That's it. It's never a good sign for a sport when you can play it at the highest level smoking cigs and wearing dress pants, a sweater vest, argyle socks, and Ray-Bans.

As with relief pitchers, conditioning is a major question mark with golfers. Anyone who's ever seen "Big" John Daly, Craig "The Walrus" Stadler, or Phil "Jigglin' Tits" Mickelson in action would be hard-pressed to say there's any kind of conditioning involved. For all the noise the media has made about golfers getting buff to keep up with Tiger, these guys look less like athletes than most professional eaters.

Adding to the embarrassment, golf is the only sport where a sixteen-year-old girl can, even for a day, beat a seasoned professional—something that hasn't been seen in the wide world of sports since 1973 when Tiffany Dixon made a series of fateful wrong turns and accidentally led the Daytona 500 for a lap before having her learner's permit revoked.

The golf swing is a complex action, made even more complex by the countless number of people trying to simplify it. But like the football kick, it is a repeatable motion that can be learned. Success, in many cases, has as much to do with having the money and time to hit balls for eight hours a day from an early age as with natural ability. This is in part because in golf, the talent pool is remarkably shallow. Like polo or yachting, golf draws from a very small and specific group of people—almost exclusively middle- to upper-class white guys. That holds true on both the PGA and European tours. (You go, Vijay!)

It's also clear from searching through player bios that most golfers didn't play much of anything besides golf growing up. When the guy who is the most revolutionary "athlete" in the history of your so-called sport is asked whether he's ever played anything besides golf and he says, "I've done other things—I've thrown a baseball a few times and thrown a couple of coins here and there," that may be immediate disqualification from the sporting landscape.

Pros: To be good at golf requires a great deal of skill and a lot of practice, something most people don't have the discipline to do. Great athletes like Michael Jordan have been unable to pick up golf and reach the level they've hoped to achieve. Pro golfers deal with high levels of pressure that most people couldn't handle. Golden Tee is fun.

Cons: Golf is the only major sport that requires virtually no physical exertion at any point. Besides, my grandmother is the club champion for her age division and can beat me. Though I'm very proud of her abilities on the links, I'd venture to say that there aren't any other sports where she can beat me. In fact, I'll lay down the gauntlet and say there aren't any grandmas who can beat me or any other able-bodied and reasonably coordinated man in his twenties in any sport.

Verdict: So that's where the line gets drawn. If there's a sport where a grandma can beat you, then that is not a sport, it is a game. And that makes golfers gamesmen—skilled gamesmen, surely, but not athletes.

DO ATHLETES THINK ABOUT THEIR STATISTICS WHILE THEY'RE PLAYING (OR, CAN I TRUST THESE GUYS TO PUT MY FANTASY TEAM ABOVE THEIR REAL TEAM)?

On the football field, Eddie George was the ultimate warrior. The Tennessee Titans' Pro Bowl running back was not only a workhorse but also, according to teammate Yancey Thigpen, "a guy who thanks you for throwing a block, who is one of the first to run downfield sixty yards after you have scored a touchdown to say congratulations—I could go on and on and on."

It goes without saying that a team player like this wouldn't care much about his personal statistics.

Isn't that right, Eddie?

"We definitely think about stats while we're playing," George told me. "If you lose the game and you have great stats, it kind of offsets itself. If we lost, it's like, *Ahh, at least I had great stats.* You keep it in your head and you check. Especially if your team is having one of those days where you're down by thirty. You're like, 'Where am I at? One fifty [yards rushing]? Okay, let's get to one seventy-five and I'm good."

The pursuit of personal honors can create friction on a team. At the end of the 2004 season, Seattle Seahawks coach Mike Holmgren called a QB sneak instead of letting running back Shaun Alexander go for the 1 yard he needed to tie for the NFL rushing title. A furious Alexander said that he "got stabbed in the back" by Holmgren (an accusation that was dismissed out of hand in a court of law). Besides Alexander, players as diverse as Keyshawn Johnson, Boomer Esiason, and Tiki Barber have demanded the damn ball.

Former NFL quarterback Rodney Peete told me, "Of course guys think about their stats while they're playing. You've got so many incentives in your contract and a lot of them are based on stats. You catch a hundred passes and you get an extra million dollars. Anybody who tells you they don't think about their stats on the field is lying."

Compared to NBA players, though, NFL players are as unselfish as the foot soldiers at Normandy. Former New York Knicks coach Larry Brown said of point guard/black hole Stephon Marbury, "I don't know why you play a team sport [if you are not] concerned with making your teammates better and helping your team win games." Well, old man, look at what it's done for Starbury. While being constantly criticized for hogging the ball and sabotaging his teams' offenses, he has put up the individual numbers that have earned him enough contract and endorsement money to feed his great[3]-grandkids.

Marbury isn't alone in worrying about getting his, as I learned when I spoke with the stars of the disgraced USA Basketball team.

Carmelo Anthony insisted, "No, I don't pay attention to my stats. I ain't like D-Wade."

Dwyane Wade laughed and responded, "You mean like Gilbert Arenas."

Anthony: "Yeah, I ain't like Gilbert Arenas. Gilbert knows. Woo, Gilbert knows. Gilbert knows if he's got ten or he got twenty. If he tells you he doesn't, he's lying."

When I relayed the conversation to Arenas, he shook his head and smiled. "See, they say that because I always put those points on them and then let them know about it. They all keep track too."

Per usual, Agent Zero confused the issue by clarifying his position.

"The way I keep stats in my head for me to have a good game is make two layups, make two free throws, hit a jump shot. That's how I think of it. Like a series or a little task. Get me two assists, have two rebounds. And I have someone chart it. They'll tell me I need to get three [of each] next time."

So like a true superstar, Arenas not only keeps stats in his head, he has a lackey charting his individual progress and keeping him updated throughout the game.

The quest for individual stats can lead to even further insanity, and nowhere is that more apparent than in the quest for the triple double—a coveted but ultimately meaningless personal statistic. According to reports, LeBron James once checked with a Cleveland Cavaliers media relations staffer late in a critical playoff game to see how many rebounds he was from this elusive brass ring. But it's not just the megastars who feel embiggened to behave in such a cromulent manner. On March 16, 2003, at the end of a blowout win against Utah, Ricky Davis, then of the Cavs, was about to intentionally miss a shot at the *wrong hoop* to try to get his tenth rebound when he was fouled hard by Jazz player DeShawn Stevenson. Atlanta Hawk Bob Sura purposely blew a layup at the buzzer for the same reason. With his team up by 20 against the Pistons, Orlando Magic guard Anthony Bowie called a timeout with 1.4 seconds left in order to secure his tenth assist. The NBA ultimately disallowed Sura's rebound, but Bowie got his precious assist, celebrating by going on to live a life of quiet shame.

Even the outcome of the games themselves can become secondary when statistical honors are at stake. On the last day of the 1978 NBA season, David Thompson and George Gervin completely took over their teams' games as they fought for the scoring title, jacking up a total of eighty-seven shots between them. More recently, Spurs center David Robinson scored 71 fake-o points on the final day of the 1994 season to beat Shaquille O'Neal for the scoring title. Robinson called it "the most memorable game of my career"—a quote that may begin to explain the beatings he took at the hands of Hakeem Olajuwon in the playoffs.

We've seen similar late-season maneuvering in baseball, the sport where individual stats carry the most weight. Sometimes players won't even step on the field for fear of messing up their numbers. Hall of Famer Wade Boggs—frequently accused of putting his own stats ahead of the team (the accusation being that he wouldn't ground out to move a runner over or risk hurting his batting average by trying to hit home runs)—sat out the last couple of games of the 1986 season to protect his average and win the batting title.

Sometimes players sit out games to avoid statistical embarrassment. The Detroit Tigers "shut down" Jeremy Bonderman in late 2003 so he wouldn't reach twenty losses. Free swingers like Preston Wilson and José Hernández sat down at the end of the season to avoid breaking the single-season strikeout record. Derek Bell went into "Operation Shutdown" to protect himself from an entire season of embarrassing statistics.

The baseball equivalent of the triple double is hitting for the cycle—that is, racking up a single, double, triple, and home run in a single game. A number of hitters have held back to secure the base they need for this lightweight accomplishment. Most recently, Toronto's Jeff Frye turned a double into a single by stopping at first base to secure his place in fake history.

The chase for statistics can become so involved that the other team is pulled into it. Detroit Tigers pitcher Denny McLain grooved a fastball to Mickey Mantle to let the Mick pass Jimmie Foxx on the all-time home run list. For this, along with racketeering, extortion, narcotics, conspiracy, theft, money laundering, and mail fraud, McLain's reputation suffered.

In 1971, the University of Florida football team pulled a move now known as the Gator Flop, lying on the ground to allow Miami to score a touchdown late in the fourth quarter so quarterback John Reaves could get the ball back and set an NCAA-career-passing-yards record. Similarly, Tampa Bay Buccaneers coach John McKay ordered his team to onside kick at the end of a blowout against the Jets and then lie down on defense (which had to be really obvious to be noticed given the way they normally played) in a failed attempt to get running back James Wilder the single-season yardage record.

Green Bay Packers quarterback Brett Favre changed a play at the line of scrimmage late in a game to allow his golfing buddy Michael Strahan to set the single-season sack record. Packers offensive lineman Mark Tauscher, who had had the gall to stop Strahan all day, said it was "disappointing" that the record was broken in such a fashion. Doesn't this Tauscher guy like to see history in the making?

University of Connecticut basketball player Nykesha Sales ruptured her Achilles tendon her senior year when she was one point shy of the school scoring record. For UConn's final game, her coach arranged with the opposing Villanova Wildcats to let Sales, who was wearing a cast, stand under the Villanova basket at tip-off. Villanova allowed UConn to win the tip and didn't guard Sales so she could get her record-breaking basket and ruin sports forever.

I had planned on finishing this chapter with a touching story about Nate Haasis, a kid who had fifteen minutes of fame for giving up a record he said he didn't deserve. Late in a blowout loss, the high school quarterback threw a 37-yard pass to set the conference career passing record at 5,006 yards. A few days later Haasis wrote a letter to the athletic conference's director indicating that he hadn't been aware his own coach made an arrangement with the other team to let him get the record unopposed. The story was picked up nationally and a media frenzy ensued. The national writers who covered it were appalled that Haasis's coach would do such a sneaky thing and praised Nate for relinquishing the record. ABC named Haasis "Person of the Week," *Sports Illustrated*'s Phil Taylor said, "I can only think of one name for a kid like Nate Haasis: Sportsman of the Year," and the *New York Post*'s Phil Mushnick briefly let go of his erection to write, "When Haasis is done playing football, he'd make a great president."

The writers of the puff pieces were so busy trying to get included in the *Best American Sportswriting: Earnest and Awful Edition* that they didn't bother to check out what really happened. In my first and probably last case of investigative journalism, I made a few phone calls to speak with some of the people who were actually at the game and found out Haasis's story was as bogus as the record itself.

Robert Burns, a reporter who covered the game for the *State Journal-Register* (Springfield, Illinois), pointed out to me that everyone in the stadium knew there was an arrangement long before the pass that set the record. Coach Neal Taylor seconded this, telling me that he informed Haasis *before* the game "that if we weren't winning, we'd do anything we could to help him get his five thousand yards." Taylor lived up to his word. Once the game was out of reach he practically announced over the loudspeakers what he was doing for Nate, turning the end of the game into a "Let's get Haasis the record!" party.

Having burned all of his timeouts, Taylor realized that the clock would run out before Haasis got the ball back. Since the game was out of hand, he yelled across the field to the opposing coach, Antwyne Golliday, to call a timeout so they could figure out a way to hook Nate up. Golliday agreed, and Taylor huddled with him and the officials in the middle of the field to devise a plan that would make Nate's dream come true. "This was about as obvious as can be to anyone," Taylor said.

Per the conversation, Haasis's team's defense took a knee to let the opposition score quickly and get Nate the ball back (with the ball carrier's own teammates even yelling at him to run to the end zone faster because time was running out). While his defense was giving up the score, Taylor made sure Haasis was on board by asking, "Do you want this?" With all systems go, Haasis's accommodating opponents then intentionally kicked the ball out of bounds to make sure Nate had enough time to run a play.

Haasis not only noticed everyone's efforts but, understandably, was moved by them. When Taylor turned to send him onto the field, Nate "was crying because he was going to reach his goal of five thousand yards." After all this work to get him the record,

Haasis left nothing to chance, deciding to make the throw easier by "bring[ing] our best receiver, the best receiver in the conference, into the slot." Coach Taylor then stood at the precise spot on the field the receiver needed to run to for Haasis to get his record. Subtle.

So after the game, Haasis must have been pretty pissed off about the lack of sportsmanship, huh?

Not quite. He told Burns that the record "means a lot to me. A lot."

Nate didn't change his tune until after he started getting slammed in the local media. The next day a story ran in the Springfield newspaper headlined "5006*?" and a flood of callers to area sports-radio stations began spewing bile at Nate and Coach Taylor. Even after that initial scrutiny, Taylor said, Haasis was steadfast, maintaining that he deserved the record and wouldn't back down to media pressure. Only after three days of nonstop criticism did Haasis finally write the letter giving up the record. In it, he separated himself from the incident by throwing his coach to the wolves, saying, "It is my belief that the directions given to us in the final seconds of this game were made in 'the heat of battle' and do not represent the values of the athletes of the Southeast football team." He put more blame on Taylor by saying that he hadn't known what was going on until right before the final pass.

While this was a great PR move for Haasis, as you might imagine it didn't turn out quite so well for his coach. For his attempt to help out his player, Taylor was eventually fired, in no small part because of the negative publicity that resulted from Haasis's letter.

Haasis was just a kid at the time, so we probably shouldn't be too hard on him. Most kids (and adults) love stats, records, and anything that can quantify their individual accomplishments. The same can't be said for all those columnists who rushed to hold up Nate as the symbol of everything they think is good about sports, a combination of Barbaro, David Eckstein, and Jason McElwain. Unfortunately for readers, there are no statistics to quantify these writers' contributions to the world.

CAN I DO THAT? IF I PRACTICED, COULDN'T I BE AS GOOD AS THE PROS?

You probably know the answer to this question already; otherwise you'd be doing whatever it is you think is so easy and getting paid to play a sport professionally instead of working your nine to five. So quit asking dumb questions.

Okay, okay, if you didn't have to work and had time to practice, could you do it then?

Well, slow down, slugger. The fact of the matter is you probably already have time to practice but end up watching *Becker* reruns instead. All right, the *Becker* comment was a cheap shot, but being able to practice is a skill unto itself. We can all say, "If I studied/worked/Jazzercized harder, I'd be great." To actually be great, however, you have to emotionally accept the fact that you may put in all that time and effort and not have what it takes. This is a pretty scary proposition when you're talking about dedicating a significant portion of your time to anything, let alone, say, the luge. It may not be as fun as criticizing from the couch, but the only way to know is to pull yourself up by your bootstraps and try practicing anything for hours a day. Once you've done that and developed a mastery in *anything* ("Madden" does not count), you can laugh at how easy any game or sport played at its highest levels is. And stand up straight and get a haircut while you're at it. [*Editor's Note:* It might be worth noting here that Todd is remarkably lazy himself, and could probably use a haircut. For the record, though, I do not believe he watches *Becker* reruns.]

That's not to say you can't become a pro just because you aren't one now. But if you're going that route, be aware of hurdles each sport presents and what is involved. If you really want to give it a shot and are willing to put some serious work in, follow this helpful guide.

The Real Sports

Football and basketball have a few players who were able to pick up the game late in life and become professionals, largely because the nature of those sports allows untrained freakish athletes to move into positions where athleticism can make up for a lack of experience and skill deficiencies. In basketball, these people are usually unpolished big men who move to the United States to play college basketball and then become pros—for example, Michael Olowokandi (who started playing around age seventeen), Hakeem Olajuwon (seventeen), and Yinka Dare (sixteen)—or superb athletes who go through late growth spurts, such as Dennis Rodman, who went from 5'10" to 6'6" in two years after graduating from high school.

Similarly, in football, being big, strong, and/or fast can sometimes be enough to catapult a guy to the NFL: Nick Hardwick of the Chargers and former pros Dan Neil and Carlton Haselrig grew up as wrestlers and made it in the league as linemen, while Rashod Kent was signed as a tight end after an undistinguished college basketball career at Rutgers, although he hadn't played football since his freshman year of high school.

These two sports are great options if you're so athletic that people marvel at you when you play anything, you are over 7 feet tall, you can run as fast as your friends even though you're 300 pounds, you can respond to a question regarding your potential by saying, "Would I be good? Come on, I'm LeBron James!" (which is what LeBronathon said when I asked him about playing in the NFL), or you resemble former WWF star Mr. Perfect in that you can throw a football 100 yards downfield, catch it yourself, *and* literally make every single shot you take on a basketball court. Otherwise scratch them off your list.

Baseball is even more difficult. A few players have picked up the game late and still made the majors, like Hard Hittin' Mark Whiten, who began playing as a high school senior, but these guys had extraordinary natural talents that almost none of us can claim. If an athlete as gifted as Michael Jordan struggled trying to make it in Double A, you're probably not going to learn the sport as an adult and end up on a major league diamond. But if you broke your arm and can now throw a ball 103 miles per hour, by all means go for it; the Cubs could sure use you.

Hockey is a sport you can forget about unless you grew up on skates, and by the time you master it, there may not be a professional league for you to play in. And tennis, contrary to common belief, is the hardest sport of them all to begin in adulthood. The level of reflex, skill, and athletic ability it requires makes it almost impossible to even become very good, let alone a pro, unless you start at a very young age and put in countless hours on the court. If you're older than twelve and aren't already nationally ranked, forget it.

The Fake Sports

You have your best chance of becoming a paid professional athlete by dedicating your time to one of the activities in which you will be considered a "nonathlete." That is to say, the ones dismissed as "games" in the "sport vs. game" argument (see Question 21). These games require no great size or strength and involve no running and jumping (golf, bowling, pool, darts). Or they're just plain ridiculous (luge).

But even with these games, don't think you're going to get a free pass just by having good hand-eye coordination and being a better athlete than your buddies. Many pro athletes in the holy trinity of basketball, football, and baseball love to play these (again, with luge being the exception) and none are pro caliber. Of course, you may find you're a savant at one of them, but even if you are, you'll still need to spend countless hours developing the skills to get to the point that you can try to turn pro.

Also, being good enough to have a real shot at success when you enter a pro event, which is incredibly difficult in itself, is not the same as *staying* pro, which means making enough money to live. You'll have to enter tournaments all over the country (or even the world), so you'll end up spending thousands of dollars a year out of your own pocket on tournament entry fees, plane tickets, gas, and hotels and restaurants. And unless you're an immediate sensation, have a financial backer, or are comfortable selling your body or bodily fluids for money, you'll need to do it all while working a second job.

Pool

Financial incentive: Moderate. It's all over the board. In general, the top pros earn between $50,000 and $150,000 per year. The real money is on the international scene, because the game is much bigger overseas than in the United States. The best international players can earn up to $500,000 or $1,000,000 a year through earnings, appearances, and endorsements. This can be supplemented, or reduced, by hustling and money games depending on your level of betting savvy and degeneracy.

Fame incentive: In places where they don't speak English, you'll be a god. In the States, unless your name is Allison Fisher or Karen Corr (which I know it isn't because you'd be playing a match on ESPN2 right now instead of reading this chapter), you're screwed until *The Hustler 3: Breakin' All the Rules* comes out and everyone again pretends for a month or so to care about pool.

Work required: Heavy. It's a lifestyle, and you'd better love hanging out with people you wouldn't want to normally.

Most people who have run a couple stripes or once banked in an 8-ball are under the impression that with a little work and maybe even a little instruction, they could be a very good, if not pro-level, pool player. Most people, as usual, are wrong. For the average person who just likes to play when he gets drunk with his friends on the weekends (as an aside, you do not play better drunk, so quit saying that to everyone when the subject of pool comes up), even becoming the best player at a local pool hall would take a considerable amount of time and work.

I spoke with Jeanette Lee, the "Black Widow," about how to get to the top. Like another black widow, Faith Evans Smalls, her rise to superstardom was not without hard work.

Jeanette's ascension in the world of pool was remarkably quick: she started from scratch at the age of eighteen and became the world's #1 player only five years later. Thinking this was a good sign for the aspiring pros, I asked her how long it would take to turn a protégé who had never played into a pro-level player if the pupil were willing to practice eight hours a day.

"Well, I think that I had a good amount of talent. I also played closer to eighteen to twenty hours a day. And I did that pretty solidly for five years."

Wait, did you just say you'd practice up to twenty hours a day?

"Not up to. At least. There were times where I ended up playing for twenty-four, twenty-six, twenty-eight hours in a row. I think the most was thirty-seven hours."

How long did it take you to get good enough to play at a pro level?

"It took me three years to turn pro. A year and a half from that to become number one in the world."

So let's say we took a novice who was only moderately obsessive as opposed to completely afflicted with OCD. How long would it take to get him or her to pro level?

"As far as playing eight hours a day, I think someone could develop the skills to be a very good player in three or four years, but that's not to say they will be good enough to be a pro. . . . You can be a very proficient player or athlete and not be a very good competitor."

Then I asked her to kiss me, at which point she hung up the phone.

Bowling

Financial incentive: You can make $2 or $3 million for a career if you're one of the best. Being in the top twenty on the PBA tour will typically net you over $100k a year, with the high end being around $500k, but for everyone else, paying bills is a concern. You're working for the weekend.

Fame incentive: Earl Anthony, Dick and Pete Weber . . . for every generation, there's room for one name that you may have heard of to emerge from the bowling world, but that's about it.

Work required: Less than being a coal miner but more than being Billy Baldwin.

Like pool, bowling is played in conditions that are fairly static, so it would seem feasible to make the jump to the pro ranks by putting in some hours on the boards. The legendary PDW (see Question 16) gave the straight scoop:

"When they made the movie *Dreamer* way back when, Tim Matheson had a little bowling background but not a whole lot. My brother Rich coached him into about a two hundred, two twenty average bowler in about two months. But this was constant bowling every day, all day, thumb blistering, thumb bleeding, him acting just like a professional bowler, doing the same things we did.

"Now, that was on one condition. Going to the other conditions [pro bowling lanes are set up in a way that most amateurs would find more difficult] and practicing different releases, different angles—probably another year or so at least. You're just not gonna get that good that quick. Maybe two years if you have some real ability to get in the mix. You need to practice, practice, practice, four, five, six hours a day, constant bowling, and trust me, it hurts. It hurts."

Can you handle the pain of bowling, pussy? If so, you may have a shot.

Darts

Financial incentive: Low. On par with video game players.
Fame incentive: Lower. No one will know you in the USA. Ever.
Work required: Lowest.

Darts is the easiest game to develop pro-caliber skills in, given the unchanging conditions. True, there's a deep talent pool since players come from all over the world (including from countries where throwing darts is the highest possible form of entertainment), but the consensus among dart players I interviewed was that with eight-hour-a-day training plus instruction, a person can reach professional-level scores very quickly.

Our good buddy Paul Lim (see Question 8) weighed in:

"If you're talking about someone with [good hand-eye] coordination, I can teach them how to play darts and do it properly in— shit, I would say an hour? But it can take a long time with someone uncoordinated. It's all about coordination of stroke, and muscle memory, just like any other sport."

To get a coordinated beginner to a high level?

"With eight hours a day? Three months."

This is quicker and less work than becoming the assistant manager at McDonald's. How much more goes into training to be a real pro?

"It's about how collected you are. It's about how you are able to transfer your practice routine to an actual match. A lot of people can't do that. . . . If you actually analyzed them in a match, you'd find their gesture, their pause, everything slows down. They become too careful, they become too tentative. They don't do this when they are practicing."

Paul pointed out that "not a lot of people" have the necessary composure. "There are thousands and thousands of scratch golfers in the world, but how come there are only a handful of top pros? They're all scratch golfers but they all can't consistently excel and have the right mind frame under pressure."

In darts the pressures are similar. Paul won the first major tournament he ever entered, the Singapore Open, because he did it "on a lark" and wasn't thinking about the pressure. For his next event he was flown out to a big tournament in England and lost in the first round, in large part because he was suddenly aware of the stakes. "You know the saying 'To become a champion is easy but to stay a champion is hard'? That's what can happen. There are different steps mentally you need to go through . . . Some people have it more than others."

It is universally said that this really is the great variable. In the words of darts writer Paul Siegel, once someone has what it takes, the separator is having the "courage to hang in there when the darts start falling on the wrong side of the wires. In a game of millimeters, these 'little things' are every bit as important and in my opinion more important than the basics."

If you feel comfortable using the word *courage* in describing throwing a dart at a board, this may be the game for you.

Luge

Financial incentive: Janitorial. $30–$50 grand a year on the high end.

Fame incentive: Less than ideal. Can you name one? Ever?

Work required: Stay on the couch . . . it's not worth it.

You would think a sport with as small a financial payoff and as scarcely participated in as luge (there are only thirteen luge tracks in the entire world) would be fairly easy to climb to the top of. Think again. Lugers are recruited into the U.S. training program at a very young age and typically take a long time to reach a high level. Jon Lundin, media and public relations manager for the U.S. Luge Association, recommends that kids start at age ten. According to Jon, it takes "eight years before a lightbulb will go off in an athlete's head and they can start to understand all of the technical aspects that go into being successful. Luge is the most technical of the three sliding sports, the other sports being bobsled and skeleton, and takes the most amount of time to learn. After fourteen, we really consider potential candidates too old to end up being successful." Think gymnasts, only colder.

The U.S. Luge Association travels nationwide during the summer trying to recruit ten- to fourteen-year-olds (during recruiting the program has to use sleds where the skates are replaced by wheels). "We're not looking for an X-Games, risk taker, speed junkie type," Lundin said. "We're looking more for someone who can remain composed and controlled at high speeds because of the level of technical expertise that's needed. They're steering the sled at ninety miles per hour with just their legs and their shoulders, so for a man we're looking for a long, lean-cut individual, very aerodynamic. Strong upper body, very good balance. Very good coordination throughout the whole body." Sounds hot!

If you get good enough to do well on the World Cup circuit, you can make a very modest living at luge. Another consideration in becoming a total luger is that races are timed to $^1/_{1000}$ of a second, so even the smallest of slips can make a difference (in the 1998 Olympics, gold and silver were separated by $^2/_{1000}$ of a second after a 3.5-minute race), meaning that you may end up blowing your brains out over forgetting to clip your toenails the night before the Olympics.

Golf

Financial incentive: Better than whatever you're doing right now.
Fame incentive: Might actually get you laid.
Work required: More than you're used to.

Golf is the crown jewel for aspiring pro athletes. To be a pro golfer, you need not be particularly big or strong, and there are players on the PGA Tour who picked up the game late in life. Unlike most other games in which it is possible to become a pro as an adult, golf provides the opportunity for real fame and riches.

The aspiring pro golfer's patron saint is Larry Nelson. The 5'9", 150-pound Nelson didn't play golf at all growing up in Fort Payne, Alabama. At the age of twenty-one upon his return from military service in Vietnam, he started teaching himself to play using Ben Hogan's *Five Lessons: The Modern Fundamentals of Golf,* perhaps hoping the game would bring some much-needed boredom into his life. By the time he was twenty-seven, he had made the PGA

Tour, and he went on to win three majors, earn more than $15 million, and get elected to the World Golf Hall of Fame. Now on the Champions Tour (formerly known as the Senior Tour), Nelson illustrates another of golf's many benefits: the opportunity to play, and earn money, into old age. It's a pretty good way to spend your golden years.

Another pro, Rocco Mediate, started playing when he was fifteen and hardly entered any junior tournaments. He wasn't good enough to get a scholarship for golf so he went to California State and made the team just as a walk-on. From there he improved and transferred to Florida Southern University, where he played on the golf team with future PGA pros Lee Janzen and Marco Dawson. At the age of twenty-one, after playing for just six years, he tried the PGA Tour qualifying school and ended up making it as a pro. "I certainly didn't expect it, and I certainly didn't expect that if I did make it to last," Rocco told me. "I just wasn't that good. I played decent in college, I won a couple of tournaments, but I wasn't a prodigy or anything. But I got better when I was out there."

Things have changed over the past two decades, though. According to Rocco, the quality of play has skyrocketed and there are far more good players in the field. "Nowadays," Rocco said, "if you're not ready to play the moment you hit the tour, it's over."

Writer Tom Coyne had a simple explanation for that: Tiger Woods. "Tiger's changed everything," he said. "If you don't have a club in your hand by the time you're three now, you're behind." Coyne knows from experience. As he described in his book *Paper Tiger,* at the age of thirty, Coyne devoted himself full time to the game in an attempt to become a professional. Coyne had been a 3 handicap golfer coming out of high school, but after taking a number of years off he was a 14 handicap when he started training for the tour.

After a year working on his game nonstop with professional instruction, Coyne did end up as a scratch golfer but he didn't make it as a pro. PGA golfers play at another level entirely, Tom learned. "I hit my 6 iron anywhere from 165 to 195. These guys on the tour, they hit their 6 iron 178 yards and they know that. Not 179 or 177."

To fine-tune to the level of the pros takes a lot of time and effort, more than just developing a scratch handicap at your local club. Rocco thought someone who had never played could master the fundamentals of a good swing, but as we know, there's more to golf than smoking heaters and sticking iron shots. Rocco said, "Working with a short-game specialist, it might take you a good year to become a pro-level putter." Beyond that, you have all the other short-game shots: "long bunker, high bunker, getting up and down consistently from all distances and types of lies." All told, he said, "you're looking at a minimum of three years" to get a beginner good enough to compete with the pros.

And then, don't forget, there's the mental part of the game. Hitting the shot on the range or even in a practice round is a hell of a lot easier than doing it in a tournament, Rocco said. "How will all of that practice translate to the course? To get to the point where you can actually compete on the course, that might take up to five years, but some guys have that killer instinct right away."

As for all those forty-somethings on the range who are telling everyone in earshot they're going to try to make the Champions Tour when they turn fifty? "The Senior Tour guys just came off of *our* tour," Rocco said. "They're really, really good." Try breaking eighty first, MJ.

Throwing a Knuckleball

Remember when I said to forget about baseball? Well, there's a caveat. If you really have such a taste for the big time that the games above won't solve, here's one more possible option:

Financial incentive: Don't be fooled by his inability to properly groom himself; Tim Wakefield has made about $40 million in his major league career. As the kids say, there's Jared Fernandez money in this one.

Fame incentive: Does the name Steve Sparks mean anything to you? Thought so.

Work required: Quit your bitching. If forty-seven-year-old men can do it, so can you. This is a good gig, as long as you're willing to accept the risk that you may have to work with Doug Mirabelli at some point.

The knuckleball is effective because it is thrown with almost no spin so that the stitching on the ball catches the air, causing the pitch to wobble during flight. Fear not, that's as close as we're getting to science. To be a knuckleball pitcher, you don't need to be big, strong, fast, or young. You don't even need to have a cannon for an arm or a wick for a collarbone. A major league knuckleball can go as slow as 45 miles per hour, a speed that can be reached by any almost armchair athlete or even Jamie Moyer. You also can be almost any age. Throwing this requires very little athleticism, which is perfect for anyone who is reading this chapter for actual advice.

Even more encouraging for the weekend warrior, the transition to being a major league knuckleball pitcher can happen very quickly. Tim Wakefield, who has won more than 150 games in the majors, was a first baseman languishing in the minor leagues before he was converted into a knuckleball pitcher; just two years later, he was starting in the playoffs for the Pittsburgh Pirates. That may seem hard to believe, but it's the truth; the Pirates were actually once in the playoffs.

That doesn't mean throwing a knuckleball is easy, though. Look no further than famed author Jose Canseco's attempt to transition from juiced-up power hitter to effete knuckleball pitcher. I caught up with Canseco during his stint with the Long Beach Armada of the Golden League. He was doing a bullpen session a week before his first starting pitching assignment of the season, and amazingly, he had a pretty decent knuckler. He claimed to have been throwing the pitch for more than twenty years. From my vantage point the ball did sometimes move and dance the way a pro's should. He just wasn't consistent. Many of his knucklers flattened out and were very hittable. There were also some control issues that would clearly need to be refined in order to pitch competitively, but overall, it seemed like he was close.

Canseco took the mound the following week and struggled, hitting four batters, walking five others, and giving up a home run in $4\frac{1}{3}$ innings . . . an improvement on his last mound appearance on May 29, 1993, when as a member of the Rangers he gave up three runs in one inning against the Red Sox and blew out his arm, forcing him to miss the remaining hundred games of the season.*

Knuckleball guru Charlie Hough, who won 216 games in his twenty-five-year major league career, said it took him only a year to go from a struggling pitcher in the Dodgers' minor league system to a knuckleball pitcher on the big league club. He explained that some basic tools were involved in mastering the knuckleball. While you don't necessarily need a "strong arm," you must have good control and "the ability to throw the ball where you want

---

* This may come as a surprise, but the same man who said he ran the 40-yard dash in 3.9 seconds at the age of thirty-five was a little off when it came to his pitching abilities. After throwing thirty or so knucklers, he started showing off his other "stuff."

"I've got a little sinking fastball I throw, too. Something just to keep the guys off balance. I start it inside to jam the guy most of the time." Big smile. "I'm a hitter so I know what these guys don't like."

So pro hitters don't like 70-mile-per-hour fastballs on the inner half of the plate?

Nothing says masculinity like throwing a knuckleball while wearing a half-shirt and spandex shorts.

when throwing it straight. If you can't consistently throw a fast-ball for a strike there's no way."

So if the last game you pitched was in T-ball, you can probably stop working on that knuckler right now. As Charlie said, you've got to have excellent command to throw strikes against major league hitters—not to mention the mental makeup to throw a 60-mile-per-hour pitch to an enraged Travis Hafner with the tying run on base.

Jose appeared to have the ability to throw a mean knuckler, and he looked pretty good in his bullpen session to me, once I got past his half-shirt, overuse of skin bronzer, and incubating mullet. Charlie said that the consistency issues I noticed were what was keeping Canseco from making the next leap.

"One thing about the knuckleball that makes it tough to judge how good a guy is," Hough said, "is that a good knuckleball doesn't vary much from the best that's ever thrown to just another guy throwing one. What makes someone a good knuckleball pitcher is control and consistency. Narrowing your misses, your bad pitches, into a range where you aren't walking guys and making mistake pitches that professional batters aren't going to miss."

I asked Hough what the best way was to learn how to get to that point then, if twenty years of practice didn't do the trick: "Learning how to throw it and being able to throw it are totally different. . . . It's very, very hard to do. All kinds of people try it and only a few can do it." He added that almost every player in major league baseball has messed around with the knuckler (although not many have made a concerted effort).

Explaining how much work was involved and how very difficult the pitch was to learn, Hough pointed to a student of his who can throw his fastball in the high 80s with good control but whose knuckleball, by Hough's judgment, is not good enough to even pitch in a low-level minor league game. The student said that while the results may not be ideal yet, it took an extraordinary amount of time and energy to even get refined to that point: "It took me about a year of throwing it every day. I'd throw until the other person gets tired. I'd throw at least one hundred pitches a day of just the knuckleball, not counting other pitches like the fastball or anything."

Further making this a difficult skill to learn, according to Hough, is the fact that "if the ball doesn't fit your hand, [you can] forget about it." Some guys have "absolutely no chance to do it no matter how much they train."

Good Lord, why even bother? This must be the hardest thing in the world to do.

Hough disagreed. "It's not like it really requires any special skill; you either have it or you don't."

So you have to be a natural and you can't get good by just practicing. Well, wait, you also have to practice a lot if you're a natural. But didn't Wakefield take just a year to make the majors after switching? And didn't Hough do the same? And why is this kid practicing so much if he's already done it for a year and isn't very good? I thought "you either have it or you don't." Isn't Hough's point that it's easy if you're a "natural"?

I think what Charlie was trying to get across, so very, very inarticulately, is that throwing a knuckler well does take some talent and ability. If you have enough talent and ability and pick it up right away, you can be good very quickly. However, if you just have *some* ability for throwing the pitch, you can put in a ton of work and you might get good enough to throw it effectively.

So if you want to throw a knuckler, you do need to be able to throw a baseball with some control, but it doesn't take a ton of athletic talent and you might be great very quickly if you put some work into it. You also might suck no matter how much work you put in. Or you could fall somewhere in between, like Jose. In summation, go try throwing one and anything might happen. Or not.

You Can Do It! Maybe!

All of this is to say that becoming great at any of these takes a lot more work than most people realize, and some people who develop the physical abilities might not have the mental strength to make it in the pros. (I'm looking at you, Ian Baker-Finch. You thought no one could see you anymore?)

But it is possible. A coordinated person can, with practice and hard work, get to a professional level of skill in a game that doesn't require amazing natural athletic ability. In fact, one of the great things about these games is that they are meritocracies. Unless you're trying to become a major league knuckleballer, which has the added peril of your brain exploding if you're trying to learn it from Charlie Hough, you don't need to beg for a chance or have the right connections to get a tryout or hope the coach sees the value you have as a player. If you're good enough, you can pay your entry fee and start making a living.

Just don't think it's going to be easy. And regardless of the path you choose, for the love of God, please quit watching those *Becker* reruns.

DOES A SIX-FINGERED PITCHER HAVE AN UNFAIR ADVANTAGE?

Antonio Alfonseca is a typical pitcher in many ways: he's from the Dominican Republic, a righty, and over 6 feet tall; he has a good fastball and an occasional changeup; and he played a lot better before he became a Cub. But he is a rarity in major league baseball. What's different about this marginally effective setup man? He has twelve fingers, six on each hand. He also has twelve toes. His nickname is "El Pulpo" ("The Octopus").

His condition is known as polydactylism. It's a congenital abnormality that gives a person more than the usual five digits on each hand and/or foot. In this regard Antonio belongs to a club that includes Anne Boleyn, Hannibal Lecter, and the pianist from *Gattaca*.

Unfortunately for Alfonseca, an extra finger doesn't do anything to help him pitch, as anyone who has seen him pitch would surmise. In fact, only four fingers are really needed to grip most pitches. Look at Hall of Famers Mordecai "Three-Finger" Brown and Winston "Weird Hands" McElheiney, both of whom had great success in the days before people of their kind were driven into the circus.

So for a better base runner, look for a player with legs that could double as stilts. For fielders, try to get a guy with hands the size of dinner plates. But for pitching, don't ask your local six-fingered man.

Or, in the more trained words of Detroit Tiger third baseman Brandon Inge, "I have no clue if it'd be useful for a new pitch, but I could think of some other things I could do with it."

Pitcher Justin Verlander seemed to agree. "It'd be a hell of a shocker."

Which we can only assume means that it would be a shocking pitch indeed to any hitter who faced it!

HOW EASY IS THE TRANSITION FROM SOCCER PLAYER TO NFL KICKER?

As part of one of my own personal get-rich-quick schemes, I met up with Matt Reis, goaltender for Major League Soccer's New England Revolution, on a rainy day at the practice facility adjoining Gillette Stadium that the Revolution shares with the New England Patriots. Reis had been considering getting into field goal kicking and, like most professional soccer goalies, had a very strong leg. Teammate Kyle Brown, for one, thought Reis had a chance at making the transition to NFL kicker. Brown's scouting report read, "Reis can kick the shit out of the ball."

A field goal kicker coming from a soccer background is a fairly common occurrence. Most of the kickers in the NFL at least played soccer growing up, some at a very high level, most notably Morten Andersen, Gary Anderson, and Seabass Janikowski. Pro Bowl kicker Nate Kaeding told me, "Usually we were on the soccer team, and the football team needed a kicker, so we got into it that way."

But why, you ask, would a professional goalie, who has played for the U.S. national team and twice been a finalist for the MLS Goalkeeper of the Year Award, consider leaving a sport he excels in for one he's never played? Well, if you sit in the Foxborough parking lot and look at the cars the Patriots players drive up in, which, admittedly, would be a very odd thing to do, you'd get an idea pretty quickly.

"It's something that my wife's been on me to do, because obviously football kickers can make a lot more than soccer goalies," Reis told me. His wife certainly knows her business. The MLS doesn't disclose player salaries, but the higher-end guys like Reis make between $80,000 and $100,000 a year. Good money, but the average NFL kicker pulls around $1.5 million a year. Even the NFL rookie minimum, $275,000, is big-time compared with MLS salaries.

The San Diego Chargers' director of college scouting, Jimmy Raye, thought for these very reasons that the soccer world was ripe for the picking. He told me, "I'm kinda surprised with the money disparity more guys haven't tried to transition into kicking in the NFL."

My thoughts exactly, Jimmy. From my perspective, the fact that I had a motivated pro ready to make the leap offered a great opportunity to:

1. See how difficult the transition is for the education of you, the reader.
2. Get a gauge as to what kind of kicking talent there is in the soccer world for my own financial purposes. If I could mine it for clients and set up shop, untold riches awaited.

But back to reality, or whatever this is—there were some hurdles to overcome. Namely, Reis had no idea what he was doing.

"I've just messed around kicking the [foot]ball, but I've never been taught technique or been out there and actually worked on it at all."

I lined up Reis from 30 yards. Afraid that one of these soccer goofballs might have something against Football Americana and

And to think, all Charlie Brown needed was a better holder.

pull a Lucy Van Pelt on my meal ticket, I operated as the holder. The 30-yarders were layups for Reis: four for four. I moved him to 40 yards out. Reis effortlessly kicked three in a row right through the middle of the uprights. After his fourth kick was again perfect, Reis turned to me: "Is this supposed to be hard?"

In the words of noted financier Damon Wayans: Mo' money! Or, in laymen's terms, "more money."

But when I backed Reis up to 50 yards, my caviar dreams were rudely interrupted as the private jet to Monaco crashed into the Atlantic. Reis's first kick was a duck hook that barely got ten feet off the ground. He shanked his second kick horribly, stubbing his toe on the grass and crushing my fingers in the process. The third try was, again, poop. Reis was trying way too hard. He had more than enough distance and accuracy on the 40-yard kicks to make it from 50, but his mechanics started breaking down from trying to put extra juice on it. I tried to take the pressure off by saying, "You've already done better than Tony Meola," but on his fourth attempt, he again missed badly.

Reis blamed the poor conditions: "You know, it's really hard to get good footing right now. I wish we could have done this on a different day." At this point Revolution broadcaster Brad Feldman chimed in: "I'm not sure the Patriots would go for that one when it's snowing in the playoffs."

My next thought was to see how much cash I could make by turning Reis into a punter. While punters don't usually make as much money as kickers, the motion for punting both balls is very similar. Reis explained, however, that the shape of the football and location of the sweet spot were entirely different and that it might not be as easy as I thought. Concern was growing that I was going to have to write another one of these books.

It turns out Reis knew his limitations. His punts were a lot like Terrell Buckley—short and terrible. His best punt had a decent hang time of 3.7 seconds but was end over end, and overall Reis showed virtually no directional control.

Okay, so getting rich off field-goal-kicking soccer players wasn't going to be as easy as scratching a lotto ticket or marrying Roseanne, but it still had the potential to be better than working.

Though I wasn't going to make any immediate cash off of Reis, he did fairly well, all things considered, even if he was a bit of a baby about the weather. He was as good as a lot of college kickers, and with some work, he could probably at least earn a tryout with an NFL team.

If the one soccer player I tried out was decent, as Reis was, certainly out of all the players in the MLS there would have to be a few ready-made for the NFL. Maybe the scope of my business plan needed to be expanded.

To unlock my unlimited earning potential, I contacted former NFL punter, kicker, and kickoff specialist Louie Aguiar, who now owns the Aguiar Kicking Academy (his previous proprietary claim to fame was being the owner of the finest mustache in the NFL). Louie also made the transition from soccer to football, and he regaled me with stories of countless other soccer players who made it in the NFL. Kicking great Pat Leahy, he said, got a tryout with the NFL's St. Louis Cardinals based purely on his success as a soccer player at St. Louis University, where he won three national championships. "He gets out there the first day and says, 'I've never kicked a football.' The coach looks at him and says, 'Go back three, over two.' He says okay, goes back three, over two, and starts kicking the ball through the uprights. And eighteen years later, he retired. It can be that seamless."*

Sounds like we're in business, Louie. So let's get into some real wealth building. What's the first step to vaulting soccer players into the elite kicking fraternity of Jan Stenerud, Kathy Ireland, and Gus the Mule?

---

* Jimmy Raye and Reis's soccer teammate Daniel Hernandez, who was a kicker at SMU and had a tryout with the Patriots, agreed that this was a very doable transition. Soccer players would just need to make some technical adjustments here and there, and get used to the pressure of nailing a kick with a game on the line.

"Well, find some soccer players and give them lessons on how to kick the ball."

Okay, I got that part.

"We should probably focus more on kicking. As you saw [with Reis], it's harder for soccer players to become punters than field goal kickers."

Come on, brass tacks here, Aguiar: Which soccer players would we want to target? Should we just go down the list of the MLS leading scorers and make cold calls?

"A lot of the scoring forwards, guys like [David] Beckham and Ronaldo, their technique is around the goal. I think most of the guys who play fullback or goalie actually have the bigger legs and have a better chance to go on and kick field goals. I think what we'd do is put a call into the MLS and see how many guys would come to an open workout. I have a pro tryout at my camp where over twenty-five pro scouts show up from NFL and CFL teams. The rub is that there are a lot of MLS jobs and only thirty-two place-kicking jobs in the NFL."

Wait, there's a rub?

Actually, there were several rubs . . . and these rubs were rubbing away my dreams of riding polo ponies, sitting in a box at the opera, and doing other things rich people pretend to like. The first obstacle would be getting players on board with the plan. This would require going through the MLS, not the players' agents, who wouldn't want to lose their clients to the world of football. But even if we got the players on board, Louie and I would have to bring in an outside agent and split the agent's fee on the contract, since the NFL requires player agents to be licensed by the league. If we had to cut in the player's soccer agent, we'd need to split the fee four ways. This was no way to run a fake business.

I consoled myself with the fact that the top kickers in the league make around $3 million a year. There was still cash money to be made. But, as it turns out, NFL agents can charge only a 3 percent commission (much lower than the 65 percent rate I proposed). So I'd be looking at a less-than-1-percent cut. We had moved from private jet to Monaco to bus trip to Branson.

Louie, my empire is in ruins. What is our Plan B here? There has to be money to be made outside of the NFL.

"You have Arena Football, and they make about what some of the MLS guys do. One of the top placekickers in Arena makes forty thousand plus incentives; he ended up making seventy. In the CFL you can make a living too."

One percent of $70,000? Poverty! Hooray! Do you have *any* good news?

"A lot of teams go for a veteran guy. The Atlanta Falcons started the [2006] season with a young guy who was handling both the punting and the placekicking [Michael Koenen] and they ended up having Morten Andersen kicking for them, and he's forty-six years old."*

Wait, that's not good news at all. I mean, is there any news that's good for me, not for Morten Andersen?

"One of the advantages we'd have in landing our players on teams is that teams can save six hundred thousand dollars by signing a rookie over someone like me who's a ten-year vet. They're required because of the collective bargaining agreement to pay the veteran players more, but what practically ended up happening in a lot of cases is the teams said, 'Well, we can go find someone younger for a lot less money.'"

That helps . . . me, not Louie's kicking career. Greed is good!

---

* Glenn Schwartzman of Alliance Sports Management, who represents kickers such as Jay Feely and Kris Brown, told me the same thing: "There's a lot of teams who are only looking for veterans, let alone not wanting a guy who has never kicked field goals before."

So, aspiring NFL agents, take note: instead of getting Mr. Rosen-haus his coffee or making payments to Reggie Bush's family, make your own way in the world and start prowling the soccer pitch for talent. For all your efforts, you may only be able to afford a noose to hang yourself with, but if you're going to really go for the gusto by jumping into the world of kicker agenting, just remember the oldest business axiom in the book: stay away from the Gramaticas.

WHAT WOULD HAPPEN IF THE NBA RAISED THE BASKET TO 12 FEET?*

Basketball has changed drastically over the years and has become almost unrecognizable from the simple game that teacher James Naismith invented for kids in his gym class in 1891. Naismith's thirteen original rules stressed passing and teamwork, but in the eyes of many basketball purists, those rules have since been overtaken by the more popular values of SLAMMING AND JAMMING. And as the game of basketball has advanced and players have gotten bigger and more athletic (the average height in the NBA as of 2005 was 6'7", which was considered a giant in Naismith's era), many feel we have moved so far away from the vision of Dr. James Naismith that the game now is reflective of the vision of Dr. Jerome James.

Now, basketball has always been a game that lends itself to ball-hoggery, as anyone who saw Oscar Robertson back down his defender for twenty seconds every possession will attest, but things have gotten worse lately. Where it was once limited to Hall of

---

* This question was submitted by Sam Walker, author of *Fantasyland: A Season on Baseball's Lunatic Fringe*.

Dr. James Naismith's Thirteen Original Rules

1. The ball may be thrown in any direction with one or both hands.

2. The ball may be batted in any direction with one or both hands (never with the fist).

3. A player cannot run with the ball.

4. The ball must be held in or between the hands.

5. No shouldering, holding, pushing, tripping, or striking in any way the person of an opponent shall be allowed.

6. A foul is striking at the ball with the fist, violation of Rules 3, 4, and such as described in Rule 5.

7. If either side makes three consecutive fouls, it shall count as a goal for the opponents.

8. A goal shall be made when the ball is thrown or batted from the grounds into the basket and stays there.

9. When the ball goes out of bounds, it shall be thrown into the field of play by the person first touching it.

10. The umpire . . . shall have power to disqualify men according to Rule 5.

11. The referee shall be judge of the ball and shall decide when the ball is in play, in bounds, to which side it belongs.

12. The time shall be two fifteen-minute halves, with five minutes' rest between.

13. The side making the most goals in that time shall be declared the winner.

Dr. J-Nais's Rules 2007—Da' Remix

1. The ball may be thrown, but only really needs to be if there is the possibility of a triple double.

2. The ball can be hogged.

3. A player can palm the ball if his salary is greater than the net worth of the head referee's hometown.

4. The ball should be SLAMMED AND JAMMED.

5. Only Shaq may be tackled. Also, don't touch Dwyane Wade or he might break.

6. A foul is to be contested and cried about.

7. If either side has Kobe, he is allowed to make Stink Face.

8. Making one goal shall be considered better than defending three goals.

9. When the ball goes out of bounds, it shall be watched rather than pursued. If any player shall hustle after said ball, the participants may look at each other and snicker.

10. The umpire shall have power to disqualify men unless said player is LeBron, in which case the foul shall be assessed to Eric Snow.

11. The referee shall determine the outcome of the game per the instructions of David Stern and the Nielsen Rating Corporation.

12. The time shall be two twenty-four-minute halves, but that just seems too damn long when you'd rather be out poppin' corks.

13. The side making the most money shall be declared the winner.

Famers who could get good high-percentage shots and not turn the ball over, this selfishness has extended to everyone and anyone who's ever made a reverse layup. The end result is that the NBA has turned into an ugly, flawed game—one big tug of war for shots, ball control, and respect. When a U.S. national team with a starting lineup of LeBron James, Dwyane Wade, Carmelo Anthony, Elton Brand, and Dwight Howard loses to a Puerto Rican team whose best players are Carlos Arroyo and Daniel Santiago, something has gone very, very wrong.

While no one is suggesting a return to two-handed set shots and a jump ball after every basket, many fans want to shift the emphasis away from dunk-happy, one-on-one play and put it back onto teamwork and fundamentals. Some, like the *Wall Street Journal*'s Sam "Sky" Walker, have an innovative solution to bring the game back into balance. Ironically, it's to change one of the rules that has remained in place since Naismith put up peach baskets in his PE class more than a century ago: to raise the hoop from 10 feet to 12.

Sam is a smart guy, a great writer, and a fantasy baseball savant, so if he had a way to make the NBA more watchable I was willing to listen. When he asked me to explore the 12-foot-hoop idea, he said he figured it would make scoring more difficult, which would force NBA players to use elaborate plays and cohesive teamwork to create good scoring opportunities. In other words, it'd cut down on games filled with four guys standing around watching one teammate trying to beat his man one-on-one.

Interestingly, this is nearly the exact same argument forward-thinkers were making fifty years ago, when one player's size and talent were allowing him to easily make baskets on his own that once required . . . well, elaborate plays and cohesive teamwork. That player was the Lakers' George Mikan, the NBA's first dominant center.

The 6'10" Mikan was the biggest player, literally and figuratively, of the early NBA, where 5'7" guards were often seen launching set shots from 25 feet and dunking was almost as rare as a four-minute mile. He was such a force that his teams won championships in seven out of the nine years he played. Many fans loved Mikan, but traditionalists of the 1940s and '50s didn't want him dominating the game without the help of his teammates, and in a fashion they considered artless. The league tried a number of rule changes to slow him down, but stopping Mikan from dominating was like stopping Stuart Scott from yelling "Booya." However, unlike how everyone has given up trying to prevent Scott from screaming stupid catchphrases, the NBA tried another, more radical measure to keep Mikan from winning titles.

On March 7, 1954, the NBA raised the baskets to 12 feet for an official league game between Mikan's Minneapolis Lakers and the Milwaukee Hawks. The idea was that raising the hoop would make shot-making more difficult and keep Mikan from playing above the rim, meaning he'd become like everyone else . . . just a lot taller and with dorky glasses.

To the uninitiated the experiment could be seen as a success. The Lakers barely won the game, 65–63, and even with the help of his vaunted drill, Mikan missed twelve of his fourteen shots. Given that this was the NBA's seventy-third rule change to try to make him worse, it's not surprising Mikan wasn't a fan of the raised hoop: "It threw the whole game out of sync." But the problem was that nobody else liked it either. That's because *everyone* had trouble scoring, not just Mikan. The Lakers shot only 28.6 percent from the field, and the Hawks hit a paltry 31.7 percent. Hawks guard Bob Harrison said, "It's screwy; it's terrible. I'll take the old game." The 6'7" Vern Mikkelsen (father of PGA star Phil), who led the Lakers with 17 points, called the experiment "a horrible flop." The NBA quickly abandoned the 12-foot hoop, and the Lakers-Hawks snore fest turned out to be the only NBA game ever played under these conditions.

But as we know, the game has changed a lot in the past half century. For one, nobody wears dorky glasses (dorky face masks, however, are now en vogue). More important, players are much bigger, more athletic, and offensively advanced than in Mikan's day. Players of Mikkelsen's size typically play two-guard rather than power forward, and guys taller and far, far, far more athletic than Mikan can play facing the basket and have skills superior to those of the best point guards of his era. Some players, like Dwight Howard, can actually dunk on a 12-foot hoop. Really, the only similarity to the Mikan era is that Kevin Willis is still playing. So if we brought back the 12-foot hoop, would Sam Walker's crazy-enough-that-it-just-might-work new/old plan bring back team play and improve the overall game?

Not likely. A 12-foot basket makes shooting, and in particular outside shooting, more difficult. That's what the Mikan game showed ("Nobody could hit the darn thing," said Lakers' Hall of Fame coach John Kundla), as did a 1961 study conducted by Stan Morrison and a game played on an 11-foot hoop that former NBA assistant coach Tom Newell put together in the summer of 2007. Even though players would adapt to the raised hoop over time, overall misses would still remain high; as University of Washington physics lecturer emeritus Charles E. Robertson told Newell's people, a shooter's "margins for error are lessened as the hoop is raised."

Both Newell and Morrison say that it becomes harder to shoot from in close on a higher hoop. This is true. But it's also harder to shoot from everywhere else, and especially from outside. For example, the players in Newell's game, which included many pros, shot 8 for 48 (17 percent) from the *college* three-point line.

Any rational person would take that as an imperative to work for a better shot, but that doesn't mean NBA players would adopt this mindset. Even now there is a very close correlation between a team's offensive field goal percentage and winning, yet many NBA players, like Antoine Walker and Gilbert Arenas, still take low-percentage, off-balance jumpers with fifteen seconds left on the shot clock. So why would they stop if all of a sudden everyone else's shooting percentages went down?

Even if the 12-foot hoop got those guys to rein it in a little, which seems highly unlikely (bordering on "absolutely no chance in hell"), the net result would be an uglier game than the one we currently have. All the missed shots the raised hoop produced would muck things up enough, but even worse would be the brutal wrestling match under the boards that'd result—exactly what we saw in the Mikan game. Vern Mikkelsen made it clear that the players who would benefit the most from a raised hoop aren't the skilled types most fans enjoy watching: "It helped me—the big, strong rebounder—because it gave me another tenth of a second to get set [for a rebound] after a shot."

With the outside shot an ineffective weapon and overall misses skyrocketing, teams would cram their front courts with Vern Mikkelsen 2.0 big men—and mostly unskilled ones, since there's always a dearth of decent 4s and 5s to begin with. These bruisers would be positioned on the interior to try to scoop up all the missed shots, which even great jump shooters like Michael Redd would be hoisting, and congest the middle defensively. So instead of skillful jump shooters and athletic wings in teams' starting line-ups, you'll be treated to backup centers filling out the forward positions to bang with the stiffs in the middle. Sorry, Jason Terry and Josh Howard, now we need to make room for D. J. Mbenga and DeSagana Diop.

A fast-break attack would be out of the picture completely as a countermeasure because your team's oafs aren't going to be able to run up and down the floor all night. The game would devolve into a slow, grind-it-out war of attrition with minimal skill, the ball being pounded down low to the biggest guys on the court, and tons of missed shots. Think of the nauseating games Alonzo Mourning's Heat and Patrick Ewing's Knicks played in the 1990s, only more physical and less fun.

Oh, and it gets even worse. Mikan pointed out the biggest problem: "It just makes the big man bigger." The fact is that for all his misses on the 12-foot hoop, he was actually even *more* dominant overall because he grabbed every rebound and clogged the middle on defense. So beyond aesthetic considerations, the 12-foot hoop would accentuate the fundamental problem the NBA has always had in maintaining competitive balance: the dominance of the big man. Just look at who wins NBA titles: almost exclusively teams with Hall of Famers in the middle. Mikan, Arnie Risen, Dolph Schayes, Neil Johnston, Bob Pettit, Bill Russell, Wilt Chamberlain, Dave Cowens, Willis Reed, Wes Unseld, Bill Walton, Kareem Abdul-Jabbar, Moses Malone, Robert Parish, Hakeem Olajuwon, Shaquille O'Neal, and Tim Duncan have accounted for forty-eight of sixty-one championships.

The fact of the matter is that well-balanced teams like the Bad Boy Pistons (or even their 2004 version) winning titles or spectacular players like Michael Jordan leading their squads to championships without the benefit of a Hall of Fame center are very rare sights. But with a 12-foot hoop those exceptions would be a thing of the past, as you'll be watching Tim Duncan raise the championship trophy for the next ten years.

Back to the drawing board, Sam. If you can figure out a way to win Tout Wars in fantasy baseball, I'm sure you'll devise a plan to stop Allen Iverson from destroying the NBA in no time. Just do me a favor and run it by Mike and the Mad Dog first.

Five Easy Steps to a More Exciting Game

1. Shorten the shot clock to eighteen seconds.

With a shorter shot clock, feeding the post will be too time-consuming, and getting from under their own hoop to under the opponent's means the big men, typically the slowest players with the lowest stamina, have the most running to do. Look for the Lakers to thrive, as Kobe Bryant, acting in the best interests of the game, has been shooting as quickly as possible for years.

2. Expand the court.

A larger court will give players more room to work and make athletic guards and forwards more effective. But many fans with premium courtside seats will be forced to defend the high pick and roll.

3. Widen the lane.

A trapezoidal lane, used in international play, forces big men to set up farther away from the hoop. The only obstacle will be explaining to NBA fans, players, coaches, and writers what the word *trapezoidal* means.

4. Allow a traditional zone defense/eliminate the defensive three-second rule.

If pro teams are allowed to pack in a 2-3 zone the way college and high school teams do, it will make life much harder on big guys. Teams will run more so as not to allow the defense to get set up, which would be a huge advantage for players like Steve Francis, who don't get back on defense to begin with.

5. All donkey basketball, all the time.

This measure will, at the very least, bring more donkeys onto the basketball court. Practically, this means the skill of riding a donkey will supersede all other abilities or size considerations. However, big men will be at a further disadvantage, as many are simply too heavy to ride these proud and noble beasts.

IS IT AS EASY TO CHEAT AT POKER AS THEY MADE IT LOOK IN ROUNDERS?

In 1972, John Ciotti, a lifelong poker player who doubles as my grandfather, saw something that he'd never forget. No, it wasn't a Wings concert, it was the ease with which card players can cheat.

"One day, before anyone showed up to our game, a friend of mine pulled me aside and started dealing the cards around an empty table. But as he dealt each card face down he was calling out the number and suit of each card. He explained that he had his eyes trained to see each card just by turning it up ever so slightly before he dealt. He said to me, 'Johnny, please don't tell anyone I can do this. I never use it in games but when I win people will start to wonder.' I never told anyone. But he's dead now so it's fine."

Do you think he ever cheated?

"Well, probably if he was really in the hole. He knew every way to cheat and I don't think you'd spend that much time learning how to do those kinds of things and never use them. We were all friends at the table so after everyone had a few drinks and was laughing and having a good time, I think it'd be pretty easy to pull it off."

According to Sal Piacente, a consultant who specializes in cheating protection for casinos, what my grandfather's friend did is a move common among experienced poker cheats. It's known simply as *peeking*.

"Most people screw their friends," Piacente told me. "They *like* to screw their friends. The easiest people to screw are the ones who trust you. . . . There's people who cheat in their house game their entire life and never tell a soul. It happens in golf clubhouses, ski lodges, everywhere."

Piacente made a DVD called *Poker Cheats Exposed* that documents all the various ways to fix a game and the ways to identify these same cheats. Depending on the circumstance, cheaters can deal any cards they want to themselves, create any flop they desire, mark cards, palm cards, you name it. They can completely dictate the game, and while these magicians may not be able to do this while levitating in a block of ice over the Grand Canyon, they can sure as hell do it in your basement.

These moves are difficult to execute, requiring hard work and skill to master, but according to Piacente most of the really fun tricks, like having a mechanical device under your shirt to hide cards, are unnecessary. "The best moves are the easiest ones to pull off," he said. That's especially true in house games, where "the dealer is not going to be counting down the cards a lot, so you can just hold a card out—take an ace and keep it in your hand."

All of these moves will work as long as the players don't know what to look for . . . and almost no one does. Each cheat has a cue or "tell" that gives it away, but to notice these in a game requires hours upon hours of study and extensive experience at the table. When asked how many people can pick up on cheaters, Piacente replied, "Not many. Not many at all. We made the DVD because all of these young kids think they're professional poker players, and very few of them know how to protect themselves or how cheating works. Even not many of the professional players know the moves. You gotta know the moves and have a lot of table hours to even think about trying to defend yourself. It's a shame, it really, really is."

These warnings would come as a surprise to all those guys who think they're Johnny Chan just because they won some money at the Palms during their buddy's Vegas bachelor party, who loudly complain about all the "fish" who don't know anything about poker, or who might have successfully used the term *the river* a couple of times. Most guys like this don't even suspect that they can be taken, despite the fact that, as Sal pointed out, cheating goes on all the time. And if they do suspect it, they usually think they're knowledgeable enough to pick up on it.

But it's not so easy; even when Sal showed me the moves, I couldn't pick up on them without repeated viewing. It was a little like high school Trig, in that I knew something bad was going on but couldn't understand how it was happening. When he mixed the different cheats together, I was completely baffled.

It only gets worse. The most effective way to cheat is also the simplest and requires no real expertise: collusion. For cheaters, collusion is "the best way to go," Sal said. "You're not manipulating the cards so it's hard to get caught. By signaling, we can protect ourselves from getting burned or draw other players in to lose more money by what's called *crossfiring*. You get together with your partner, come up with some signals, and that can be done with no problem whatsoever. If you have a game and we're friends, I'd just say, 'Hey, Todd, I've got this friend who's a really good guy and looking for a game, you mind if I bring him over?' Then we'd work together and *boom*, it's over."

To see this firsthand I planted two cheats, whom we'll call "Tex" and "Mr. Sandman," into my friends' regular Texas Hold 'Em game. I followed Sal's tip and introduced my ringers as "buddies from out of town." Like a lot of guys who play poker, my friends consider themselves solid players, and to be fair, I had, on drunken occasion, lost money to them. But they're nothing more than skilled amateurs. To Tex and Sandman, this was easy pickings. After showing me their signals for indicating to each other what hand they had, when to raise the stakes, and when to draw the suckers at the table into betting, they went to work.

I'd like to say it was really dramatic like in the movies, but to the untrained eye, it just looked like a regular boring game of cards. Tex won a couple of big hands but that's about it. Since I knew the signals, I did pick up on some visual clues, so I pretty much knew what hands each one had and when they were working together. Also, I saw when Tex and Sandman passed a card between each other. Of course, Tex got up to grab a drink before the hand and told me that they were soon going to do this.

Afterward, we let my friends in on the stunt and discovered that absolutely none of them had suspected that something was going on. My pal Mike was utterly baffled: "I had no idea whatsoever. When your friend [Tex] won that big hand with a pair of aces, I just assumed he got lucky. I mean, he didn't even win a ton of hands. And the other guy you brought ended up losing money."

Tex had a laugh at that one. "The big hand, the pair of aces, actually *was* on the up and up. They were just dealt to me. But what happened was I checked and had [Sandman] raise for me before he got out of the hand. We ended up getting a lot more money out of it that way. There were a couple hands where I held back cards, but mostly we just signaled to each other. Either way, it would have been hard to get caught even if we wanted to with how much they were drinking and not paying attention."

Sandman had a similarly dim view of the competition: "Well, first thing is these guys are bad players, so a lot of the hands we could win just because they don't know what the hell they're doing. But they aren't so bad that they can't bust you out if they get lucky. With what we're doing, we improve our odds and take out most of the luck."

Piacente backed up the claim that my friends were outmatched even without the cheating. "Some of the best cheats were outstanding players before they started cheating. And that helps because not only are you going to win more but you can talk the talk of a player who would win."

The point Mike brought up is a fair one, though. Why did Sandman lose money then?

"That's poker," said Tex. "You can't win every time. We split everything and I walked away up four hundred and sixty bucks, so why risk it? You said you wanted to see how it really would go down, and we'd never risk getting caught over a couple bucks. You want to string games like this out for as long as possible."

Piacente seconded this approach: "All you need to do is win one or two big hands. If you're winning hands left and right, it starts to get suspicious. I mean, how many times can you lay down the ace of spades before they start asking questions?"

That raises the question: What does happen if the cheats become sloppy or greedy and get caught?

"I don't know, it's never happened to me," said Tex. "We're pretty careful about where we play and who we play with."

Piacente, however, has seen the shit go down.

"Usually the player is just asked to leave."

That's not what happened in *Rounders,* Sal.

"In a private game there may be a small threat of violence, but usually the player's back is covered by who they came in with. Or you just go to a casino; two people colluding at a casino is easy. Casino cheating, there's no violence at all. Everybody thinks the casinos are so sharp, but they're not as sharp as you'd think. And remember, they don't put as much of an emphasis on poker as they do on other games because they get their rake either way."

So there's no real deterrent to cheating? Is there any kind of prosecution at the casinos?

"No, not at all. I've never seen it."

What's the solution for someone who loves to play cards? Maybe go play in a tournament?

According to Piacente, these are overrun with fraud as well. In tournaments, some players sneak in matching chips they secured at lower buy-in tournaments. Others collude; two or more dirtbags will intentionally lose hands to a single player they're working with to build up his chip count.

Online gambling? No, not safe either. There is software that allows you to see what cards your opponents have, and although the best sites have computer algorithms in place to detect collusion, as long as cheats don't get too greedy, chances are they're not going to get caught.*

Okay, so cheating is supereasy to pull off, but can you make a living off of it? Are we talking the Bret Maverick life or something more like Joey Knish's?

"You can make a living, but it's slow," said Sal. "They have their down seasons, they have their good games that come and go. Sometimes they blow their money as fast as they make it. Even cheating you still get burned and a lot of times you're splitting the money you make with other people who are setting up your games."

That's why, Sandman said, he and Tex "pretty much just do this for fun and for a few extra bucks." Trying to make a living as a card sharp is "a real grind," he added. "You can't just keep cleaning out the same games. Eventually, they won't invite you back."

But make no mistake, cheating is rampant in the poker world and it goes on more than you're probably aware of. The crazy shit

---

* It should be noted that you might be losing at all of these things just because you suck at cards, too.

you think you've seen since you started playing after Chris Money-maker won the World Series of Poker in 2003 experienced players have seen a hundred times over.

If you don't want to get abused in poker, you've got to know your stuff. Gramps dispensed some wisdom: "If you really want to make money at poker, you have to master both the honest and dishonest ways. Not only do you have to know all the odds, which not a lot of people do, but you have to know all the cheats, every-body's personality, and how desperate they are."

Sure, you can just play poker with your friends, but as Sal pointed out, even that's not much protection. Remember, most people like to screw their friends. You could also just play for fun, but my grandfather thought I was a sissy even to suggest such a thing: "You can do that, but what're you gonna do, play for pen-nies? The excitement is in playing for real money."

Grandpa was starting to scare me a little, but then he gave this sober piece of advice for those of us who are easy marks at the poker table: Quit altogether. "Pick something to do where your in-telligence rewards you and that you can actually succeed at con-sistently without cheating."

Maybe not the kind of advice that will get an adrenaline junkie salivating, but following it means at least you'll be able to pay rent without having to hang out with guys named "Worm."

COULD A NON-BASKETBALL PLAYER BEAT AN NBA PLAYER IN FREE THROWS?

"My friend Gene Weingarten claims that if he practiced for a year, he could become a world-class free-throw shooter, and could beat any professional basketball player in a free-throw shooting contest for a very large sum of money. I say Gene is an idiot. Who is correct? Bear in mind that Gene may well be an idiot even if he is correct about the free-throw shooting. But he is not."

—Dave Barry

This was the question Pulitzer Prize–winning humor columnist Dave Barry posed to me when I began working on this book. While I had neither the time nor the resources to ascertain whether Gene is an idiot, I did my best to settle the sports part of the debate. Finding a man to practice free-throw shooting full-time for a year for a gentlemen's bet between two writers was not realistic, so to wrap my head around the question, I looked for a guy who had never played basketball before but who was willing to shoot one hundred free throws a day for three months.

After scouring the yacht club at Martha's Vineyard, conducting interviews outside of a Kenny G concert, and placing ads in the back of the Brooks Brothers catalog failed to land my great white whale, I called my editor, Jed Donahue, and shared the dilemma.

Much as Napoleon sailed around the world in search of Curly's Gold before realizing that it was buried in his backyard all along, it turned out Jed was just the man I was looking for.

Jed is most famous for defeating Olympic gold medalist Maurice Greene in the 100 meters in an untelevised made-for-TV event called The Battle of the Century (detailed in Question 6). But amazingly, for as accomplished an athlete as Jed is [*Editor's Note: This "accomplished athlete" hasn't been to the gym since Bill Clinton was in office*], it turned out his basketball experience was virtually nil.

Jed's first practice session, filmed and documented in the now famous "Soul Man" sessions, was a sight to behold. Airballed threes from the corner, awkward attempts at Teen Wolf–style between-the-legs dribbling, and reverse layups with both feet nailed to the ground served as the appetizers for a main course that included him making thirty out of a hundred free throws. It was reminiscent of one of those movies where scientists unfreeze someone from the past and the Neanderthal can't figure out how to use a can opener. Clearly, professional help was needed.

To that end, I considered a couple of shooting coaches used by NBA teams—both of whom were utterly incompetent and remarkably overpaid—as well as a clueless NBA assistant, before deciding the best person for the job was USBL scouting director Mark Argenziano. Argenziano, who has worked in virtually every capacity in basketball, is a uniquely talented shooter (as a high school player he shot 96 percent from the line and once hit seventeen three-pointers in a game), and more important, he's skilled at conveying his knowledge to others.

Mark met with Jed for a two-hour tutorial. He immediately fixed many of Jed's fatal flaws, including not bending his knees, not following through, and closing his eyes during shots.

After a week, Jed was already shooting better than four-time NBA all-star Ben Wallace.

After two weeks, he was shooting better than Shaquille O'Neal, the only active member of the NBA's Fifty Greatest Players team.

By the end of the first month, he was shooting better than five-time all-star Chris Webber.

By the end of the second month—and after another session with Mark—he was shooting better than two-time MVP Tim Duncan.

By the end of the third and final month, Jed went on a two-day kick where he hit 76 percent over the course of 467 foul shots—identical numbers to what Kevin Garnett put up in his 2000–01 all-star season.

A common refrain from NBA players is that they are much more successful from the line in practice than in actual games. (Similarly, I can dunk when no one is looking.) To erase any doubts, I decided to put ol' Jed to the test in a competitive environment. Off to Washington he went to go head-to-head against Wizards' shooting guard DeShawn Stevenson, a career 69 percent foul shooter.

Now, Stevenson is not your run-of-the-mill 69 percent shooter. The guy can really shoot. At the time of the contest he was hitting 49 percent from the three-point line in NBA games (he later dubbed himself "Mr. Fifty" when his overall shooting percentage rose above 50 percent), and the week before he had made sixty-eight of ninety-six threes (71 percent) in a contest against teammate Gilbert Arenas with $20,000 on the line.* Jed literally cannot make an NBA three-pointer. Or a layup.

---

* The Stevenson/Arenas battle was one for the ages. The bet was that Stevenson couldn't make as many NBA threes as Arenas could make college threes shooting *one-handed*; $20,000, winner take all. Arenas made seventy-three out of one hundred to win the contest. Both DeShawn and Gilbert claimed that no money was

Whoever blinks first still sucks at foul shooting.

The rules would be simple: fifty free-throw attempts, most makes wins.

The race was on, but one horse came out lame, and possibly should have been euthanized. Jed stumbled out of the gate with a dreadful 2 for 10. Jesus, Donahue. Having never shot a basketball in a competitive situation before, Jed was choking. There were questions as to whether he could even reach the 30 percent he was making before he had ever practiced.

DeShawn calmly made 7 out of 10.

The next round J-Town got his sea legs a bit, making 6 of 10.

DeShawn made his 8. It was only round two and the match was almost out of reach. 15–8.

Then Jed started rolling. 8 for 10.

---

exchanged, meaning either there was never a bet to begin with and the whole thing was a big publicity stunt, or the more logical conclusion: Agent Zero was waiting until the season ended to kill DeShawn Stevenson and claim his winnings.

DeShawn answered with his own 8 for 10.

23–16.

8 for 10 for Jed again. He was starting to heat up.

DeShawn only managed to put up 5 for 10. He tried to play it off: "I like to make it close." But now nerves were starting to affect both parties.

28–24.

This is where things got interesting. DeShawn, sensing he might actually be in trouble against a guy who had never played basketball before in his life and who had made 2 out of 10 to start the contest, responded by pulling out all the stops—yelling "Hey!" and snapping his fingers when Jed would shoot, waving his arms under the basket, and even taking a page out of Michael Winslow's book and simulating crowd noise.

But nothing could stop the machine. À la *NBA Jam* the ball had a trail of smoke coming out of it. 9 for 10.

Donahue had taken the lead for the first time: 28–33.

It all came down to this. With Jed's poor first round, the contest had started out as such a joke that halfway through DeShawn asked the scorekeeper, "Do I even need to shoot anymore, or have I wrapped it up?" Now the question was more serious: "How many do I need?" The answer was 5 to tie, 6 to win. A repeat of his previous round and DeShawn and Jed would be dead-even and headed to overtime.

DeShawn made four in a row to start, and thinking he was tied due to a scorer's error, went for the win—calling out "Glass!" to teammate Caron Butler. Miss. Two more banks missed. Badly. "How many shots do I have left?" Three. He drilled one for the apparent win (actually, the tie)—and then two more Cartwright-style for good measure.

"Ha ha, I won! Yes I did!" yelled Stevenson.

Final score: DeShawn Stevenson 35, Jed Donahue 33.

Pretty damn close. After Jed's horrific choke job to start, he took two of the last three rounds and tied the third. But DeShawn was not done chirping.

"Hey, you have a friend that wants to challenge me?" he taunted. (DeShawn, I'm ready when you are. Bring cash, please.)

"How about a rematch?" said Donahue.

"No, I don't do rematches," replied Stevenson, who himself had begged Arenas for a rematch of their contest. He quickly took off.

Gene Weingarten was in attendance to witness the match and settle his bet with Dave Barry. He spoke with Jed about what had transpired.

"I'm amazed you did as well as you did given the fact that you weren't practicing for a year. I heard him say he practices by shooting one hundred free throws a day. So basically, you were practicing the same amount that he does ordinarily for a game. . . . You essentially beat him the last three rounds."

DeShawn screamed from the gym's exit. "Yeah, I won! Chicken and grits, grits and chicken!"

Having absolutely no clue what this meant, Jed ignored him and went back to the conversation with Gene: "I've only been doing this for three months. If I did this for another six months and got another session with my shooting coach, I could really refine my form."

"I contend you proved my point," said Gene. "Give you another year of practice . . . can we all agree that even though you lost, I won?"

Well, not necessarily, Gene-o. The original question was actually whether you could "beat any professional basketball player in a free-throw shooting contest for a very large sum of money." When it comes to beating the best of the best—pros who have been shooting with flawless technique since they were young kids—it gets a little more complicated. Argenziano indicated that he could take any spaz and make that person a very solid shooter over time—70, 75, maybe even 80 percent. But the freakishly good foul shooters not only have put in hundreds of thousands of repetitions over the course of years and years, but they're also blessed with certain natural talents that not everyone has. So it is by no means a foregone conclusion that with nine more months of practice, even nonstop practice, Jed would be able to beat Ray Allen or Steve Nash. In fact, it's rather unlikely.

Dave Barry was even less charitable to Gene's position: "So, as I understand it, you are encouraged because a guy who practiced 'only three months' got beat by a mediocre NBA free-throw shooter who was not taking it seriously. Okay! My feeling is that you could practice for ten years and still not beat a good NBA free-throw shooter who was trying, any more than you could practice pole vaulting for ten years and beat a good pole vaulter. Also, you are—let's not kid ourselves here—a loser."

No one is doubting that Gene's a loser, but despite what Dave said, DeShawn was really trying and Jed still gave him a real battle. So the bet wasn't settled definitively, and never will be until Gene stops yapping and shoots the free throws himself. But we learned all we needed to. While there are going to be varying degrees of success based on individual talent, without question it is possible to be better than all but the best foul shooters in the NBA with some practice—even if you're so bad at basketball that you can't make a layup.

Hey, so there's your answer! Goodnight, folks!

Okay, okay, okay . . .

Why Can't NBA Players Shoot Free Throws Better Than Some Editor Guy Who Just Started Playing Basketball?

This is the more interesting question, and although it wasn't submitted by any bickering columnists, it's what's at the heart of the debate.

A good way to examine this question is to look at how someone who is as good an overall shooter as Stevenson could be so mediocre at the line. Before the match we gained some insight when Jed spoke with Wizards center Brendan Todd Haywood. The BTH, who was Jed's first choice for an opponent, is a career 59 percent shooter from the line, or where Jed was after a few weeks of practice.

Asked to predict how DeShawn would do in the contest, Big Brendan Todd said, "Out of fifty shots in practice? The pressure's not really going to be on him and he's a pretty good free-throw shooter. I think he'll knock down forty."

This was right in line with what Stevenson said he makes in practice. For a guy who can knock down 71 percent of his shots from the NBA three-point line with Gilbert Arenas screaming in his ear, 80 percent from the foul line isn't great. Yet this is still considerably better than what DeShawn shoots in a game. Where is the disconnect?

"In games it's different because everybody's watching," said Haywood. "In practice, you're by yourself, so if you miss, you just miss. But in game situations you've got twenty thousand fans watching. Sometimes the time and score of the game dictates how tough the free throw is going to be. You've definitely got to look at fatigue, having a rhythm, did you make your last one, did you miss your last one. Stuff like that always factors in."

Stevenson had a similar explanation.

Some objects in this picture are larger than they appear.

"I think a free throw is all mental. You get there, everybody is watching you, and you've got to knock it down . . . compared to a jump shot where you just catch and shoot." He chalked up many of his misses to "not being focused, not taking my time."

There are certainly psychological factors (see: Anderson, Nick), but a free throw being all mental? If playing under conditions where everyone was waiting on you to perform a shot is that difficult, we'd never even have a pro golf tour . . . which might be for the best, but that's besides the point. Where was the fatigue when the bed-shitting Donahue almost beat Stevenson head to head? And is it even conceivable that DeShawn was less prepared for the "pressure" of a free-throw contest with no one watching than Jed was?

This was enough psychobabble for me coming from two guys who don't even shoot their free throws that well in practice. There must be more to foul shooting than they were saying. Like, say, technique.

Told of Brendan's and DeShawn's analysis, Mark Argenziano said, "I think the mental aspect does come into play—slightly, but much more when your technique is not efficient and simplified. If you have the technique down, it's really simple. The fewer parts there are to the shot, the fewer things there are that can go wrong. The proper shot is so simplified you're almost doing it without thinking." So you can talk about pressure and mental lapses all you want, but if you don't have proper technique and don't practice over and over to make it second nature, what you're thinking at the line might be the least of your problems.

So why can't more NBA players get the correct technique down? One definite component of the problem is either a lack of coaching or, worse, bad advice. DeShawn, for one, said he doesn't work with any coaches on his free-throw technique. Maybe that's not such a bad thing, though, considering the alternatives. To try to improve, Haywood works with Harvey Grant, a former NBA player who was only a career 71 percent foul shooter. The other Wizards coaches with NBA experience are Mike O'Koren (65 percent), Phil Hubbard (dubbed the club's unofficial "free throw coach") (71 percent), and head coach Eddie Jordan (76 percent). I may not have the NBA credentials of these fine fellows, but I did coach in the USBL and can shoot free throws better than those guys with either hand, and I can tell you that the technical term for this kind of an arrangement is the blind leading the blind.

To teach something it sure does help to at least know the basics, and unless a physical impairment is involved, anyone who can't make at least 80 percent of his free throws doesn't understand the basics and should not be teaching anyone. At practices leading up to the 2006 World Championship I watched Dwight Howard, a career 61 percent free-throw shooter (who has actually gotten worse at the line each year he's been in the league), working on his foul shooting with one of the USA Basketball coaches. Every day Dwight would stay after practice to try to improve, and was clearly listening to the instruction. Unfortunately, the coach had no idea what he was talking about and kept insisting that Dwight get "more arc" on the ball without going into detail as to how. Dwight's coach allowed him to launch shot after shot with the same abbreviated follow-through that had also plagued Jed.

Let's contrast Dwight's instruction with Jed's.

Jed's coach, Mark Argenziano, immediately recognized the glitch, explained the problem to Jed, and walked him through specific ways to fix it. Heady stuff.

"It's pretty astonishing, isn't it?" said Rick Barry, NBA Hall of Famer and former MVP, who has the second highest free-throw percentage in NBA history at 89 percent. "They have all of these millions of dollars invested in these athletes and they have these people who absolutely allow them to continue to do things incorrectly. It's incompetence basically. You have to know what is fundamentally sound and what isn't. I've watched players working with coaches who allow them to shoot incorrectly time after time."

Former NBA center Chris Dudley—who has the second-lowest career free-throw percentage in NBA history at 45 percent and the lowest single-season percentage at 31.9 percent (remember, Jed *started* at 30 percent)—agreed about the lack of quality coaching. "Baseball has batting instructors. For as much money that's in the game it certainly would help to have an instructor who just focused on shooting." Only recently have teams like the Dallas Mavericks started to hire coaches specifically for shooting.

But you can't blame it all on coaching. Even on teams that have shooting coaches, not all players elect to take the help, and some of the NBA's worst bricklayers stubbornly stick to the same failed approach. Shaq is a career 53 percent shooter who due to a childhood wrist injury would be a perfect candidate to switch to the underhand "granny" style Rick Barry used. But he wouldn't take Barry's instruction (although he did experiment with various techniques). "He said he was ready to do it after the Olympics but the Lakers didn't want me to get involved," Rick told me. "But obviously he wasn't serious enough because if he says yes they'd go along with it." Dudley worked with Barry very briefly on the granny style but ultimately declined to use the remarkably uncool shot in an NBA game.*

No matter what style you use, you have to be willing to put in the effort, which in many cases is the real problem. Mark Argenziano said that he became an outstanding shooter by making between 1,000 and 1,500 shots every single day in high school.

---

* It's hard to imagine how anything could be more embarrassing than Chris Dudley's double-pump shooting stroke, which looked somewhat like a seizure, but the granny shot probably is. Believe it or not, that could be a legitimate problem, especially for a borderline player, which Dudley was when he started out. Unless Barry's style brings the player up to a high level, the scrub will only be calling further attention to his free-throw struggles, and the resulting media and fan scrutiny could embarrass not just the player, but the entire organization. Avoiding all that attention—even if it means continuing to go one for two from the line in garbage time—could be the difference between a multiyear contract and a one-year deal, or between making a team and being sent to the NBDL. For the more accomplished players, like Shaq, the motivation is simply to not look like a nerd.

According to Barry, many NBA players just don't work at foul shooting enough: "Well, they say they practice. A lot of them aren't really willing to put the time in." The only teammates he could recall practicing as much as he did were Calvin Murphy and Mike Newlin—who for their careers shot 89 percent and 87 percent from the line, respectively.

Although it's far easier to improve if you don't have ingrained bad habits, the record is clear that if players are willing to put in the work and get proper instruction, they can go from being awful free-throw shooters to very respectable or even excellent. Tony Parker, Shawn Bradley, Josh Howard, and Dale Davis have talked about how working with a good free-throw coach helped them improve at the line, and Hall of Famers Karl Malone, Magic Johnson, and Moses Malone all dramatically improved their foul shooting from when they came into the league as well.

As to why some players don't work harder at free throws, part of the reason is clearly a lack of incentive. DeShawn Stevenson, for example, spent countless hours in the gym to become a good three-point shooter. He didn't come into the NBA as a three-point threat, so developing that talent made him a valuable starter for an NBA playoff team and should earn him a good multiyear contract. But like many players, especially jump shooters who release their shot at its peak, his technique doesn't translate at the free-throw line. And since he only goes to the line once or twice a game, how much time is it worth investing in a skill that he is barely going to use? Even a jump from 70 percent to 90 percent would raise his overall points per game only marginally.

The point isn't that shooting free throws well is easy (although it is). It's that while Jed's close contest with an NBA player would appear to the untrained eye as a miracle of modern athleticism, it was not. Jed had some things going for him that many NBA players don't. He had a coach who knew what he was doing, had 0.0

percent of his ego tied up in his ability to play the game, and didn't have the pressure of his own history of personal failures at the line. He was not burdened with years of practicing god-awful technique, and he never had to deal with the eyes of a nation staring at him when he clanged a shot off the side of the rim.

With all of that said, I asked Rick Barry how long he thought it would take a man who never played basketball before to be better than the worst foul shooters in the NBA. Rick responded immediately:

"One day."

HOW LONG BEFORE NASCAR DRIVERS ARE REPLACED BY AI (ARTIFICIAL INTELLIGENCE, NOT ALLEN IVERSON)?

Putting a computer in control of a race car is a serious decision especially if you consider a possible future where race cars conquer the planet. Those who fear the rise of the machines (I, for one, will welcome our robot overlords) must face the unnerving possibility that these robot cars could soon climb the first rung on the ladder of civilization: NASCAR racing. Could eliminating 200 pounds of useless weight from the average stock car give enough advantage to outweigh the loss of skill, training, determination, and firesuit ad space that the best NASCAR drivers possess?

David Stavens is one of the lead designers on the Stanford Racing team, a group that competes in the Defense Advanced Research Projects Agency (DARPA) Grand Challenge. The U.S. Defense Department puts on this series of races, in which autonomous vehicles attempt to finish designated courses, to further its goal of having one-third of ground military forces autonomous by 2015. The first race, which took place in 2004, was an utter disaster, as no car even finished the treacherous 142-mile desert course. But improvement, as it often does with technology, came rapidly. In the span of eighteen months, five vehicles finished the same course, with Stanford taking home the $2 million first-place prize for their winning car, the cleverly named Stanley. Who said computer types aren't creative?

Stavens was helping prepare a vehicle for the 2007 DARPA Urban Rally when I spoke with him. The Urban Rally is the most challenging DARPA race yet, requiring the driverless vehicle to operate in a mock urban environment and handle most traffic situations—i.e., merge into traffic, turn corners, interact with other cars, stop at stop signs, and park in parking spaces—all while obeying California driving laws. This is remarkable advancement; within three years, Stanley will have gone from driving worse than Toonces to better than Billy Joel. With the next leap in mind, I asked Stavens, whose expertise is in Artificial Intelligence and Robotics, how far away the good ol' boys of NASCAR were from being bested by our future metallic masters.

"If you didn't need it to race with other cars, we can do it right now," he said. "We could take Stanley, the robot we made for the desert challenge, set it at any speed you want, and it would zip around the circle all day."

So you're saying Stanley could already beat Tony Stewart in a time trial?

"Oh yeah, I mean, that's a gimme. Now, Stanley would need to have knowledge of the track beforehand, so we would have to use GPS wavelengths to get the coordinates of the various areas of the track, but once that was set, then a robot could certainly drive the track at very, very close to the fastest speed possible in a time trial. In fact, right now there are already research cars in Formula One racing that are able to beat human drivers. And the reason why is because all the vehicles are able to calculate very precisely the exact way to get around a turn and the precise physics of it so they can do it at the maximum speed possible." He added: "Also unlike a driver, once it's perfected, the computer isn't going to make any mistakes. At least we hope not."

Okay, so the robots would start every race in the pole position, but as we've seen with Ryan Newman, that doesn't always ensure victory. Are we going to reach a point where an AI car could beat a NASCAR driver in an actual race?

"I would say that probably within five to ten years you'd be able to solve most of the technical challenges, and then after that it would be an issue of, do people want this and are they willing to pay for it, are they willing to accept the liabilities that come with it?"

Holy shit. So you're saying there are going to be robots winning NASCAR races before I actually watch a NASCAR race?

"Yeah, I think it's coming. . . . The actual racing once they get on the track and running isn't really the main problem. If you have a bunch of cars zipping around a track at a hundred and fifty miles per hour, then you don't really need to see all that far ahead. The biggest thing is merging back into the speedway. Coming out of the pits, if you need to be able to merge into cars that travel a hundred and fifty miles per hour, then you need to have a very long range perception, which is still very difficult to achieve. And all of the necessary technology is going to be expensive. It's really much more a question of what the marketplace is going to demand and what consumers are going to want."

I want it now! Give it to me now! How much money would I have to give you, right now, for this to happen?

"If there is a real demand for a robot NASCAR, we could probably build one here at Stanford, but it would probably take a million dollars to really do it."

Whoa, slow down, Stavens. I'm keeping my book advance for myself. Maybe I'll help you get it from Bill Walsh or one of those other Stanford richies, but before we try to get Phil Knight or Fred

Savage to cough up that million, let's back up for a second. You had said that you "hope" the robot won't make mistakes on the track. What if this thing got into an accident? Even if the robot was a safer driver and lowered fatality rates, if it pulled a *Maximum Overdrive* and killed Dale Jr., that may not go over so well.

"We're going to make it as safe as we can make it, obviously, but at some point in time you're going to have someone that's going to be injured or someone is going to lose their life, just like in a real NASCAR race. Then there are big questions out there, such as whose fault is it? Is it the robot's fault? Is it that no one's really at fault? Is it the manufacturing company's fault? It's a very difficult question. I think that is actually going to be one of the challenges. At this point, that is a bigger barrier than the technology itself."

Besides the obvious advantage of intelligence, what other edge will a robot have over these car jockeys?

"At least over the course of a long race, a multihour race, maybe the driver is getting fatigued for any reason or because of the heat or because of the sound of the loud engine and therefore makes a bad decision or two; the computer is never going to do that. The computer is always going to make the right decisions."

When you say "right decisions," will a computer do a robot run onto the track and throw his robot helmet at a fellow driver the way Robby Gordon did? Or will it ever use its robot arm to punch out another driver?

"People really enjoy the human aspect of athletics. Computers may be able to drive a car in a technically flawless way, [but] it's not clear if that will still be satisfying to the fans in a way the human element is. But part of the allure of sports for people is the personalities."

Okay, so we know a robot could be a better driver, and we know the people who like the personality of Denny Hamlin aren't going to be into it, but how far off are we from being able to cut humans out of the process entirely? When will a computer be able to go around and raise sponsorship money? From what I understand, that's the most important part of being a NASCAR driver.

"Well, uh, the Stanford team does use sponsors, and a lot of the events that we do to attract sponsors use our cars to—"

No, I mean the way a NASCAR driver would glad-hand people and kiss the sponsors' ass at a corporate function.

"To completely solve that problem is very hard. In some ways, that's the holy grail of robotics. You need to be able to do speech recognition, you need to be able to do natural language understanding, you need to be able to have very high cognitive function like social skills, you need to be able to look and evaluate who is the most likely person to sponsor me and who is the person that I'm going to spend my time crunch with. . . . Maybe fifty, a hundred years. Hopefully I'll see that in my lifetime, but maybe I won't."

No, no, we don't need anything with high cognitive function. Just good enough so the robot could go in with a plastered-on smile, tell the same jokes over and over again, and slam some Bud Light.

"Oh, well, that is attainable now. There is definitely work going on in humanoid robotics, particularly in Japan, where they're investigating that kind of robotic scenario, that could be applicable to what you're describing. They've done some pretty realistic stuff. Frighteningly realistic. Again, there's not a lot of interaction going on there, it's just something that looks like a human that's talking and moving like a human. It'd have to be programmed and there would be very little artificial intelligence to it. Up until the point where someone interacted with it, or tried to ask it a question, someone may think it's a person."

That would be fine for our purposes. We're trying to replicate Bill Elliott, not Bill Hicks.

"If it's just telling stories and jokes, it's possible people may be fooled, but the question for that scenario is the cost to implement something like that. It could be quite expensive. . . . You'd have to hire a dedicated team of researchers, and I would guess you could hire any celebrity in Hollywood for the day for less money. You'd have to ask yourself if it would really make more sense than just hiring a spokesperson."

Yeah, but it'd be better to turn off a switch when you're done.

"Well, someday the robots are going to replace us all. Except for the poets maybe."

Initially I thought this was a question we'd have to revisit in the 2075 edition of this book, along with *How many Zolaxians would it take to defeat the Lakers? Is Billy Bonds taking ectoplasm?* and *Why is* Around the Horn *still on the air?* However, the technology needed to run a car like this may be available as early as 2012, and a system could hypothetically be put together a few years after that. It's possible right now to make a machine that could play golf better than any human,* but we don't do it. Why? Well, because Deep Blue looks extrastupid in plaid pants. But also, it would remove the human element of the games that sports fans enjoy.

On some level, even if NASCAR drivers aren't true athletes, part of racing's allure is the personalities inside the cars (the other part being watching these personalities crash into each other and walls at 200 miles per hour). So although in auto racing it looks like robots will soon be able to dominate the track, no robot will ever be able to conduct interviews while simultaneously thanking God and its ten sponsors with the flair and panache of these good ol' boys.

---

* Real estate mogul Al Czervik and his business partner Mr. Wang of the now defunct Wang Laboratories were the primary trailblazers in this particular field.

COULD ANDY RODDICK BEAT AN AVERAGE TENNIS PLAYER WITH A FRYING PAN?

Andy Roddick is a twenty-five-year-old professional tennis player with twenty-four ATP titles to his credit, including the 2003 U.S. Open. He finished that season ranked #1 in the world and since then has consistently been in the top five. Having spent his entire childhood training on the tennis court, sometimes for as many as ten hours a day, he now has the ability to strike shots at speeds and with a level of accuracy that are almost impossible to comprehend. Andy has hit the fastest serve ever recorded, at 155 miles per hour. His second serve is better than the first serve of almost anyone who is not a professional tennis player. If you had never played tennis before and hit with Andy, you would immediately understand that you were dealing with an incredible athlete. You wouldn't win a point and would possibly get injured by one of his serves.

I play tennis, too! While Roddick was the world's #1 player, I made it to #2 on my high school team the season I played. Like Roddick, I can hit all of the shots. Unlike Andy, I can't hit any of them particularly well or with any kind of power or placement. I hit my first serve around 105 miles per hour, which is slower than his second serve, and it doesn't have anywhere near the kind of action Andy's ball does. I pray to God the first one goes in, because if it doesn't, I could easily double fault. Also unlike Andy, I'm not going to dominate a game on raw athleticism (will, desire, and talent, maybe). If you had never played tennis before, I would beat you but you almost certainly wouldn't come away impressed.

The best way to make the comparison is to say that there's no comparison. Roddick spends his time plowing through opponents in major tournaments, while I spend too much time on my couch watching him do so. Still, like Roddick, I am a tennis player and a competitive guy, so although I never had the dedication or the talent to play at his level, I wanted to know what a win over a player as great as he is felt like. In my heart I knew that I had what it took to beat him. I just had to figure out an unfair way to do it.

As to how unfair, well, that would take some thought. While someone with no tennis experience would not win a point from Andy in a set, I probably wouldn't have a prayer of winning more than a point or two either. This is, in part, because I'm not that good, but also because the difference between a recreational player and an actual pro might be greater in tennis than in any other sport.

Tennis isn't played by a ton of people in America and is therefore not the most competitive sport on its lower levels. I was a pretty good local player growing up despite playing only a couple times a month, and some of the people on my high school team played even less often than I did. To further illustrate the point, my father took up the game in his forties and within three years of playing regularly could occasionally beat me. For more information on his occasional wins, simply make eye contact with him.

Even though virtually anyone can become a decent high school player (at least in western Pennsylvania), to become very good at tennis takes an insane amount of work. Typically this grind starts at a very young age. Pro Scott Draper says that because tennis is so skill oriented, no matter how talented the athlete, a major commitment must be made. "It's not unusual for aspiring young tennis players to spend four to five hours per day on the court. Of course for the top players, practice and fitness become a full-time job."

Kids aren't just playing but *training* for four to five hours a day, with real coaching. You don't find that kind of forced dedication in childhood outside of tennis, except with gymnasts and mathletes. The incredible skill level required of tennis pros is, as Scott said, one of the reasons that the game can't just be picked up by a good athlete late in life. I learned the difference between people who play tennis and people who *train* to play tennis the hard way. At the age of seventeen, I went to a low-level tournament and could barely win a point off of kids who weren't the finest of athletes but did bring more than one racquet and did not wear Sambas.

I would venture to say that Andy Roddick is significantly better than the players who beat me so easily in high school, so if I wanted to be able to beat him and make it feel like a real win, I would have to come up with a handicap that seemed reasonable enough, on the surface at least, to make Andy emotionally invested in the match. Also, if I defeated Roddick, I wanted the victory to boost my ego, and him playing blindfolded and strapped to a gurney wouldn't impress my friends much.

The first thought was to make Andy play with one hand tied behind his back. This would weaken his serve, limit his range of motion, and affect his balance. But pro athletes can be extremely effective with one hand (major league pitcher Jim Abbott was the best at this parlor trick, winning eighteen games one year for the Angels; and Ismael Paez whipped my ass one-handed in pool [see Question 20]), and in tennis, this particular disadvantage wouldn't mean much. Even with one hand, Andy would have an unimpeded forehand, could put a nasty slice on any ball to his backhand or run around it and crush a forehand back at me, hit serves hard enough and with enough action that I would have trouble returning them, get to the net and knock off volleys at will, and easily run down every shot I hit. Good Division I college players probably would be able to take a game or two off of a one-armed Andy, but the handicap wouldn't do me much good. I would need something more extreme to give myself a chance.

Okay, so what if we made Andy wear an eye patch? An eye patch, though exceedingly cool, would hurt both his peripheral vision and depth perception. It would also be extremely annoying to him. But while Andy would be worse with an eye patch, even in conjunction with his left arm tied behind his back, he would still probably prevent me from winning a game. A good college player may be able to get a set from him, however. We were getting closer.

What if Andy gave me the use of the doubles alleys? Well, in a pay-per-view match in 1992 Jimmy Connors gave Martina Navratilova half the doubles alleys (and was only allowed one serve) and still smoked her, and I don't think my game is quite up to par with one of the greatest players in the history of women's tennis. The doubles alley combined with a pirate patch and a hand tied behind Roddick's back? Eh, still not enough.

After more head scratching, I thought I found a simple solution: ask Andy to play lefthanded. Anyone who plays tennis knows that even routine shots become chores when you're hitting with your off-hand. For those who don't play tennis, go outside and try to throw a baseball with your nondominant hand. Unless your name is Greg Harris, I bet you look like a total spaz. A perfect way to level the playing field.

Only one problem: Roddick is (to borrow a malapropism from Yogi Berra) "amphibious" and can play at a level far beyond your typical club player with his left hand. Playing with his off-hand, he can beat a friend of his who is a former college tennis player. Andy also has regular lefty-on-lefty battles with his brother, who was a top-ranked junior player and who, playing lefty, beat the dreadlocked guy from Dave Matthews Band 6–0, 6–0. Back to the drawing board.

My thoughts went to the Kurt Vonnegurt short story "Harrison Bergeron," where a futuristic government put hindrances on its citizens to make everyone "equal." Under this scenario, we would make Andy wear weight boots to take away his blazing speed and jumping ability, incorrectly prescribed glasses to distort his vision, layers upon layers of clothes to make his movements laborious, or an earpiece that produced a loud clanging sound before he hit his shots. Would he agree to drinking heavily before the match? Could I fly the hockey fat suit to Florida? After too many hours of thought, finally I gave up and said, "Fuck it, make him play with a frying pan."

This was a risk. Changing an instrument on an artist doesn't always produce inferior results. Some high-level trumpet players are so skilled at their craft that they can masterfully reproduce the sound of their instrument just by buzzing their lips. On the other hand, another great artist, Freddy Sanchez, showed that sometimes even the slightest change in equipment can make all the difference in the world (see Question 4).

But the iron frying pan would be more than a slight change. First, even a player as great as Roddick would be hindered by having to lug around this heavy, cumbersome piece of hardware. Second, the skillet would severely limit his booming serves. Third, only one side of a frying pan can be used to strike the ball, meaning that he would have to flip over the pan every time he switched to his backhand. Fourth, a frying pan has no strings, taking away Roddick's ability to use a variety of spins that help him hit powerful and well-placed groundstrokes. Lastly, it would force him to expend a lot of mental energy to resist making bad "out of the frying pan . . ." puns when he won a point.

I put the call into the Andy Roddick Foundation and spoke with Andy's mother, Blanche. I explained I was doing a book and this could be a great promotion for it and the charity. She came back a week later with the okay. All was well in the world: I had managed to convince even Andy's mother that the pan would level the playing field, when in reality I had tilted the playing field in my favor.

Or so I thought. A week before the event, a television executive told me that he had just heard of something that would make for a great event for the book. His brother, an avid tennis player, had two weeks earlier played doubles with Andy Roddick . . . and Roddick had used a frying pan. I had never mentioned to the executive that I was already lined up to play a pan-wielding Roddick, so this wasn't a put-on. Only one conclusion could be reached: Andy Roddick was indeed practicing to beat me with a frying pan.

This was not part of the plan.

There was good news, though. Roddick was emotionally invested in our match, just as I'd wanted, and now everyone around me would be even more impressed if I won.

The bad news was that if Roddick was practicing, I just might lose. Even worse, my dad saw through me entirely. He refused to accept that someone playing with a frying pan could beat a tennis player who was using a real racquet: "I don't care if he's practicing or not. If you don't shut him out, that's a loss." Given that the wasted money on rackets and court time in my youth came out of his pocket, this seemed like a reasonable position for him to take.

On the appointed day I arrived in Boca Raton, Florida, ready for battle. When I spoke to Andy directly he claimed he had never played with a frying pan (a detail I'd conveniently leave out when I told the story to people back home). "But it's funny," he said,

Howard Hughes and the lead singer of Blink-182 prepare for battle.

"Phil Helmuth asked me last night at my charity poker tournament if I could play with a frying pan and he didn't even know we were doing this." This was turning into an episode of *The Twilight Zone*. Too many coincidences.

We started rallying, and Roddick was, unfortunately, amazing. He was able to center the ball on the pan immediately and consistently put his shots deep in the court. Considering that a frying pan is heavier than a racquet, has a smaller surface area, and has no strings, that he could hit the ball right away with no trouble is beyond belief. Although Ichiro might disagree, top tennis players, more than other athletes, have this kind of hand-eye coordination. I was getting a little concerned.

But as we continued to hit, it became clear that Roddick had major difficulties to overcome. The main one was his inability to put spin on the ball. Hitting every shot flat may not have been a problem for his coach, Jimmy Connors, who struck everything on a line, but for any other tennis player in the world, not being able to use spin to control your power and depth is a real issue. It also meant that Roddick had to abandon his typical grip on his strokes, going from western to continental.

The backhand was a beast unto itself. Making solid contact with a frying pan is hard enough, but once you have to flip it over and coordinate the grip change, you're getting into unmanageable problems. Any shot to his backhand made for just too much work. This was an even bigger issue on volleys and the net game, where I was worried Andy would take control. In fact, volleying was eliminated entirely because of the shorter amount of time he had to make the flip to the backhand.

To Roddick's credit, though, he fought through these problems. Almost immediately he identified the need to stay at the baseline, and after only a couple of minutes of warmups he recognized that the backhand had to be avoided at all costs. Playing from the backcourt, he made a concerted effort to run around any ball hit to his backhand—no simple feat, since I kept putting the ball to that side. "I see what you're trying to do, and I'm not going to let you do it," the defiant Roddick yelled to me. If not for his footwork, speed, and anticipation, he would have been shanking backhands into the stands all day. As it turned out, the entire time we played he ended up hitting all but two shots with the forehand.

But ultimately, while Roddick consistently put the ball in the court, he wasn't able to hit shots with enough speed or accuracy to control points, which in this matchup would be a particular problem. I'm what in tennis circles is called a "push," or what the mulleted players in the Pittsburgh area call a "pussy." Players of my style simply "push" the ball back to their opponent without any particular power, the idea being that if you keep the ball in play long enough, your ADD-riddled opponent, who wants to pretend he's Andy Roddick and hit the ball hard, will do something stupid and miss.

Roddick, however, actually was Roddick and was more concerned with winning than with being a tough guy on the tennis court (a ridiculous premise to begin with). Recognizing that the pan limited his options for aggressive shots, he attempted to match me at my own game.

The best tennis player in America did an impressive job keeping rallies going, but I didn't bail him out by making errors. My handicapping was on the money. Andy was good enough to think he had a chance, but I was in the driver's seat. As hard as he tried to keep the ball in the court, the frying pan I had saddled him with eventually did what I wanted it to. He started missing, and pretty soon I was cruising. But thinking of my dad, I didn't just want a victory; I wanted a shutout.

I was closing in on finishing Andy off when the unthinkable happened. Wanting to put on a show for the adoring (my word, not theirs) crowd, I let my ego get in the way and went for a big shot down the line that missed by inches. It was only one point, but I knew what my dad would say when he started giving me a hard time: Andy Roddick beat me with a frying pan.

Still, no matter what kind of nonsense I'd have to hear, I knew that if I closed out the game without further incident I'd show the world the full extent of my abilities . . . in other words, that I was just competent enough at tennis to defeat a man who was using a frying pan.

On match point, Roddick slapped a forehand wide and the guy with the racquet won. Oh, and the guy with the racquet also did some exaggerated fist pumps and gave high fives to the crowd, yelling something about the "heart of a champion." Of this display it was later said, "That was an appropriate victory celebration for someone who had just won Wimbledon." I finally knew what it was like to beat Andy Roddick: embarrassing.

But I didn't care how embarrassing it was; I finally had my win over a top player, and even better, in the process I drew blood. Defeated, Roddick slammed the pan to the ground in frustration, breaking the handle. Andy, don't you realize a good artist never blames his instrument?

(As an aside, the match where I used the pan and Roddick used the racquet wasn't quite as close.)

I'd like to say my sensational victory was a testament to my greatness, but really it was just my brilliant strategy. With a frying pan, no player, even one as great as Roddick, can hit the shots needed to defeat a decent player who keeps the ball in the court at all costs. There are just too many ways to make an error with a frying pan, and our points ended with Roddick either being caught in an incredibly awkward hitting situation or being forced to go for

You should see him with a waffle iron.

an aggressive shot that he didn't yet have the feel for making. However, against a more aggressive/dumb player who made unforced errors, even someone on the intermediate level, Roddick would have taken over. He'd have patiently dinked his opponent to death and run down balls until the player went for too big of a shot and missed.

You may find this hard to believe, but as impressed as I was with myself, I came away more impressed with Roddick. Even using a frying pan, he could make almost any high school tennis team and be considered a solid player at all but the best of programs . . . although this would unquestionably be very awkward given the age difference and his insistence on using the pan and all. That he was this good after just fifteen minutes of practice (or a week, depending on who you believe) was remarkable.

Afterward Roddick alluded to a rematch and put the fear of God in me when he said he hadn't reached the height of his pan powers. "I think if I had more time to practice, I would improve. A lot of the shots I didn't quite know how to hit with the frying pan. You saw on that volley I hit that went flying. The adjustment to the backhand was the biggest thing. I kept running around it but you can't do that forever. If I could fiddle around with it, I'd be okay."

Allow me to translate: *I'd be okay = I would crush you.*

This veiled threat of vengeance begs the question of what strides Roddick could make if he practiced for the fictitious rematch, assuming the broken pan could be restored to its original form. Would those forehands that went sailing out when he tried to hit a winner start dropping in?

Probably so. I grew even more concerned about the prospect of a rematch when I later learned it's possible to play at a very high level with a skillet. The late Bobby Riggs, the U.S. Open champ of Battle of the Sexes fame, used to hustle amateur players for money using a pan as a handicap. Both Riggs biographer Tom LeCompte and Hall of Famer Pancho Segura, a good friend of Bobby's, seemed to think that Riggs with a pan was able to play around the level of a Division III men's player.

This seemed a touch ambitious but not that far off. Roddick within a week would most likely start limiting his errors and punishing floaters. In a month or so, he'd be keeping most every ball in the court that he was willing to play conservatively. Pretty soon he'd adjust to the loss of his biggest weapon, his powerful serve, and learn to minimize the problems with the backhand, returning serves, and dealing with hard-hit balls.

And if he became so obsessed with beating me in a rematch that he dropped off the tour for a year to spend hours a day hitting forehand after forehand, learning to use the edges of the pan to slice the ball, mastering how to flip that pan quickly enough for volleys, learning whether a nonstick pan would be more effective than a traditional one . . . he would be declared criminally insane and possibly institutionalized. And is finally being able to beat me really worth all that, Andy?

WOULD A TEAM OF MIDGETS BE THE GREATEST OFFENSE IN BASEBALL HISTORY?

On August 19, 1951, between games of a doubleheader involving the St. Louis Browns and Detroit Tigers, the 3'7", 65-pound Eddie Gaedel popped out of a papier-mâché cake to celebrate the fiftieth anniversary of the American League and as a tie-in promotion for Falstaff Brewery. This was very similar to a publicity stunt that Browns owner Bill Veeck had done many times before, and almost everyone in attendance considered it a major disappointment because he had promised a "festival of surprises." The people of Falstaff Brewery, who sponsored the game, were especially unhappy. Veeck had sold them on participating by guaranteeing that they would receive national publicity, and a midget popping out of a birthday cake clearly wasn't going to bring it.

The legendary showman Veeck apologized to all involved.

But when game two rolled around, it became clear that Veeck hadn't lost his touch and had just been suckering everyone in for a big payoff. With Bob Cain on the mound and Bob Swift catching for the Tigers, Gaedel, the midget in the cake everyone was so disappointed with, went to the plate for the Browns, a miniature bat in his hand and a uniform proudly sporting the number ⅛. As Browns staff presented papers to the umpire documenting that

Gaedel had officially been placed on the Browns' active roster before the game, the Bobs, Cain and Swift, huddled to devise a strategy to face Veeck's secret weapon.

Their solution was for Swift to make a low target behind the plate by getting on his knees, but it was no match for Gaedel's minuscule strike zone and Cain delivered four consecutive balls. Gaedel took his base to thunderous applause, stopping multiple times to bow and wave to the adoring crowd. When he finally reached first base, he was replaced by a pinch runner and given a standing ovation.

The following day, American League President Will Harridge voided Gaedel's contract, and later unsuccessfully tried to have Gaedel's at-bat stricken from the record books. A rule was created that contracts needed to be approved by the commissioner's office before a player could suit up for a major league team. The league told Veeck in no uncertain terms that midget ballplayers would not be allowed to participate in major league games. The Browns' owner, who said he had gotten the idea from Hall of Fame manager John McGraw, protested. He threatened to request an official ruling on whether diminutive Yankees shortstop and reigning MVP Phil Rizzuto was a short ballplayer or a tall midget. In his memoir Veeck recalled, "If baseball wanted to discriminate against the little people, I said, why didn't we have the courage to be honest about it, write a minimum height into the rules, and submit ourselves to the terrible wrath of right-thinking Americans."

Gaedel's at-bat was the most famous PR stunt in baseball history and a tribute to Bill Veeck's marketing genius, but had history taken a different course, it could also have been the defining moment of professional sports' ultimate game break.

In the modern era of baseball, with an ever-increasing value being placed on the ability to get on base by any means necessary and with teams constantly looking to get an edge on the competition, the time is right to answer the question that fans have wondered about ever since Gaedel drew that famous walk: Would a team of men with a strike zone smaller than a baseball mitt be the most effective offense in baseball history?

It made sense to begin the evaluation process by talking to the men who would have to combat this unstoppable force: major league pitchers. Surprisingly, not all of them thought the miniature mashers would be so unstoppable. I talked to pitchers from A (Bronson Arroyo) to Z (Joel Zumaya), and almost every one believed facing the midgets would be no challenge at all. Even when presented with the dimensions and the major league precedents—Gaedel's at-bat and Lenny Dykstra's entire career—they stayed confident.

"It comes down to the ability you have to throw pitches for strikes," said two-time AL Cy Young Award winner Johan Santana. "If you can command the strike zone, that's all that matters."

I indicated with my hands exactly how small this strike zone was. Santana was undaunted.

"If you can throw strikes against major league hitters, you can do it anywhere. It doesn't matter how small the strike zone is. You're just putting fastballs in there."

All-star closer Joe Nathan had a similar but more measured view.

"I think if anything, it would just take a while to get used to throwing down at that level. Once you get your release point down, I think it would actually even be easier because you don't have to supply as much power or hit the corners. I'm sure they're going to have some walks but I think major league pitchers should be able to be pretty successful doing that."

Granted, Johan does have two Cy Youngs under his belt, and Nathan is one of the best closers in the game, but putting the ball through an area not much bigger than the ball itself almost every time would seem harder than they were representing.

When told of the utter confidence that most pitchers displayed, and the ease at which they believed that they could strike out the mighty mites, Pirates hitting coach Jeff Manto thought some false bravado was responsible. "If you asked those guys if they could throw the ball into a keyhole, they'd say 'No problem.' That's the kind of confidence you need to be a big league pitcher."

So what did Manto think would really happen?

"Well, first off, I don't think the umpire would know the strike zone down there. But the real question is if a pitcher can throw a strike that low into that small of an area consistently. I don't know, there's a lot of leverage you've got to talk about, all kinds of mechanics for them that don't usually come into play. If it's done like the Bill Veeck thing, where they just send them up there to take [pitches] until they walk, it could be the best offense of all time."

Manto laughed.

"It'd be the best offense without a hit."

Giants slugger Ryan Klesko saw Manto's point and raised him a ridiculous idea: "You'd have to pitch your best guy like Greg Maddux who can throw a lot of strikes to have a chance . . . but they're going to give up a lot of runs because their pitching probably isn't very good."

Interesting theory, Ryguy. Of course, the midgets will only be an offensive weapon. A full lineup of them could put up a ridiculous amount of first-inning runs before being subbed out at the bottom of the inning, but also, a midget could be used as a designated hitter, or as a pinch hitter to open a game with a walk or in a critical situation where a walk could swing the game's outcome.

When I explained this to Cleveland Indians second baseman Josh Barfield, the son of cannon-armed former all-star and Soul Glo impresario Jesse Barfield, he was psyched. Josh agreed that midgets should be given their fair turn at bat. "That's the Moneyball approach right there," Barfield said. "I think it'd be very interesting to see. I know I'd pay to watch it."

With that blessing from baseball royalty, I knew it was time to put the miniature offense to the test.

Right away I brought the idea to the St. Paul Saints, a professional team in the American Association whose owners include comedian Bill Murray and Mike Veeck, son of the great Bill. In an amazing stroke of luck, the Saints already had a promotion planned for July 22 titled "Saints Smallball—A Tribute to Eddie Gaedel." From the word go, the Saints were enthusiastic about the concept, and they agreed to try to stop a batting lineup composed entirely of midgets in an exhibition lasting three half-innings.

Midgets *vs.* Little People

The players asked to be identified as *midgets,* as they think the term *little people* sounds ridiculous. The LPA (Little People of America) disagrees and says that the term *midget* is offensive, but that *dwarf* and *little person* are acceptable designations. I'm going to respect the wishes of the players I worked with, but if you're reading this book in the year 2080 and you guys have it figured out by then, please understand I'm just a product of my time. That goes for the offensive stuff in most of the other chapters, too, especially the fifty gratuitous fat jokes. Sorry, fatties of the future.

The midgets I selected, while not baseball players, were a group of outstanding athletes who tour the country as part of the Tiny Trotters basketball team. One of their members is even a midget wrestling champ. They were perfectly capable of running the bases (probably faster than David Ortiz), and if a pitcher wanted to discourage their participation by hitting one with a pitch, they not only would be able to take the pain, but could possibly charge the mound and put the guy in a camel clutch. There would be four of them, enough to rotate through the order as many times as needed.

The Lineup

Remarked Saints color man Kris Atteberry of Murderers' Row 2.0—or rather, Murderers' Row 0.5—"What's interesting, too, is the batting order of the midgets. They go from the tallest to the shortest, with the shortest being the cleanup hitter."

Justice—4'4"
The Dynamite Kid—4'2"
Blix—3'7"
Leroy the Phone Guy—3'4"

The Saints countered with pitcher Dana Kiecker, once a promising rookie for the Boston Red Sox with pinpoint control. Kiecker was certainly well past his prime but pitching regularly, and if everyone I spoke to was to be believed, the game would be easy pickings for him. Atlanta Braves veteran catcher Todd Pratt, for one, thought it would be a total mismatch.

"They're definitely not gonna hit, but it does depend on how high level of a pitcher if you want a real test."

When told that Dana Kiecker was the pitcher, Todd became extremely confident that the midgets wouldn't score.

"I played with Dana. He'll definitely do great. Excellent control. He should strike them all out with no trouble."

Not so fast there, sonny. . . .

Kiecker was laboring. He'd already thrown twenty-eight pitches, two runs were in, there were no outs, and the bases were drunk

Rick Ankiel's greatest nightmare.

with midgets (although drunken midgets would always be preferred). If he were facing Ken Griffey Jr., he'd try to snap off a nasty slider on the outside corner; against Barry Bonds, a fastball up and in; but with the 4'2" Keith "The Dynamite Kid" Kearns coming to the plate, he had no answers.

So Kiecker did the next best thing: he gave up. With the count 3–0, the one-time Red Sox Rookie of the Year tossed the ball underhand and yelled, "Here you go! Hit it!," praying that the diminutive dynamo would bail him out. But The Dynamite Kid was too wise, and the bat never left his shoulder. "Ball four," the umpire barked, and Kiecker slammed his glove to the ground. TDK took his base.

Dana eventually got through the inning, but it was a bloodbath. He walked seven batters and gave up four runs, throwing a total of fifty-seven pitches. (A starting pitcher usually only throws about a hundred pitches in an entire game, and Carlos Silva walked only nine batters in 188 innings in the entire 2005 season.) He was so worn out by the little bruisers after just that one inning that we called it a day.

Kiecker did improve greatly from the start of the inning to the end. After walking the first five batters, he struck out three of the next five (with two more walks mixed in). But despite his excellent control, it took him a lot of pitches to start getting near the zone. And to even get to that point he had to switch to throwing sidearm to flatten out the angle of his pitches.

I asked Dana whether he thought a current major league pitcher could consistently throw strikes to a midget. "I don't think there's too many pitchers around, either in the American Association or the major leagues, that can consistently put it there three times each at-bat."

That's especially true of trying to pitch to the smaller midgets. The only batters Kiecker struck out were the two midgets over four feet tall: The Dynamite Kid (twice) and Justice (once). Dana never figured out the 3'7" Blix or the 3'4" Leroy. Even worse news for pitchers is that as unstoppable as Blix and Leroy proved to be, there are many, many midgets smaller than them.

Kiecker really thought the midgets could make an impact in the majors. "Look, if they're going up there one after another, a pitcher might be able to strike some guys out by getting in a rhythm, but even then it's going to be tough. If you just sprung one on a pitcher, forget it. That's too hard a slot to hit."

This fell more in line with what I had heard from Angels all-star closer Francisco "K-Rod" Rodriguez, one of the few pitchers I spoke to who didn't think the midgets would be as easy to strike out as Adam Dunn: "First of all, I'm not going to be able to throw strikes. No way. My target for the hitter is very different so my approach would be completely messed up. He's going to get a walk immediately. I'd rather face Barry Bonds in the bottom of the ninth."

Having concluded that the midgets would be effective, I wanted to figure out just how effective they would be and how best to use them in a major league game. As there is still no book written on a "Smallball" style of play I consulted with Nate Silver of Baseball Prospectus. Baseball Prospectus is a collective of nerds (and some geeks) who present interesting new theories on the game by studying stats and data. Major league executives typically mock these

Leroy the Phone Guy describes what it's like to stand there and do nothing.

theories until they eventually co-opt them and claim them as their own. The kind of cutting-edge work the Baseball Prospectus guys are doing was exactly what was at the center of the debate generated by Michael Lewis's *Moneyball*. To give you an idea of the general comprehension of the baseball establishment, ESPN's Joe Morgan thought this was a book Billy Beane wrote about computers, and he frequently criticized it even though he never read it.

My interests in talking to Nate were twofold:

1. Would the late Nelson de la Rosa ($1\frac{1}{2}$ feet tall) have been more valuable than his sidekick Pedro Martinez?

2. What would be the best application of his skill(s) during a game?

Silver's e-mailed response:

> Here's one way to look at the "midget" problem. Suppose that you have your midget be the DH in the game. He hits in the leadoff spot, draws a walk to lead off the first inning, and then exits the game.
>
> Based on historical win expectation tables, a walk to lead off the first inning increases a team's probability of winning the ballgame by about 4.6%. Multiplied by 162 games, this translates to an extra 7–8 wins versus an average player ($162 \times 4.6\% = 7.452$).
>
> In other words, this is one valuable midget. A hell of a lot more valuable than Marco Scutaro.*

---

* And that's if you had to pinch run for him. There are midgets who are faster than some major league baseball players, so a pinch runner may not be necessary. A player who walks four times a game and can run the bases would be the best player in the history of baseball.

Marco Scutaro, eh? Scutaro plays for the forward-thinking Beane's Oakland A's, and we just unearthed a talent worth seven to eight wins more than him. All-star territory! Get Beane on line one! Hell, get Sandy Alderson on line two! We'll start a bidding war for The Dynamite Kid!

Okay, so since I didn't have an assistant, or even a phone that could do a three-way call, I went to the buyers one at a time, starting with Alderson. Alderson is the CEO of the San Diego Padres and the chair of Major League Baseball's rules committee, so he was uniquely positioned to talk to me about rules concerning midgets. Also, Alderson is famous for being the first baseball executive to emphasize Bill James's principles—he was Beane's boss in Oakland in the 1990s—and is known as a man willing to take a risk. I figured he would jump at the chance to have his offensively challenged Padres lead off every game with a guaranteed walk.

I was wrong.

"The reason no one has pursued the use of a person of less-than-normal stature on a major league team," Alderson told me, "is that it was tried before and the commissioner's office essentially outlawed the practice to keep the sport from becoming a carnival."

I asked the man of normal stature if his outlook would change if the "less thans" were allowed to play.

"If it was allowed, I don't see the use. With the limited roster space in the game and how many pitchers teams carry, we'll sometimes only have four or five positional players available at any one time. To have a player whose only function is to draw a walk, you're limiting yourself too greatly."

When I told him the numbers that Baseball Prospectus worked out and that the midget player would clearly have a great deal of value over a traditional bench player, Alderson was not pleased and made up a reason that I'm pretty sure even he didn't believe.

"I don't think you can simplify the issue to a number like that. You would have to work out a lot more angles than you've laid out. Is a player who is assured to steal two bases every time he's on first worth less than a guaranteed walk even? There was a player who had that singular a purpose and that was Herbie Washington for the Oakland A's."*

While I understood that roster flexibility would be a factor, would it not make sense to look into using midgets if they provide such a valuable starting point? I told him I could further work out the angles and numbers, but Alderson was about done. "I'm having a hard time taking this question seriously. Do you have any others?"

Yes, how could any midget be worse than starting a thirty-nine-year-old Eric Young in left field?

Click.

Isn't Alderson supposed to be a stat guy or something? Maybe I should have reread *Moneyball*.

Speaking of which, next I went to ol' Billy Beane. Certainly *he* would be willing to take a chance at anything that could give him a competitive edge. I mean, through the years half the 'roided-up sluggers he's put on the field have been less athletic than Justice. After literally two months of being told by the A's front office that Beane was out of town, busy, or unavailable, I finally heard from publicist Jim Young that the GM simply was not interested in discussing the matter. Innovation knows bounds.

So maybe the superserious stat-heads weren't the right guys to talk to. My next move took me to Beane's nemesis, the affable

---

* I'm pretty sure there has never been a human being who would be guaranteed to steal two bases every time he got on. Herb Washington, who was the world record holder in the 50- and 60-yard dash, absolutely 100 percent stunk as a pinch-running specialist. He was caught stealing seventeen times out of forty-eight attempts.

Kenny Williams, general manager for the Chicago White Sox, who was similarly not thrilled by my offer.

"I've acquired quite a bit of a sense of humor working in the Chicago market. It's a necessity to keeping your sanity. But this is out there."

It was actually done in a game, though! Baseball Prospectus drew up the numbers, and they showed that a team could gain a big advantage by using this strategy.

"Well, Baseball Prospectus says I should have been out of a job a long time ago, so I don't hold their opinion too high."

I was starting to get the feeling that the Baseball Prospectus angle was not a good one to take.

But if you could lead off every game with a walk, that would be a big advantage, right? (Not a rhetorical question, since the White Sox leadoff hitter at the time of our conversation was Darin Erstad.)

"Well, I can't argue that."

Long pause.

"It's ridiculous."

Long pause.

"I don't even know what to say."

Say you'll sign him, Kenny!

Long pause.

So you really don't think a midget would be useful on a team, or is it more the stigma of being the guy who signed one?

"I really don't want to get into this," he said. "Okay, let me answer this question this way: I pray to God this year that the Detroit Tigers field a team of midgets." Me, too! I have four clients looking for a job!

My last hope was to find an executive who was just an all-around good guy. I identified the thoughtful, intelligent general manager of the Astros, Tim Purpura. Tim had just signed the 6′2″,

280-pound Carlos Lee to a six-year, $100 million deal, so he clearly was someone who valued production over whether a ballplayer looked "normal." Still, to have a shot at getting one of the midgets signed, I needed to show Tim that even though you could fit five of them into the frame of the rotund Lee, you might be able to get ten times the production at 5 percent of the cost. (These numbers not verified by Baseball Prospectus.)

Without tipping my hand, I asked Tim how he would value a player who could be guaranteed to get on base every time he went to the plate yet didn't play the field.

"It's an interesting thought," he replied. "I guess my question is how is it guaranteed?"

I explained our game with the Saints and how there are players who are in the two- and three-foot-tall range. He was intrigued.

"Certainly I would think a player like that would have value. As you're probably aware, Bill Veeck did that years ago with Eddie Gaedel, and the commissioner banned him from the game. My guess is that someone would find a way to get the guy banned. But is a guy with a perfect on-base percentage attractive? Heck yeah. You've just gotta find a way to get it done."

Now this is what I'm talking about, a GM who places a high enough priority on winning to embrace basic logic. I pushed the obvious merits of midget batters further and suggested that a midget who walked every time at bat would immediately be one of the most valuable players in Major League Baseball. The science was too tight. Tim couldn't find it in his heart to see it any other way.

"Sure. It takes up a roster spot, and that would be the tough part on a twenty-five-man roster. Typically we operate with thirteen or fourteen position players, so you're taking up one of those position player's spots, but there's clubs that operate with guys who are only pinch hitters and don't ever really play the field. This is not so far away from what you're talking about."

Then I popped the question: Would he take Blix?

"Again, it goes back to the point, how do you guarantee it?"

I assured Tim that this was a sure thing and even offered a money-back guarantee.

"While I might want to consider it, my guess is that baseball would not permit it. They would find a way to outlaw it."

How right he was. When asked in 2001 whether a midget could play today, Commissioner Bud Selig told the *New York Times*, "I don't like to deal in hypotheticals, but the answer is no." Selig said that the Gaedel incident "was clearly not in the best interests of the game. It was so aberrational it turned the game into a farce."

This from the guy who tried to put Spider-Man logos on the bases and allows players to use pink bats. I called Major League Baseball to see if that was an official stance or simply an off-the-cuff remark. Pat Courtney, a publicist for MLB, told me, "From the guys I've talked to, nothing has changed since then."

I tried to explore the issue further, but MLB was absolutely terrified. Every person I talked to, from PR people to lawyers, had no clue how to respond and ran me in circles for weeks.

Finally, the curtain was pulled down entirely. Selig declined an interview request and employees would no longer comment on the issue.

In any other job setting this kind of discrimination probably wouldn't hold up in a court of law, so I went the legal route and spoke with attorney Roy Reardon. Reardon (no relation to Jeff or Jimmy) is a member of the Simpson, Thacher & Bartlett litigation department and is best known for handling the Casey Martin case. Martin, a golfer who suffered from a birth defect in his right leg known as Klippel-Trenaunay-Weber syndrome, successfully sued the PGA Tour under the Americans with Disabilities Act for the right to use a golf cart during competition. Although the ruling frustrated right-thinking sports fans across the nation, it was a huge win for disabled athletes with wide-ranging implications; most notably the precedent later allowed an injured Ray Lewis to carry a battle-ax in short-yardage situations. I asked Reardon whether this case spoke well for the chances of a midget ballplayer, since he wouldn't even be asking for special treatment, just the opportunity to play a sport like everyone else.

"I think a midget that is barred has a litigable issue," Roy responded, "because he's not asking to change the game. The Americans with Disabilities Act is there to give those who are handicapped an opportunity to participate. That's the whole purpose of the act. And if you deny them the opportunity to participate, you've got a problem."

Echoing a point Bill Veeck had made years earlier, Reardon added, "Let me ask you a question. How short is a midget? Eddie Stanky, who was very short, he got a hell of a lot of walks. No one ever said, 'This guy's too small.' Where do you draw the line? Is it three eight, is it four two, is it five one? It's a distinction that Major League Baseball isn't going to be able to answer. If you take a healthy midget who wants to play, they're going to have a fight on their hands."

Although the point is well taken, according to the Little People of America's website, dwarfism is a "medical or genetic condition that usually results in an adult height of 4'10" or shorter" (which, as an aside, seems like a pretty arbitrary height; that's only four inches shorter than Prince) and is recognized under the Americans with Disabilities Act by the U.S. Department of Justice. Some attorneys I spoke with questioned whether an ADA suit would be the best route to pursue. Amy Berecek of the law firm Thorp, Reed &

Armstrong suggested that the strongest stance would be to issue challenges in areas where "certain state and local laws clearly prohibit discrimination against little people based on their height. The state of Michigan and the California cities of San Francisco and Santa Cruz prohibit height and weight discrimination, and the District of Columbia prohibits discrimination based on personal appearance. If major league baseball banned little people from playing in the league, it could face legal challenges in Detroit, San Francisco, and Washington, D.C.—all places where the league has teams. Therefore, if a little person wanted to play for one of these teams, the league cannot deny him that opportunity because of his height."

While the method of litigation can be debated, this much can be agreed upon: a legal challenge would make it extremely difficult to keep midgets out of the game. All it would take is a ballplayer being denied access to a tryout or a spot on a team due to his height, and the legal battle would be on.

The Dynamite Kid, it's your turn at bat . . . your time to be a Giant has finally come.

ACKNOWLEDGMENTS

Going into this project I knew that to do it in a way I wanted would mean cutting everything out of my life and immersing myself completely in the world of sports for a solid year. Considering that I already wondered whether it was appropriate to spend so much of my time playing, watching, talking about, and thinking about games that are, without question, a massive waste of time, this was a real concern. Yes, there were people who were more obsessed than I:

> I didn't cry when they buried my father—I wouldn't let myself. I didn't cry when they buried my sister. On Thursday night, with my family asleep upstairs, my eyes filled as Agassi and Marcos Baghdatis played out the fifth set of their moving second-round match.
> —Greg Garber, ESPN.com

But still, I was pretty knee-deep in sports craziness and was about to go deeper. Well, obviously I decided to take the plunge, and in the end, this project gave me total clarity as to how sports should properly be defined: They remain a massive waste of time.

I have a number of people to thank, and no one more than my parents, Martin and Charlotte Gallagher, and my grandfather, John Ciotti, who have always been there for me. Particularly, my Dad was very helpful in giving input on the book, and my Mom helped anytime I was in a jam, including being stuck in St. Louis with a broken cell phone and not able to get a hold of PDW. They're the best people I know.

Every time I've read the acknowledgments in a book I always assumed that the author was blowing smoke up everyone's ass. But in actually writing a book you realize how important it is to be surrounded by smart people who can augment what you want to do and curb your self-destructive instincts instead of just forcing some shitty agenda down your throat. I was lucky in that I worked with people who made the grind much easier. If not for these folks, this book wouldn't exist, which would probably be okay by any number of people and organizations, but I'm grateful.

A special thanks goes to my agent, Scott Hoffman. Unlike virtually everyone else in entertainment whom I've approached with an idea, Scott saw the merits of how I wanted to do the project and made no concerted effort to ruin it by saying, "Wow, great idea, let's try to come up with a different version that will be much worse!" or "Hmm . . . I love what you want to do, now just change everything."

Thank the good Lord I got to work with my editor, Jed Donahue. I knew we were in good shape when I made an offhanded joke about Marco Scutaro on day one and he laughed instead of staring at me blankly for making a Marco Scutaro joke. He was instrumental in making this book what it is and was willing to spend countless hours working with me to get it right. His involvement also went well beyond typical editor responsibilities and included racing Mo' Money Greene, shooting a hundred free throws a day for three months, and pulling some kind of Jedi mind trick on Ted Leonsis. I was also lucky to have the support of the rest of the staff at Three Rivers Press, especially Philip Patrick, Carrie Thornton, Robert Siek, Amy Boorstein, Dan Rembert, Lauren Dong, Linnea Knollmueller, Mary Choteborsky, Jay Sones, Shawn Nicholls, and Julie Kraut.

My friend Erik Tillmans is a very talented guy who assisted throughout the entire process, in virtually every capacity. Erik is the funniest person alive. If you brought dead people into the equation, however, he would finish a distant sixth behind the Three Stooges and Rodney Dangerfield.

Dan Zappin, Lisa Donovan, and Tony Lee were always there when I needed them on the video and photography end. (This is starting to sound like an Oscar speech.) If there's any justice in this world, they will be out of my price range for the next project I do. Actually, come to think of it, they were out of my price range for this one too, so I thank them for helping a friend out.

The lovely Jamie Greenberg made sure all of my terrible spelling and grammatical errors were cleaned up before I ever sent anything out. Per her demands, I will also mention that she helped with other things, such as finding a frat for us to play beer pong, helping make travel arrangements, finding out-of-town photographers, and possibly inventing the universe. From the beginning, she was there while I sold the book and then frantically said, "Wait, how am I actually going to do any of this shit?"

Brian Moore: We will consider my saying here that I owe you a round of golf and a dinner for your contribution as contractually binding. Hopefully, when the time comes for me to pay this off, I will be in St. Martin, happily retired and not taking your phone calls.

Tim Foley succeeded where many others before him had failed in doing research. Jed would attribute this to his Georgetown education and having worked for George Will, but I call it ol'-fashioned sticktoitiveness. He also was an amazing fact checker, but if anything is screwed up in the book it's his fault. Or Jed's. Or maybe Jamie's.

Karen Smith handled anything and everything that I've needed through the years. When something needs to be done at the last second, she always gets it right.

Chip Namias and Jordan Feagan were great with helping me get some of the more difficult interviews. Many hours were spent sitting on the couch bullshitting about this project with Jordan.

Joe Queenan, I sincerely hope giving you half of my advance for that ridiculous index pays off to the extent you've represented.

Sam Walker was extremely helpful in so many facets and helped educate me on the process of being a first-time author. Our 12-foot hoop battle awaits.

Jefferson Davis made up for seceding from the Union by selflessly helping me line up Freddy Sanchez to play Wiffle ball.

Amanda James, you brought a lot to the table with your intangibles. Late in the game, you came through in the clutch. These are all bad sports clichés, but if you look them up, I promise you will see they are complimentary.

Oprah Winfrey: You are, in the words of the great Maya Angelou, "The wind beneath my wings." Your signed copy is in the mail, and I hope we can sit down on your couch to discuss how your book club brought me from the brink of illiteracy to being a published author.

Mark Argenziano not only shared his insights for the book, but he and his brother Jeff twice woke up before dawn to drive four hours to give Jed instruction in free-throw shooting. Way to blow it, Jed.

Steve Padilla made a big contribution to humanity by filming his college classmate Jed in the famous "Soul Man" tapes. Fortunately he also got Mark's coaching on video.

Jack Smith and Melissa Cantu helped me track down some key research information.

Paul Siegel, thank you for being so helpful with the darts info. Apologies on the cheap shot, but to be fair, it was pretty funny.

Thank you to Deadspin, FJM, The Big Lead, CSTB, and all of the other great sports blogs out there for giving me something in sports worth reading.

Particular thanks go to all of the athletes who participated in the events and discussed the questions. Without them, there would have been no book. Sincere thanks go also to the athletes' representatives who facilitated this project on the shoestring budget we had: Blanche Roddick and Graham Cross, Ted Leonsis and Nate Ewell of the Washington Capitals, Jill Geer, Sara Hunninghake, Paul Cobbe, Zack Bolno of the Washington Wizards, Emanuel Hudson, Dave Hemmah, Tom Whaley of the St. Paul Saints, Kevin Outcalt of the Golden Baseball League, Polam Reddy of the cricket association, the Dr. Theodore Atlas Foundation, Robert Burns, Bill McCandless, and Jim Trdinich of the Pittsburgh Pirates.

Thanks also to the many people who took the time to be interviewed for this book, including Larry Babcock, Joe Rogan, Jim Mora, John Mafee, Bill Kutzner, Hal Shuler, Robert Spruck, Tyrone Rush, Joanie Seawalt, Bernard Gross, Franklin Rose, Lois Clement, Robert Barad, Todd Wiseman, Kevin Outcalt, Tom Nordland, Jim Dalbey, Aimee McDaniel, Nate Silver, Brad Feldman, Andrew Freund, Tim Fanning, Gilbert Geilem, Dan Steinberg, Dave Benedetto, Craig Miller and USA Basketball, Matt Hemmingway, Robert Holmes, Nate Ewell, Chris Dudley, Rick Barry, Mark Ellis, Guy

Mezger, Barry Frank, Dan Meisenheimer and all of the great people at the USBL, Damon Bingham, Scott Kravchuk, Rich O'Hallorhan, Ron Rubenstein, and Will Carroll. To any others I may have overlooked here, your contributions to this book are greatly appreciated.

Katie, Louie, Betsy, William, and Lucy Catalano; Jamie, Ricky, Quintin, Trey, and Reed Catalano; Paul, Holly, Ben, and Gabe Ciotti; Mike Gallagher; Annie Gallagher; Ann Marie and James Piper; Katie Gallagher; Reenee Gallagher; Kathy Gallagher; Jack O'Malley; Kurt Haarmeyer; Ida Hohn; Ki Arasini; Martin and Marie Gallagher; Veronica Rossi; Kevin Gaffney; Jon Reese; Josh Deblasio; Roy Bodnar; Matt Rusinko; George Stingl; Erin Beckner; Mz. Bidner; Joe Conlin; Tad Conlin; Sara Conte; Richard Harris; Jacob DiCesare and family; Logan Douds; Pat Driscoll; Dave Dupilka; Patricia Feeney; Steve Holloway; HaHu and Oscar Lemon; Mollie Milligan; Gary Potter; Bobby Rue; Ben Toth; Gregg and Simone Turkington; and my good friends in the LADS: You have all been, at some point, good to me through the years.

Fight on, soldiers of H.O.P.E. everywhere!

Special Thanks

Finally, special thanks go to the Andy Roddick Foundation for their involvement and interest in the project. The goal of the Foundation is to improve the quality of life of, and enhance educational and economic opportunities for, children based on the principles of respect for family, education, and morality. Focusing its efforts in southeastern Florida and the Austin, Texas, area, the Foundation supports programs that combat childhood diseases, care for abused children, improve childhood literacy, and encourage young people to stay in school.

For more information or to make a donation, visit:

http://www.arfoundation.org.

INDEX

Assholes, total
   Fans as, xiii et al.

Barry, Dave
   Refers to close friend as "an idiot,"
      217
   Refers to close friend as "a loser," 223
   Thoughts on shooting free throws,
      217, 223

Barry, Rick
   Reflects on shooting free throws,
      227, 228, 230
   Rejected as mentor by player who
      sucks, 228
   Ridicules NBA foul shooters, 228
   Shoots free throws like somebody's
      "granny," 228

Beer
   Wasted by author, 64
   As prop, 64
   Wasted by author, 65
   As prop wasted by author, 65

Beer pong
   And Papua New Guinea, 67
   Played with sake or scotch instead
      of beer, 70
   Origins of not explained, 64

Benitez, Armando
   Likened to other porkers, 169
   Member of clean-plate society, 160
   Referred to as slob, 161

Booger
   As nickname of man named Smith,
      121

Bradley, Shawn
   Ridiculousness of, 149

Canada
   Location called into question, 41
   Warren Moon flees to, 127

Canseco, Jose
   Pitching skills of, 185–86
   Masculinity of, 187
   Mullet of, 188

Center
   Likelihood of winning an NBA
      championship without, 208

Cocaine
   As illegal foreign substance, 102
   As pick-me-up, 102
   She don't lie, she don't lie, she
      don't lie, 102
   Snorting technique during baseball
      games, 102

Darts
   Needlessly discussed at great
      length, 64
   Needlessly discussed again,
      117–18
   Needlessly discussed a third time,
      as if it were a real sport, 179–81

Dates
Ease with which obtained if the phrase "I'm Keith Hernandez" is used, 37

Devil Rays, Tampa Bay
Existence called into question, 130

Duncan, Tim
Fans look forward to future with, 208
As provider of much fun, 208
Really fun to watch in action, 208

Eagles, Philadelphia
Break with long-standing tradition of excellence and sign complete scrub nobody ever heard of, 127–28
Sign free-agent bartender who did not actually grow up in Philadelphia and who they will later cut just as soon as the team stops sucking, 127–28
Subject of film about total amateur bartender who wanders in off the street and breaks into the NFL, though he had actually already played in the World Football League and was a whole lot bigger than Marky Mark, 127

Favre, Brett
Ass-kicking threats of, 157

Ford, Whitey
Betty Ford Clinic named in honor of, 101
Drinking habits of, 101

Fox, Rick
Mercifully brief acting career of, 149

G, Kenny
Gratuitously mocked, as if that were a new idea, 217

Gerard
As middle name of Mike Tyson, 21

Golf
Legitimacy as sport challenged, 161–63
Pussy-like traits of those who play it, 161

Goodman, John
Bewildering fatness of, 2

Gramatica, Bill
General patheticness reviewed, 157

Gramatica, Martin
Patheticness of not reviewed, 157
Kick against Seahawks left undiscussed, 157
Utterly inexplicable absence from book, 1–265

Grandma, my
Defeats author in sporting event, 162
Defeats author at golf, 162
Gifts in any sport other than golf ridiculed by author, 162
Huge advantages over grandson of, 162
Ineligibility to be described as an "athlete" even though she beat author at golf, which doesn't really count, 163

Hernandez, Keith
Clever impersonations of, 37

Grizzlies, Memphis
Arrive in Cleveland without top-level, snipers-on-the-roof, Secret Service–type security, 34

Iverson, Allen
As Antichrist, 208

Jordan, Michael
Quality of golf game called into question, 149

King, Don
  Brainchildren of, 20

Kwitkowski, Ted
  Thoughts on tits, 98

Laid, getting
  Likelihood of occurring, 33–44

Legion of Tough Guys, The
  What to do if they show up, 24
  Likelihood of beating Mike Tyson,
    24–25

Manigault, Earl "The Goat"
  As playground legend, 71
  Unusual nickname of, 71

Mantle, Mickey
  Fondness for alcohol of, 101

Masturbating in Madison Square Garden
  As big-ticket event, 25

McEnroe, John
  Tasteless comments about Williams
    sisters, 112
  Failure to mention what a dud Mary
    Carillo is, 112

Midgets, the
  Abused for cheap laughs, 249–65

Mongolia
  GDP of, 58
  As Monsters of the Midway, 59
  Surprise appearance of in book
    about popular American sports,
    58
  Wrestling and, 57

No mas
  As customary phrase used to
    concede defeat, 24
  Basically what author said to his
    grandmother after golf match,
    162

Obesity, morbid
  Upside of, 1–10

Oshinowo
  Putative last name of someone
    named Babatunde, though who's
    checking? 53

Padres, San Diego
  Shut out by pitcher on LSD, 102

Pirates, Pittsburgh
  Cheap apartments and, 87
  Wiffle ball and, 27, 32

Planet Earth
  Baddest man on, 25
  Mike Tyson's relationship with, 22–25

Puck bunnies
  Attractiveness to the toothless, 38

Pulpo, El
  Nickname of Antonio Alfonseca, 191
  Not being Spanish for "The Goat," 191
  Typicality of, 191
  Six fingers and, 191–92

Pussy
  As author's alter ego, 244
  Defeated by Grandma at golf, then
    whines about it, 162–63

Roddick, Andy
  Does not actually beat author with
    a frying pan, 245–46
  Suggests rematch with frying pan,
    247

Ruffians
  Turning up at Cus D'Amato's gym,
    23–24
  As unusual word to use in a book
    about sports, 21

Slob, fat
  As ideal NHL goalie, 1, 10

Spade, Andy
    As brother of David, 34
    As date, 34
    Wow Factor of, 34

Thongs, silk
    Ditched by sumo wrestlers, 54

Tits
    As portent of trouble on the horizon, 98

Toronto, University of
    As breeding ground for hot chicks, 33

Turpin, Melvin
    As singer, 149

Tyson, Mike
    Box-office appeal of, as masturbation practitioner, 25
    Brain damage and, 22
    Compared to Icarus, for no good reason, 19
    Elected to Académie Française, 24
    Waxes philosophical, 22

Trailblazers, Portland
    Meager qualifications to work in front office discussed, 125

Van Damme, Jean-Claude
    Cited by author in somewhat sad attempt to polish friend's credentials as a groupie, 34

Dates alleged former model, 34
    Failure to appear on same page as Kenny G, 217
    Not even mentioned, 163–265

Vandeweghe, Kiki
    Solemn head-shaking of, 72

Walker, Kenny
    Mentioned in same breath as Michael Jordan, Kobe Bryant, Vince Carter, and Dominique Wilkins, 76
    Leaping skills compared to Spud Webb's, 76

Wahlberg, Mark
    As star of hokey sports film about Vince Papale, 127
    Not even Italian, 127
    Plays wide receiver 16 inches taller than him, 127

Wheels
    Likened to tits as harbinger of disaster, 98

WNBA
    General suckiness of, 108–11

Zero
    Number of times author has beaten his grandma at golf, 162